PLYWOOD
WORKING
for EVERYBODY

PLYWOOD WORKING for EVERYBODY

John Gerald Shea

 VAN NOSTRAND REINHOLD COMPANY
NEW YORK CINCINNATI TORONTO LONDON MELBOURNE

Also by John G. Shea:
Colonial Furniture Making for Everybody
Woodworking for Everybody
Antique Country Furniture of North America
The American Shakers and their Furniture
Contemporary Furniture
The Pennsylvania Dutch and their Furniture

First published in paperback in 1981
Copyright © 1963 by Van Nostrand Reinhold Company
Library of Congress Catalog Card Number 63-24099
ISBN 0-442-26429-1

Van Nostrand Reinhold Company
135 West 50th Street, New York, NY 10020
Van Nostrand Reinhold Ltd.
1410 Birchmount Road, Scarborough, Ontario M1P 2E7
Van Nostrand Reinhold Australia Pty. Ltd.
17 Queen Street, Mitcham, Victoria 3132
Van Nostrand Reinhold Company Ltd.
Molly Millars Lane, Wokingham, Berkshire, England RG11 2PY

Cloth edition published 1963 by D. Van Nostrand Company
Third cloth impression 1969

16 15 14 13 12 11 10 9 8 7 6 5 4 3 2 1

PREFACE

Plywood has become an ideal building material, not only in our homes but in countless varieties of construction. It rides the rails in thousands of box cars and coaches. It sails the seas in hulls of pleasure craft and commercial vessels. It was on wings of plywood that much of the early aircraft industry relied. Without this versatile material huge sports arenas, bridges, docks and public structures would be impossible to build on contemporary plans.

During World War II, plywood became a military mainstay for fast construction of airplanes, barracks, boats, drydocks, landing craft and other essential wartime equipment. Prefabrication of plywood was the key to crash production. Even President Kennedy's famous PT boat was constructed of plywood, as was much of the aircraft and water craft of our allies and enemies.

Plywood, as we know it, is a fairly recent product. While the process of veneering and laminating layers of wood together dates back to ancient times, fabrication of conventional plywood panels originated in this country in 1905. Since then, the manufacture and sales of plywood have expanded rapidly; forecasts of future demand indicate that by 1970 annual plywood production will have reached seven billion square feet.

It is not the purpose of this book to dwell on these staggering statistics of plywood production. Instead, we will describe the common types, grades, and kinds of plywood and illustrate many of its "do-it-yourself" consumer applications. Designs, photographs, and working drawings are included to help the craftsman at home and the student at school work with plywood.

The first chapter of the book describes the properties of plywood—its composition, manufacture and diversity in types and grades available for construction purposes.

The second chapter deals with arrangement of workshop facilities and reviews the tools required for plywood working. Sample workshop layouts are suggested with an assortment of original designs and working drawings of benches, cabinets and related shop furnishings which can be built of plywood. The background is aimed at stimulating construction of practical home workshops where the users of this book can build the plywood projects which follow.

Plywood construction is covered in the next two chapters. Here we explore in pictures and text the basic processes and joinery methods employed in making things of plywood. In subsequent chapters, you will find information on plywood finishing, covering and upholstering —with emphasis on step-by-step photographs showing exactly how some of these operations are performed.

With the cooperation of the American Plywood Association, we offer in the next three chapters an abundance of attractive *"do-it-yourself"* plywood project designs and working drawings. These range in variety from an assortment of indoor furniture designs to plans for building outdoor furniture, utility items, childrens' playthings and recreational equipment. As the photographs indicate, these projects are practical and designed with excellent taste.

Because plywood is such a versatile material —and because readers may wish to go further in their exploration of its uses—the final chapter of the book is devoted to *"Special Plywood Projects."* First, you will find illustrations and architects' plans to guide construction of more elaborate "built-in" and exterior structural designs. Supplementing this is a full photosequence, covering ten pages and showing, step-by-step, how to install plywood wall paneling. The final pages of this chapter illustrate how to build plywood boats with reference to supplementary working drawings obtainable elsewhere.

It is hoped that this book will introduce readers to the many advantages of building with plywood, that from it they will gain a better understanding of this useful material, and that they will enjoy making the plywood projects presented.

JOHN G. SHEA

Greenwich, Connecticut
May, 1963

ACKNOWLEDGMENTS

Without active cooperation of the industry whose products are the subject matter of this work, it would have been impossible to prepare a book such as PLYWOOD WORKING FOR EVERYBODY. But right from the start, this author had the good fortune to find ample cooperation.

Since the subject of this book is Plywood, its two primary sources of information were the American Plywood Association, representing the softwood plywood industry, and the Hardwood Plywood Institute, representing manufacturers of hardwood plywood. Both associations responded immediately and effectively.

There also were many others who helped. In fact, as the work progressed, the author made many new friends, all of whom were keenly interested in giving this project their intelligent support.

In view of the warm response of these excellent people, it seems fitting to thank them personally as well as to acknowledge the associations and companies they represent.

First, there is Jim Plumb of the American Plywood Association who stayed with this work from start to finish and always managed to come up cheerfully with exactly the right material for the right page. Clark McDonald and Bill Groah of the Hardwood Plywood Institute promptly made available quantities of valuable research information and illustrative material. They also coordinated (in cooperation with Georgia-Pacific Corporation) the special sequence of wall paneling photographs which the author has produced exclusively for this book.

My good friend Jerry Smith of The Weyerhaeuser Company, in Tacoma, furnished the pertinent and attractive Weyerhaeuser material. The vigorous support of Lamar Newkirk, of the Georgia-Pacific Corporation in Portland, Oregon—especially on the paneling project—did

much for the book. Fred Isley, Martha Nold and G. I. Fischer of the United States Plywood Corporation searched their files to furnish a wide assortment of photographs and information on their attractive plywood products.

Stanley Jepson of the American Forest Products Industries; A. M. Hattal of the National Lumber Manufacturers Association and R. H. Hammre of the Forest Products Laboratory of the United States Department of Agriculture can always be counted on to furnish the most penetrating research information. This book, like my earlier WOODWORKING FOR EVERYBODY, has benefited immensely from the consistent cooperation of these gentlemen.

Since plywood must be worked in conjunction with other materials and tools, significant contributions to this book also were made by manufacturers of related tools and materials.

Bill Kinderwater of DeWalt, Inc., offered the resources of his organization, providing a series of special operational photographs made to illustrate how power tools are used in plywood construction. Similar alert cooperation came from Bill Wolfe of the Millers Falls Company, with specially made photographs of power tools working just with plywood—a departure from ordinary illustrations of general woodworking practice.

Jim Downes of the Magna American Corporation furnished models for photography as well as fine photographs of his Shopsmith and Sawsmith in action. My friend D. V. Holman, President of The Adjustable Clamp Company, made his products available for special photography and furnished excellent photographs demonstrating plywood clamping techniques.

Over the many years in which this writer has prepared books and magazine articles, he has had frequent occasion to call on such companies as: Armstrong Cork, Black & Decker, Borden,

Disston Division of H. K. Porter, DuPont, Firestone Tire & Rubber, Nicholson File, John Oster Manufacturing, Pittsburgh Plate Glass, Reynolds Metals, Skil Corporation, Stanley Tools and United States Rubber. Again for this book, all of these companies offered the best of their product information and illustrative material.

A special word of thanks goes to Donald Buckwell of Stanley Tools for custom photography of hand tools. R. M. Roberts of E. I. DuPont de Nemours & Company made available extremely useful information and photographs on plywood finishing and upholstering. Eugene Moore of the Armstrong Cork Company furnished excellent photo material on plywood covering. And Donald Hunter of The Borden Company supplied detailed information on adhesives and sent subjects for photographs.

Additional generous help came from George Ashbey of the Nicholson File Company; Ralph Dubrowing of the Natural Rubber Bureau; R. O. Willis of Firestone Tire & Rubber Company; Bill Mead of Reynolds Metals Company; T. H. Randecker of United States Rubber Company and Don Broeckert of Burgess Vibrocrafters.

To all these good friends who cooperated on this book, let me express a hearty "Thank you!" At times my requests may have seemed somewhat exacting, but you were most patient. Your thoughtful response to these requirements helped to produce a better book.

J.G.S.

CONTENTS

5 PLYWOOD FINISHING

6 UPHOLSTERING AND COVERING PLYWOOD

7 PLYWOOD PROJECTS FOR INDOOR LIVING

8 PLYWOOD PROJECTS FOR OUTDOOR LIVING

9 CHILDREN'S PLAY WORLD OF PLYWOOD

10 SPECIAL PLYWOOD PROJECTS

1
PROPERTIES
OF PLYWOOD

What Is Plywood?

Wood of itself is a wonderful material. It has served mankind in countless ways through the centuries. The texture, the mellow tones, the toughness of this natural building material is hard to beat. But wonderful as it is, wood in its native state is subject to deterioration. It cracks, warps, splits, shrinks and swells.

To make the most of the inherently fine qualities of wood for his long-term needs, man has been forced to add a few refinements and improvements. He has contrived methods to redistribute the physical properties of wood and to control these properties to achieve greater structural strength and stability.

To attain an improved product, the tree was taken apart and its contents redistributed. Thin sheets, or *plys*, of wood were shaved from the tree. These plys were welded with glue into a sandwich of three or more layers. The grain of each ply was bonded crosswise to the grain of ply-veneers above and below it. The result: a composite, multi-deck sandwich consisting of an odd number of wood plys, or layers, with grain running alternately in both directions.

What are the advantages of this redistribution and reassembly of natural wood?

One decided advantage, because the strength of wood lies with the grain, is the added toughness achieved when plys of wood are bonded together in opposing grain direction. In this way, both length and breadth are strengthened. The resulting panel, made up of alternating wood plys, is twice as strong and rigid as natural, solid wood.

Other advantages are apparent in plywood's resistance to shrinkage. Solid woods tend to shrink across the grain. But in plywood this tendency is greatly minimized by the force of opposing longitudinal grain. In its overall aspects, you will find that plywood has better dimensional stability than wood and that it is less likely to alter its dimensions with each change of moisture content in the atmosphere.

WOOD IS STRONG ACROSS THE GRAIN

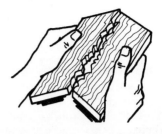

BUT SPLITS EASILY ALONG THE GRAIN

SANDWICH OF WOOD SLICES GLUED TOGETHER

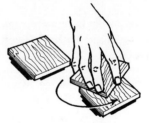

WITH GRAIN OF ONE SLICE CROSSING THAT OF ANOTHER

BONDED TOGETHER UNDER CLAMP PRESSURE

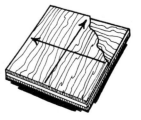

RESULTING PLYWOOD IS STRONG IN *BOTH* DIRECTIONS

Because of the balanced construction of plywood—with the grain of one ply bonding and crossing the grain of another—it has much less tendency to warp than solid wood. Solid wood also is naturally subject to cracking, checking and splitting. On the other hand plywood will resist destructive impact because of its cross-laminated construction. And since plywood has no plane of cleavage, it is virtually splitproof.

Origin of Plywood

In the historic sense, there is nothing new about plywood. Centuries ago Chinese carpenters used the shavings from blocks of wood for surfacing furniture. Antique Chinese woodwork was fabricated on the cross-laminated, plywood principle. Early Egyptian furniture built on the plywood principle has survived generations to become museum pieces. Egyptian mummies were entombed in cases fabricated of plywood and veneer.

In this country the plywood veneering technique was employed as early as the eighteenth century in fabrication of fine furniture. Daniel Webster's prayer desk, with a simulated plywood rack for holding the prayer book, is a notable American antique made of plywood-type materials.

But the first attempts at mechanical production of plywood are said to have been made in France. In the 1860's a Frenchman by the name of Garand invented a mechanical veneer slicer. The difficulty with this device was that the thickness of the veneer could not be regulated. However, in the 70's Garand replaced his original cutter with the first *rotary* veneering lathe. This machine laid the foundation for the plywood industry as it is known today. Evolution in machines since that date has been rapid.

Douglas fir plywood, the original source of this nation's expanding plywood industry, is produced principally in the states of Oregon and Washington. It is here that the giant fir trees grow from which much softwood plywood is manufactured. This wood is ideally suited for peeling (veneering) on rotary lathes as well as for other processes of plywood fabrication.

The first panel of Douglas fir plywood was exhibited at the Lewis and Clark Exposition in Portland, Oregon, in 1905. From this panel has grown an industry producing enough fir plywood alone to make a four-foot wide ribbon of

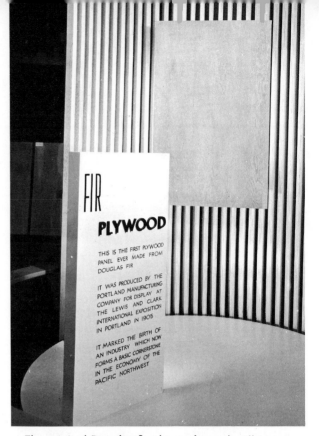

The original Douglas fir plywood panel, still intact, as displayed above, was first exhibited at the Lewis and Clark Exposition in Portland, Oregon, in 1905. Courtesy of American Plywood Association.

plywood encircling the globe almost ten times! The output of this industry is measured in billions of square feet. This is augmented by massive production of hardwood plywoods—another branch of the industry.

Evolution of Plywood—the Waterproof Breakthrough

Ever since its origin plenty of uses have been discovered for plywood. It found its way into the manufacture of numerous items for industry and the home. Because of its increased stability and ease of fabrication it was used extensively—but only for construction that would not be exposed to moisture.

In fact, this very restriction of protection against moisture was its Achilles' heel. For like the fabled Wax Man who performed great wonders until assailed by the Sun and thereby melted, early plywood could do most anything, unless it was exposed to dampness. Thus, for use outdoors, it was worse than worthless; the glueline melted and it simply flaked apart.

4

Among the first persons to observe this—to their considerable regret—were automobile manufacturers. Structurally, and because of its indoor endurance and stability, plywood was considered an ideal material for making floor boards and running boards as well as side panels for cars. The necessary surface protection was provided with numerous coats of paint and varnish. Even so, after a period of outdoor exposure surface plys commenced to bulge and flake apart. As the complaints of their customers ascended to an uproar, auto manufacturers had to forsake plywood. And thus the plywood industry not only lost one of its biggest customers but was also forced to reappraise the limitations of its product and to devise ways and means of doing something to improve it.

The trouble lurked in the glueline. Plywood was only as good and enduring as the glue which held it together. During the early years of its manufacture animal glues were brushed on each joining veneer and the assembled panel was then set up in presses for drying overnight —a slow and costly operation resulting in a product which had to be kept dry and protected indoors.

Later, starch, casein and even vegetable glues were introduced. But far from being waterproof these were not even water resistant.

Visualizing the vast market awaiting plywood if it could only be used outdoors, the quest for a truly waterproof glue became a search for survival of the industry itself. In fact, during the depression years of the early thirties many plywood manufacturers went into bankruptcy and output of the entire industry declined alarmingly. This happened largely because plywood was not qualified for exterior use.

Meanwhile, a chemical engineer by the name of Dr. James V. Nevin was working on formulae for development of truly waterproof glue. Nevin, an Irish scholar educated extensively both here and abroad, was acquainted with the early works of Dr. Leo Bakeland, the German chemist for whom Bakelite is named. Bakeland conducted experiments with phenolic resins as early as 1909—and many of these experiments offered clues followed by Nevin in his later research.

There was great jubilation throughout the plywood industry when, late in 1934, Nevin an-

nounced that he had developed a completely reliable waterproof glue. Extensive tests were conducted, and in January 1935 commercial production of the product began. First it was called "SUPER" plywood by its original manufacturer—the Harbor Plywood Corporation. Soon its manufacture became common to the industry, where it was classified as "Exterior Type"—a revolutionary turning point in the progress of plywood.

Needless to say, Dr. Nevin's discovery of waterproof glue boosted the potential of plywood to hitherto unknown heights. All kinds of exterior construction which had previously been impossible—prefabricated housing, boat building, outdoor construction—all imaginable exterior applications of plywood, were now feasible as a result of Nevin's discovery.

The automobile industry, once a prolific user of plywood, had to reject early types because of deterioration caused by moisture. Development of waterproof adhesives may herald a comeback, already started with natural wood veneer panels ("Flexwood") shown on luxury car, below. *Courtesy of U. S. Plywood Corporation.*

5

Manufacture of Plywood

In its manufacturing process, plywood represents a form of wood conservation, for little waste is tolerated in extracting the finished product from the original log. While two methods are employed to remove sheets of veneer from the log, namely by rotary lathe and veneer slicer, by far the most common—particularly in manufacture of softwood plywoods—is the rotary lathe or "peeling" method.

Logs used for plywood are literally unwound or peeled against a keen cutting edge into continuous sheets of wood. These sheets, or veneers, are peeled from the rotating log in much the same way that wrapping paper is unwound from a roll.

When the log has been unpeeled as far as the first lathe will take it, it is cut in half and the two pieces are put in a smaller lathe. Here they are unwound further to form inner plys of plywood panels. Ultimately two core spindles are left—just about big enough to make two sections of two-by-four.

The entire log is used. Even the limited trimmings are fed into a chipper and utilized for making hardboard and paper pulp.

As the long ribbon of veneer emerges from the rotary lathe, an automatic clipper, operated by a skilled technician, cuts it to desired widths, separating defective portions and obtaining as many clear sheets as possible. These sheets are then sorted and dried in preparation for the glue spreader and assembly procedures.

The dried and cut sheets of veneer, which are to form the plys of plywood, are then fed through the rollers of a glue spreader where they are bathed in a continuous flow of adhesive at uniform thickness. At the "out" end of the glue spreader, the veneers are assembled of alternate cross-grain sheets to form three-, five-, or seven-ply panels.

Then a hydraulic, hot press takes over to bond the adhesive under temperatures of 260° to 285° Fahrenheit at pressures of about 200 pounds to the square inch. Following the heat and pressure bonding, the rough panels are trimmed to standard sizes and sanded. They are then stamped with registered trademarks to certify their type and grade.

Rotary-cut plywood veneer is peeled from log as it revolves in lathe against sharp cutting knife. *Courtesy of U. S. Forest Service.*

Veneer slicer is used to obtain select cuts of surface veneer for many species of hardwood plywood. *Courtesy of U. S. Forest Service.*

1 Peeler logs are especially selected for manufacture into plywood. Sawed to working lengths, they are kept in mill pond prior to processing. *Courtesy of American Forest Products Industries, Inc.*

2 Rotating in barker lathe, the outer bark is removed to prepare the log for veneer peeling operations. *Courtesy of American Plywood Association.*

3 Turning against a sharp knife in the peeling lathe, wood veneer unwinds (like wrapping paper) to form continuous sheets from which plywood is manufactured. *Courtesy of American Plywood Association.*

4 After cutting to standard sizes, veneer is dried, mended and prepared for edge jointing prior to passing through glue spreader for panel assembly. *Courtesy of American Plywood Association.* tion.

5 Giant presses bond the assembly of cross-laminated veneers and adhesives into rigid plywood panels of uniform thickness. This operation is controlled under heat and pressure. *Courtesy of American Plywood Association.*

6 After passing through sanding machines and edge trimming to exact size, plywood panels are thoroughly inspected and stamped for type and grade. *Courtesy of American Plywood Association.*

Standards of Quality

The United States Department of Commerce has established commercial standards for the manufacture of plywood. These standards are augmented by the exacting specifications and high-level, quality identification maintained by the plywood industry itself. Such matters as the type of glue bond, species, testing procedures, grading and labeling, must conform to government standards and to quality codes established within the industry.

Many plywood manufacturers subscribe to a service which continually samples their product. Plywood panels, thus tested, are stamped not only with the name of the manufacturer (and plywood association of which the manufacturer is a member) but also with the registered marks of the testing service and labels identifying its species, type and grade. Thus green markings on a softwood plywood panel usually identify it as interior-type while red markings identify the exterior-type.

Types and Grades of Softwood Plywood

Douglas fir is the most common of the softwood plywoods and is available in panels measuring 4' by 8'. However, greater lengths may also be had—particularly of the exterior-type for use in boat building and exterior construction. Widths range from 24" to 60", with 48" being most common.

Usually, softwood plywoods are made of an odd number of plys, approximately of equal thickness. Panels are available as thin as 1/8" (for special purpose) but run in regular stock thicknessess ranging from 1/4" (3-ply) to 1 1/8" (7-ply).

As already noted, two types of softwood plywood—exterior and interior—are available. Each type is clearly labeled on the surface and edge stamping of the panel. Exterior plywood is waterproof while interior plywood is only moisture-resistant and thus unsuitable for any type of construction which must be exposed to dampness. Within each type there are several grades.

Grades of softwood plywood are identified by letters stamped on the edge and surface of the panel. The letter "A" signifies the best quality of veneer while "B," "C," and "D" indi-

Durability of various adhesives for exterior-type plywood is evaluated after a long period of outdoor exposure. In above photo, tests are being made by technicians of the U. S. Forest Products Laboratory at Madison, Wisconsin. *Courtesy of U. S. Forest Service.*

Torn apart, after baking and boiling, specimens of exterior-type plywood are studied to see how glueline held against force of torture testing. *Courtesy of American Plywood Association.*

cate decline of quality to lower grades. As an example an "A-A" grade of plywood is surfaced on *both* sides with the best quality of veneer. Only minor defects and limited patches are permitted in this quality. But since the "A" designation pertains to *surface* quality only, the inner plys may be fabricated of a patched, but structurally sound, "C" grade.

Of course, the ultimate end-use of the plywood must determine selection of the proper grade. Grade "A-A" will be selected where both appearance and endurance are required. Exterior "A-A"—and special marine versions thereof—may be used for boat hulls and other construction exposed to moisture. Grade "C-D" plywood, which foots the scale, has its place in construction of sub-floors, roof or wall sheathing, where it is covered by other materials.

The table on the facing page, lists common grades, dimensions and specific applications of each type of Douglas fir plywood. It should be helpful when ordering softwood plywood for a particular job.

COMMON GRADES AND USES OF DOUGLAS FIR PLYWOOD

Exterior Type (Waterproof Adhesives)

Grade	*Thickness* (4' x 8' panels)			*Major Uses*
	3 Plys	*5 Plys*	*7 Plys*	
A-A	¼", ⅜"	½", ⅝", ¾"	⅞", 1"	Outdoor furniture, boats, signs, fences; appearance important for both sides.
A-B	¼", ⅜"	½", ⅝", ¾"	1"	Most uses as for A-A grade; appearance of one side not so important.
A-C	¼", ⅜"	½", ⅝", ¾"	1"	Exposed uses, combinations (sheathing-siding) soffits, signs; appearance of one side not so important.
C-C (repaired)*	¼", ⅜"	½", ⅝", ¾"		Backing for wall finishes, base for thin flooring materials.
C-C (unsanded)	5⁄16", ⅜"	½", ⅝", ¾"		Truss gussets, farm buildings, combination sheathing and siding; rustic appearance.
Marine Plywood				Hulls of racing boats and larger boats.

B plies or better throughout. No butted end-grain joints permitted in any ply. Boat-hull grade requires solid inner plies.

Interior Type (Non-Waterproof Adhesives)

Grade	3 Plys	5 Plys	7 Plys	Major Uses
A-A	¼", ⅜"	½", ⅝", ¾"		Furniture, cabinet doors, partitions; appearance important for both sides.
A-B	¼", ⅜"	½", ⅝", ¾"		Cabinets, display counters; appearance of one side not so important.
A-D	¼", ⅜"	½", ⅝", ¾"		Wall paneling, displays, built-ins, counter tops, table tops.
B-D	¼", ⅜"	½", ⅝", ¾"		Backing for interior finish materials.
C-D	5⁄16", ⅜"	½", ⅝", ¾"		Wall, roof, sheathing, short-period construction barricades, nail-glued truss gussets, shipping cases.
C-D (plugged)	¼", ⅜"	½", ⅝", ¾"		Sheathing where a solid face is required.
Interior underlayment	¼", ⅜"	½", ⅝", ¾"		Underlayment for resilient floor material. ½" and thicker used as combination subfloor and underlayment.
2.4.1		(7 plys) 1⅛"		Combination subfloor and underlayment for floor systems designed with supports 4' on center. May be purchased with tongue and groove edges.
C-D (with exterior type glue)	5⁄16", ⅜"	½", ⅝", ¾"		Subfloor, wall and roof sheathing, truss gussets.

*One or both faces have been patched and touch sanded.

Hardwood Plywood

For the making of fine furniture, wall paneling and an extensive variety of other uses, hardwood plywood is regarded as an ideal building material. Like its softwood counterpart, it comes in both exterior and interior types. But, as illustrated on the facing page, it is veneered with a variety of beautifully grained and highly decorative hardwoods, including rare species of both domestic and foreign origin.

Hardwood plywood differs structurally from the softwood variety. Most hardwood panels use a solid "core," or extra-thick middle ply. This may vary in both thickness and substance, depending on specific applications of the panel.

VENEER-CORE HARDWOOD PLYWOOD

Most common is the *veneer core* panel, which is manufactured like softwood plywood but composed of a thicker core and thinner surface veneers. It is used for wall paneling, sheathing, furniture and for special applications where the panel must be curved or bent.

For the making of table tops, doors, cabinets and fixtures, *lumber core* plywood is commonly used. This contains a thick, solid wood core fabricated by edge-gluing narrow strips of solid lumber. A variation of this is the *particle-board core* plywood made of a composition, wood-particle core bonded together with a resin binder. This composition offers a maximum of dimensional stability.

LUMBER-CORE HARDWOOD PLYWOOD

Types and Grades of Hardwood Plywood

Hardwood plywoods are made of three, five, seven and nine plys, ranging in thickness from 1/8″ to 1″. Like the softwoods, their manufacture conforms to government standards. Within the industry, standards are scrupulously upheld, with markings devised for labeling and identifying each type and grade.

Four types of hardwood plywood panels are available: Type I is manufactured with waterproof adhesive for use in construction of objects exposed to moisture. Type II, made with water resistant adhesive is for interior application. Type III is only moisture-resistant which means it can be damaged by water but resists indoor dampness and humidity. The fourth type, Technical Type I, has the same waterproof qualities

as Type I, but varies in thickness and arrangement of plys.

The grading of hardwood plywood falls into five specific categories. Leading the list is Premium Grade #1 with select, matched veneer on surface, avoiding contrasts of color. Good Grade #1 also avoids sharp contrasts in color and grain. Sound Grade #2 allows some surface deficiencies such as imperfect matching of color and grain, but does not permit open defects. Utility Grade #3 allows tight knots, mismatching of veneers, streaks and slight splits. Backing Grade #4 permits larger defects which do not affect strength or serviceability of panels.

Specialty Grade SP hardwood plywood is custom made, of select matching veneers for special requirements.

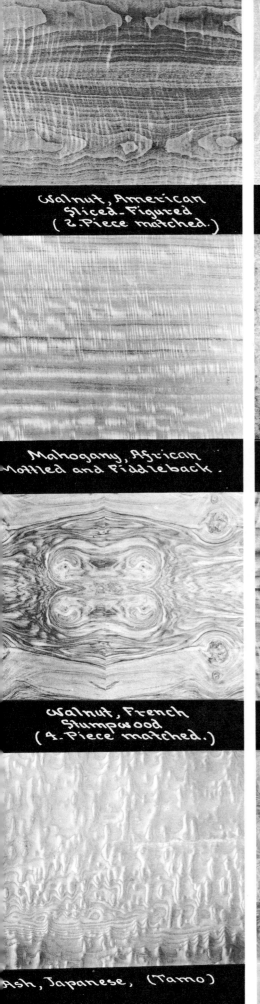
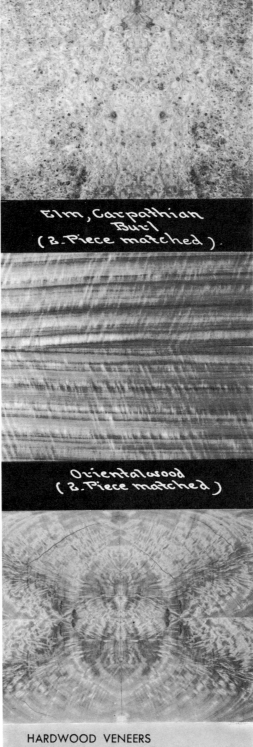

Walnut, American
Sliced-Figured
(2-Piece matched.)

Oak, Domestic
Quartered.

Gum, Red
Figured
(2-Piece matched.)

Mahogany, African
Mottled and Fiddleback.

Elm, Carpathian
Burl
(2-Piece matched).

Olive
Burl
(2-Piece matched.)

Walnut, French
Stumpwood
(4-Piece matched.)

Orientalwood
(2-Piece matched.)

Paldao
(2-Piece matched.)

Ash, Japanese, (Tamo)

HARDWOOD VENEERS
Courtesy of Hardwood Plywood Institute

Avodire,
Crotch.

Special Plywoods

The science of other industries helps to produce plywood of greater functional value. Most notable, perhaps, are the *overlaid* panels. Some of these are surfaced with resin-impregnated fiber sheets glued to one or both sides. This provides a tough, pre-painted surface, especially advantageous for exterior construction and marine use. Another type of overlaid panel is hardboard faced and sanded to extreme smoothness. Both are overlaid on fir surface plys, and they furnish an excellent base for paint by concealing all traces of surface grain and eliminating grain raise.

When it is desirable to have the beautiful graining of natural wood appear on the surface, an overlay of clear thermoplastic polyester film has been developed. This is bonded to the natural wood surface to provide a highly protective and damage-resistant finish. The resulting product, called *Permagard*, has numerous applications, particularly in places where highly decorative effects must go hand in hand with hard service.

Common among surface treatments are the grooved plywood panels used for both interior and exterior walls. These are often prefinished to eliminate the extra time and cost of painting and finishing operations.

Panels of brushed fir plywood, on which the softer grain has been removed by running the surface through a heavy wire brush, are tastefully finished for decorative impact. Striated and embossed panels are also used where special interior effects are desired.

Exquisite grain of hardwood plywood veneer is permanently sealed and protected when thermoplastic polyester film is bonded to surface. This transparent overlay, called Permagard, is stain and water resistant. *Courtesy of U. S. Plywood Corporation.*

Beautiful grain pattern of Western red cedar is accented with this exterior-type plywood siding. Traditional plank construction of early American homes is simulated with grooved scoring panels. *Courtesy of U. S. Plywood Corporation.*

Striated plywood wall paneling contributes to neatness of decorative scheme. It is made by striating the face of the plywood panel with planer knives especially ground to produce deeply scored, perpendicular lines. *Courtesy of Georgia-Pacific Corporation.*

Highly decorative, sculptured effect of brushed fir plywood is produced by running the surface through rotating wire brushes to remove soft areas of graining. Relief pattern of grain is then finished in attractive colors. *Courtesy of Georgia-Pacific Corporation.*

2

THE PLYWOOD WORKSHOP

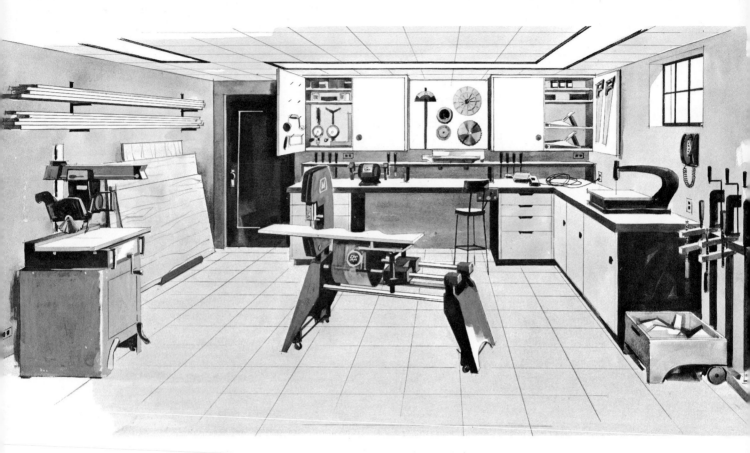

HOW TO PLAN YOUR WORKSHOP

Most home workshops start small and grow. A good "pounding place" for a working area in the basement or garage usually comes first. Then, suddenly, you find all those trips to the hardware store for tools and materials have produced a "shop."

When you start pounding be certain to choose the best location. Consider the kind of work you plan to tackle. If you see shopwork as a mild recreational pastime—for turning out tiny furniture models or craft novelties—bring your shop upstairs with compact workbench units as shown on pages 20 and 22. But if you are aiming at remodeling, rebuilding or refurnishing your home, you must count on a full-fledged plant, as illustrated above.

This is the complete basement workshop. See how space is organized here into efficient arrangement of workbenches, tool racks, storage cabinets, lumber and plywood racks, clamp fixtures and power tool working areas. There is fluorescent lighting in recessed panels overhead as well as a sound-proof ceiling. Resilient flooring saves feet and tools. Proper heating and ventilation assure comfort and easy concentration. There is a place for everything—and everything contributes to satisfying shop work.

Of course, you do not have to set up shop in the basement. A spare room upstairs may be your spot. But remember, noise and sawdust go with a productive shop. So try to soundproof your workroom in a location isolated from the areas of normal household activity.

Regardless of location, you may want to start your shop with one or more of the plywood workbenches, cabinets and accessories, shown with working drawings on the pages which follow.

A GOOD SHOP LAYOUT

Space requirements govern the layout of your shop. For example, bringing long plywood panels into cutting position on standing power tools demands plenty of "swing room."

Major power tools—circular saw, bandsaw, jointer, combination machines including the radial saw and Shopsmith—usually are mounted on casters for full use of the minimum 6′ clearance recommended on the adjoining diagram. When outsize lengths of plywood and lumber are cut, the machine should be in a position diagonal to the working area for moving up as the cutting progresses. For extreme lengths, the stock may even be fed into the machine through the open cellar door.

With the adjoining floor plan of the complete shop, plywood and lumber delivered through the cellar door is stored beside the saw or on the rack above. The radial saw stands ready to rip and crosscut the material as it arrives, accommodating outsizes of stock fed through the open door. The mid-floor area, occupied by the caster-mounted combination machine, may also be used for a single-purpose circular saw, bandsaw and jointer.

This layout ensures ample bench space for hand tool operations and assembling your work. It also furnishes mounting surface for auxiliary power tools such as drill press, jig saw, power grinder and bench jointer. Hand tools and power tool accessories are kept on the tool board and in the cabinets over the end bench. Hardware and other materials are stored in the drawers below.

Cabinets at the right hold portable power tools. End racks take assorted clamps, and a scrapwood wagon tucked underneath keeps things tidy. Of course, somewhere in one of those floor cabinets is a shop vacuum cleaner—always essential at cleanup time.

If your aims and space are limited, try the one-wall layout below. Here, a radial saw is placed in mid-position to adjoining wall benches for easy accessibility. The saw's variety of attachments furnish facilities of a complete power shop using minimum floor space. Mounted on a mobile bench stand it moves out in line with the door for lengthy cutting.

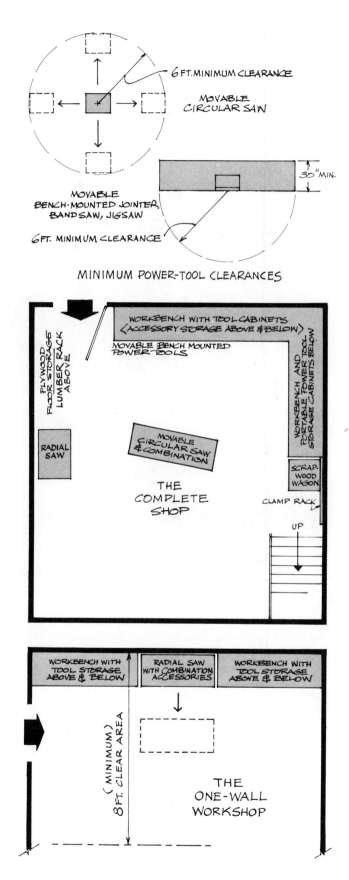

6 FT. MINIMUM CLEARANCE

MOVABLE CIRCULAR SAW

MOVABLE BENCH-MOUNTED JOINTER, BANDSAW, JIGSAW

30″ MIN.

6 FT. MINIMUM CLEARANCE

MINIMUM POWER-TOOL CLEARANCES

WORKBENCH WITH TOOL CABINETS (ACCESSORY STORAGE ABOVE & BELOW)

MOVABLE BENCH MOUNTED POWER TOOLS

WORKBENCH AND PORTABLE POWER TOOL STORAGE CABINETS BELOW

PLYWOOD FLOOR STORAGE LUMBER RACK ABOVE

RADIAL SAW

MOVABLE CIRCULAR SAW & COMBINATION

THE COMPLETE SHOP

SCRAP. WOOD WAGON

CLAMP RACK

UP

WORKBENCH WITH TOOL STORAGE ABOVE & BELOW

RADIAL SAW WITH COMBINATION ACCESSORIES

WORKBENCH WITH TOOL STORAGE ABOVE & BELOW

8 FT. CLEAR AREA (MINIMUM)

THE ONE-WALL WORKSHOP

A GOOD WORKBENCH AND TOOL CABINET

No matter how modest or elaborate your home workshop ambitions, your first concern must be construction of a good workbench and a cabinet to hold your tools. Obviously, your workbench should be sturdy. And it should be built to withstand the impact of constant buffeting, pounding and lurching which are part of the woodworking process.

A good workbench must be heavier than an ordinary table. It must be solid enough to anchor itself to the floor so that it will not move with your work. It should have a heavy pounding surface. At the same time it should not be so massive that it cannot be moved around when necessary.

Such a workbench is illustrated above. Made of plywood, with sturdy two by four framing, it brings together a variety of desirable features. For maximum strength and endurance it is assembled with bolts, screws and nails as well as glued bonding of all plywood parts. This con-struction guarantees longitudinal and vertical reinforcement.

This bench offers a number of functional advantages. For instance, all base parts are fitted flush, providing a smooth, neat appearance and an area easily brushed to keep your work surface tidy. There is ample shelf space below to house your portable power tools and their accessories along with the odds and ends of materials and hardware which always accumulate around a workbench.

The tough, double-thickness, plywood top affords adequate working surface—even for end mounting of power tools. Overlapping ends and front edge allow for clamping down surface work. If desired, plywood doors can be attached to enclose the storage space underneath.

The plywood tool cabinet, shown above, contains the normal household variety of hand tools with shelf space to spare for nails, screws and hardware.

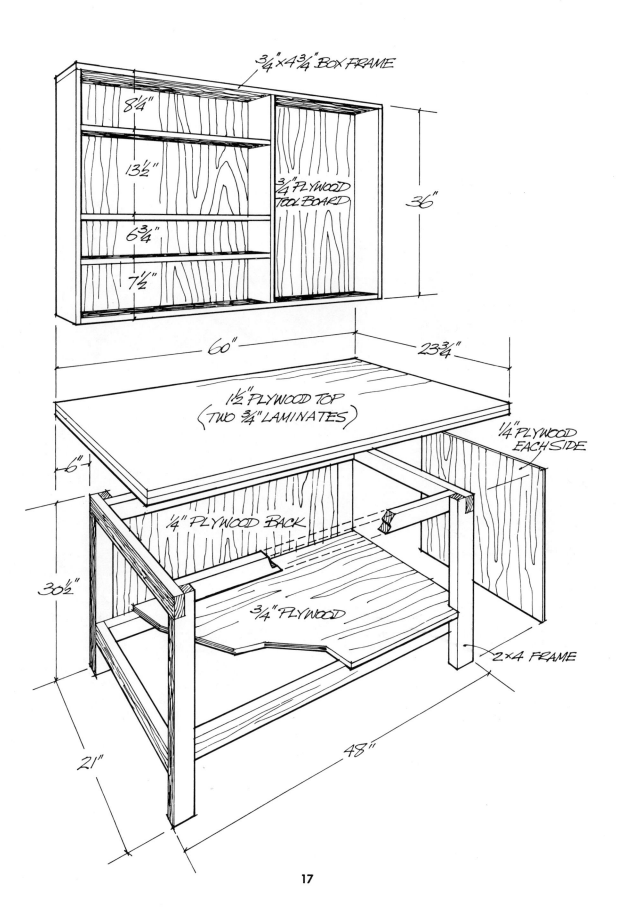

3/4" x 4 3/4" BOX FRAME

8 1/4"

13 1/2"

6 3/4"

7 1/2"

3/4" PLYWOOD TOOL BOARD

36"

60"

23 3/4"

1 1/2" PLYWOOD TOP
(TWO 3/4" LAMINATES)

1/4" PLYWOOD EACH SIDE

6"

1/4" PLYWOOD BACK

3/4" PLYWOOD

30 1/2"

2 x 4 FRAME

21"

48"

17

Original design by author

WORKSHOP FOR LIMITED SPACE

If your situation allows space in a spare room to pursue your woodworking hobby, why not choose a bright corner and build the compact workshop shown above? Here you have another special workbench design combined with a floor-to-ceiling plywood cabinet for storage of working materials. Augmented with a few combination power tools, this setup furnishes facilities for even the most advanced craftsman. Furthermore the plywood construction of these designs is not too hard.

The workbench—although strong and sturdy—is of modern, functional design. Its complement of large drawer-bins will be welcomed for handy storage of additional tools and materials, and the jumbo-sized bottom bin can accommodate a variety of portable power tools. The tool rack along the back of the bench keeps your "instruments" handy, while additional tools may be mounted on the side of the adjoining cabinet.

The plywood storage cabinet, reaching from floor to ceiling, is not only designed for storage of those extra plywood panels but also furnishes a tier of drawers for keeping nails, screws, and small supplies. The open space above, with its movable shelf, can accommodate large cans of finishing materials.

When building this cabinet it is important to keep in mind that the accompanying working drawing is based on the assumption that your ceiling is eight feet, six inches high. Any variation of these measurements should be adjusted with revised measurements of the base and top components to meet your specific requirements. Obviously, in order to accommodate plywood panels measuring eight feet long, the opening height must measure at least eight feet. However, the same design can be adapted—even for much lower ceilings—if in your finished cabinet you do not need space for storing full length panels.

18

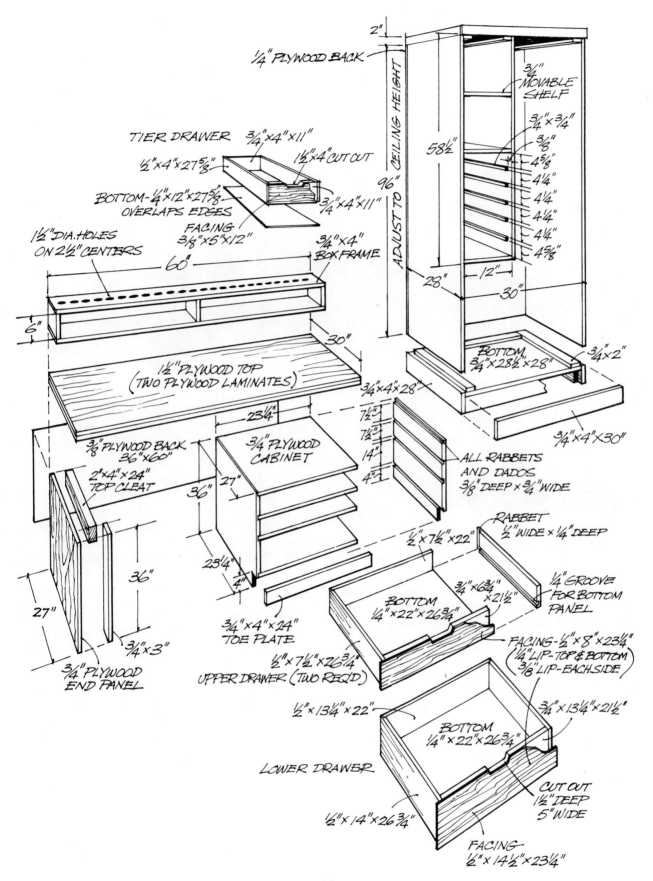

TIER DRAWER
3/4"x4"x11"

1/2"x4"x27⅝"

1½"x4" CUT OUT

BOTTOM-¼"x12"x27⅝"
OVERLAPS EDGES

3/4"x4"x11"

FACING
3/8"x5"x12"

1½"DIA. HOLES
ON 2½"CENTERS

3/4"x4"
BOX FRAME

60"

6"

30"

¼" PLYWOOD BACK

2"

96"

ADJUST TO CEILING HEIGHT

58½"

3/4"
MOVABLE
SHELF

3/4"x3/4"

3/8"

4⅝"
4¼"
4¼"
4¼"
4¼"
4⅝"

28"

12"

30"

1½" PLYWOOD TOP
(TWO PLYWOOD LAMINATES)

3/8" PLYWOOD BACK
36"x60"

2"x4"x24"
TOP CLEAT

3/4" PLYWOOD
CABINET

23¼"

27"

36"

23¼"

4"

3/4"x4"x24"
TOE PLATE

½"x7½"x26¾"
UPPER DRAWER (TWO REQ'D)

3/4"x4"x28"

7½"
7½"
14"
4"

½"x7½"x22"

BOTTOM
¼"x22"x26¾"

3/4"x6¾"
x21½"

ALL RABBETS
AND DADOS
3/8"DEEP x 3/4"WIDE

RABBET
½"WIDE x ¼"DEEP

¼" GROOVE
FOR BOTTOM
PANEL

FACING-½"x8"x23¼"
(¼"LIP-TOP & BOTTOM)
3/8" LIP-EACH SIDE)

BOTTOM
3/4"x28½"x28"

3/4"x2"

3/4"x4"x30"

36"

27"

3/4"x3"

3/4" PLYWOOD
END PANEL

½"x13¼"x22"

BOTTOM
¼"x22"x26¾"

3/4"x13¼"x21½"

CUT OUT
1½"DEEP
5"WIDE

LOWER DRAWER

½"x14"x26¾"

FACING
½"x14½"x23¼"

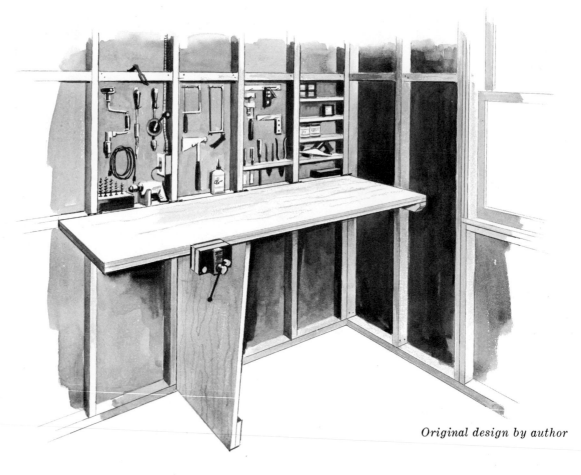

FOLD-UP WORKBENCH

Perhaps you would prefer to locate your workbench at the back of your garage. Fine idea—providing the family jalopy is a compact model. But what happens if the bumper-to-bumper stretch of your sleek new vehicle reaches practically from inside the door to the back wall? You can still accommodate both the car and workbench by deciding on the fold-up bench design shown above. With this design you can also padlock your prized collection of tools in a safe hideaway far from the grasp of inquisitive little hands.

Made of exterior-type plywood, this convenient bench is constructed to integrate with the two by four framing of your garage. It is as strong as the garage itself. Ample space is provided between studding of the wall area for hanging tools. And shallow shelves for boxes of screws and hardware can be attached between studs.

When building the fold-up workbench be sure to use waterproof glue and galvanized or brass fasteners. As indicated on accompanying working drawing, heavy hinges are required and a sturdy folding bracket is essential to hold the leg-flap perpendicular when the bench top is dropped to working position. Use a heavy folding hasp and padlock to secure the bench in closed position. A door latch may also be attached from the side.

For many do-it-yourselfers, the garage workshop offers an ideal solution, particularly if your projects are large and are used out of doors. This is the handiest place for delivery and storage of lumber and materials. Moreover, in this setting you can pursue your hobby without getting in the way of household activities. And since it is easy to move the car out into the yard during working hours, there is plenty of space. Of course, there are many other places in and about the home where the fold-up workbench may be used with equal convenience.

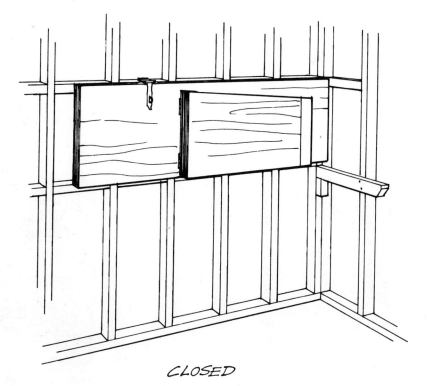

CLOSED

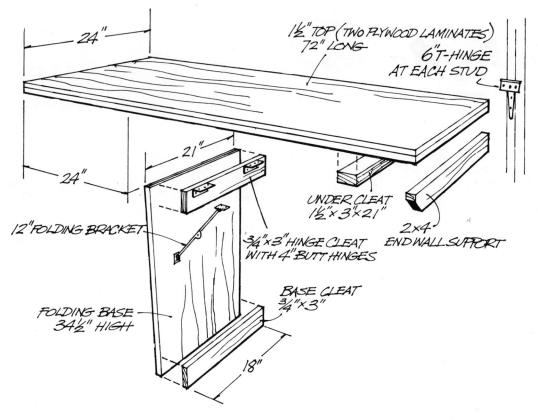

24"

1½" TOP (TWO PLYWOOD LAMINATES)
72" LONG

6" T-HINGE
AT EACH STUD

24"

21"

UNDER CLEAT
1½" x 3" x 21"

12" FOLDING BRACKET

¾" x 3" HINGE CLEAT
WITH 4" BUTT HINGES

2x4
END WALL SUPPORT

BASE CLEAT
¾" x 3"

FOLDING BASE
34½" HIGH

18"

21

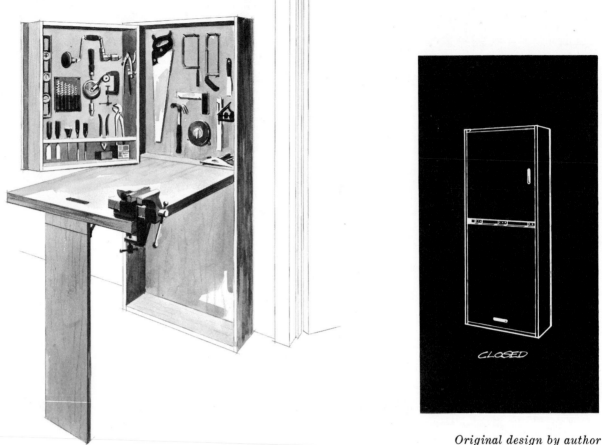

Original design by author

TUCKAWAY CRAFT SHOP

When space is extremely limited you can still enjoy your woodworking hobby, in a modest way, by building yourself a "tuckaway" shop. Tucked away, in shut position, this occupies little more then one square foot of floor space. Yet with the bench extended, it furnishes facilities for hammering, sawing, boring and all other maneuvers that go with woodworking.

Obviously, the tuckaway craft shop was not designed to serve as a base for heavy construction. But it should serve the needs of the handyman about the house. Such a shop also provides an organized, convenient place for keeping the normal household variety of tools in one compact location. Equipped with an electric hand drill (with its many attachments) and with a portable jig saw, the tuckaway may even be used to make small articles of furniture—such as some of the easier designs shown in this book.

This unit should be firmly attached to the wall with screws driven through the back and into the wall studding. As indicated on the working drawing, all hinges must be sturdy enough to support the top door when it is weighted with tools and supplies. While ordinarily this cabinet door would be opened *before* the bench counter is elevated, and closed *after* the counter is dropped into shut position, a roller glide can be attached to the under surface of the door to ease opening and closing regardless of bench-counter position.

You will find that the construction of this design is elementary. It actually requires no more than ordinary precision in sawing all parts square and to exact measurements. However, you must make certain that all these parts are firmly joined with finishing nails, screws and glue to form a strongly bonded unit. If your "tuckaway" is to be exposed to dampness use exterior- type plywood and waterproof glue.

22

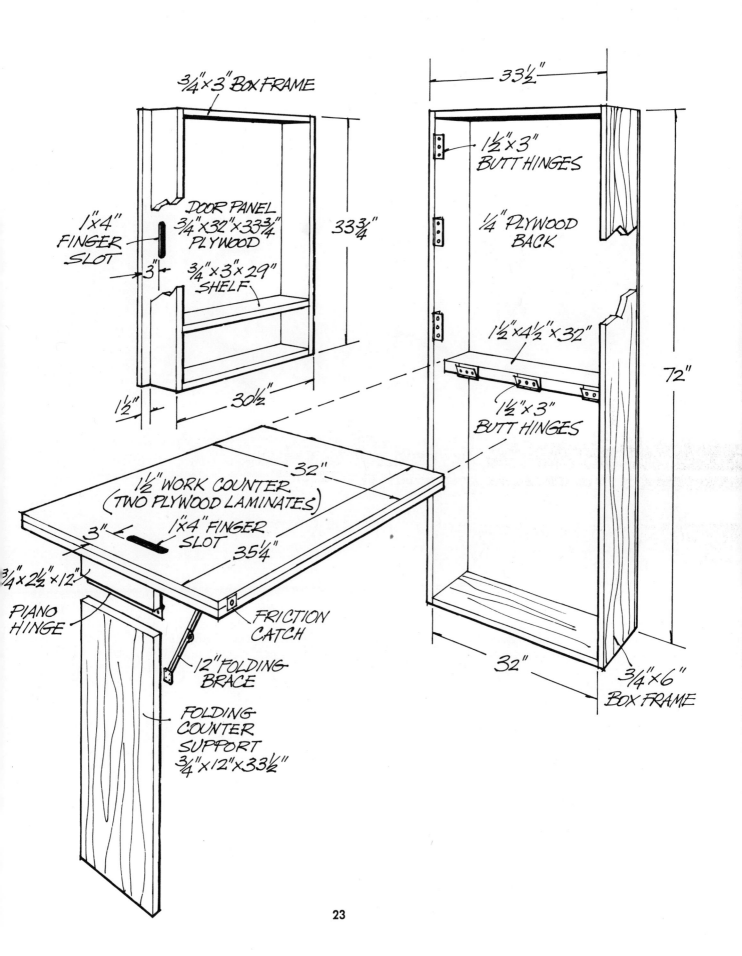

3/4"×3" BOX FRAME

DOOR PANEL
3/4"×32"×33 3/4"
PLYWOOD

1"×4"
FINGER
SLOT

3"

3/4"×3"×29"
SHELF

1 1/2"

30 1/2"

33 3/4"

33 1/2"

1 1/2"×3"
BUTT HINGES

1/4" PLYWOOD
BACK

1 1/2"×4 1/2"×32"

1 1/2"×3"
BUTT HINGES

72"

32"

3/4"×6"
BOX FRAME

32"

1 1/2" WORK COUNTER
(TWO PLYWOOD LAMINATES)

1"×4" FINGER
SLOT

3"

35 1/4"

3/4"×2 1/2"×12"

PIANO
HINGE

FRICTION
CATCH

12" FOLDING
BRACE

FOLDING
COUNTER
SUPPORT
3/4"×12"×33 1/2"

23

POWER TOOL CADDY

What is to be done with that fine collection of portable power tools you recently acquired? If you leave them on the bench top, their tails (cords) are bound to become tangled—and unless you are extra-cautious one or more may fall on the floor and get damaged. Of course, they can be kept on a shelf. But there, too, they get dusty and entangled as well as taking up space you want for other purposes.

So, why not give them their own special housing?

The portable power tool caddy, illustrated above, was especially designed to solve this problem. This mobile unit provides six separate compartments to accommodate a full assortment of power tools. Since the smaller tools, such as the electric drill and saber saw, can be bedded two to a compartment, this caddy should take care of your complete collection.

Many features of this design may interest the busy craftsman. For instance, the caddy can be moved about on 2″ casters. Thus, it can be rolled directly to the job. Since it has its own double electric outlet and plug-in cord, two power tools can be plugged in simultaneously—a feature of real convenience when work requires alternate use of two tools.

The overlapping top provides another working surface which will be welcome for clamping operations and to act as an extension for resting large panels of plywood on workbench or machine.

Beneath the top there are three handy drawers where your electric tool accessories are kept in orderly fashion.

Make your power tool caddy of a good grade of plywood. Use exterior-type if it is to be exposed to dampness or to outdoor climate.

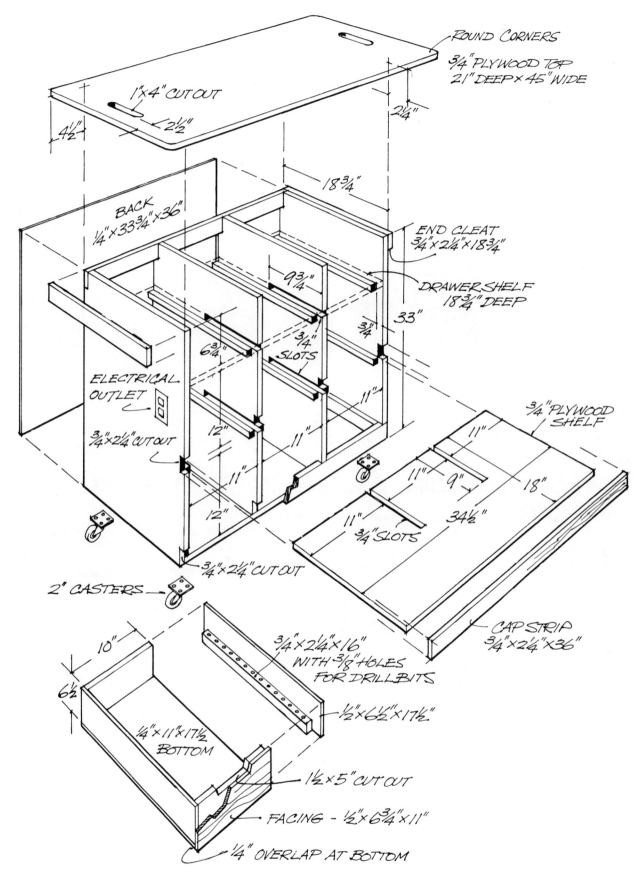

ROUND CORNERS

3/4" PLYWOOD TOP
21" DEEP × 45" WIDE

1"×4" CUT OUT

2 1/2"

4 1/2"

2 1/4"

18 3/4"

BACK
1/4" × 33 3/4" × 36"

END CLEAT
3/4" × 2 1/4" × 18 3/4"

DRAWER SHELF
18 3/4" DEEP

9 3/4"

3/4"

33"

6 3/4"

3/4"
SLOTS

ELECTRICAL
OUTLET

12"

11"

11"

11"

3/4" × 2 1/4" CUT OUT

12"

11"

3/4" PLYWOOD
SHELF

11"

11"

9"

18"

11"

34 1/2"

3/4" SLOTS

3/4" × 2 1/4" CUT OUT

2" CASTERS

CAP STRIP
3/4" × 2 1/4" × 36"

10"

3/4" × 2 1/4" × 16"
WITH 3/8" HOLES
FOR DRILL BITS

6 1/2"

1/2" × 6 1/2" × 17 1/2"

1/4" × 11" × 17 1/2"
BOTTOM

1 1/2" × 5" CUT OUT

FACING — 1/2" × 6 3/4" × 11"

1/4" OVERLAP AT BOTTOM

25

ACCESSORIES:
SAWHORSE PLATFORM AND SCRAPWOOD WAGON

Horses you will need; sturdy sawhorses to support your plywood panels during sawing operations. What easier way to come by horses than to construct the plywood pair illustrated above? These are of rudimentary notch-to-gether—knock-apart construction. They are as simple to make as cardboard cutouts. Yet they are sturdy and serviceable. Since they are easily assembled, and disassembled, with cross-lapped notches, they can be stored flat and placed out of the way when not in use.

A unique feature of this plywood team is its adaptability to be yoked together with a notched stringer. This provides a proper platform for a plywood panel measuring four feet by eight feet. If you should decide on projects which will involve working with prefinished plywood—such as the paneling shown on page 168—you can easily pad the top edges of your horses and their yoke to avoid surface damage.

Make your team of horses of ⅝" or ¾" plywood. Use exterior-type if you intend to use them outdoors. If you have power tools for this job, you can cut out the four legs in duplicate operations and notch all parts with only a few additional saw cuts. Observe that it is only with plywood that you can effectively employ this notched knock-apart construction without splitting the parts.

But after you have cut your horses, what are you going to do with that leftover remnant of plywood? As a suggestion, there is just about enough left to make that little scrapwood wagon.

The scrapwood wagon may prove to be even more fascinating to your youngsters than to the busy at-home carpenter. But this handy little item furnishes a neat bin for containing odds and ends and leftovers of wood. You will certainly have no trouble coaxing the small fry to trundle it away promptly. And they will appreciate your dividend of leftovers for building their space ships and astral artillery!

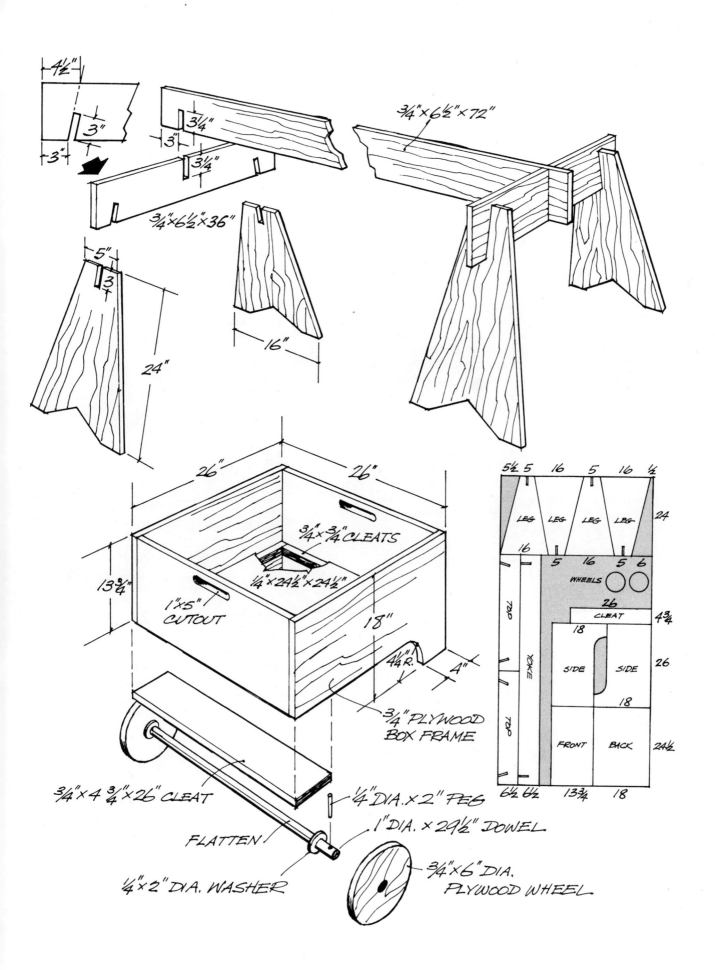

4½"

3"

3"

3¼"

3"

3¼"

¾"×6½"×36"

¾"×6½"×72"

5"

3"

24"

16"

26"

26"

¾"×¾" CLEATS

¼"×24½"×24½"

1"×5" CUTOUT

13¾"

18"

4¼" R.

4"

¾" PLYWOOD BOX FRAME

¾"×4¾"×26" CLEAT

FLATTEN

¼"×2" DIA. WASHER

¼"DIA.×2" PEG

1"DIA.×29½" DOWEL

¾"×6" DIA. PLYWOOD WHEEL

5½ 5   16   5   16   ½

LEG   LEG   LEG   LEG   24

16

TOP

5   16   5   6

WHEELS

YOKE

26

CLEAT   4¾

18

SIDE   SIDE   26

TOP   18

FRONT   BACK   24½

6½ 6½   13¾   18

HAND TOOLS

Every home has a hammer. But you will find yourself requisitioning considerably more hand tools as your interest grows in homeshop woodworking. In fact, you will soon note there is more than one type of hammer—and that a particular job usually demands an assortment of specialized tools.

Fortunately, there is no hurry about acquiring these. The hand tools shown here and on the next three pages represent an almost complete inventory. Some of these you may never need. But as you get on with your building projects you may find those trips to the hardware store increasing. For each tool has a habit of insinuating its own indispensable advantage for performing a particular job.

The hand tools shown on these pages are of the highest quality. In the long run, it pays to buy the best. The illustrations are intended to show and name what is available, and to act as an interpreter between you and your hardware dealer for identification of exactly what you want to buy.

Of course, additional tools of new design are constantly appearing on the market. But the basic items seem to remain. From those illustrated you should be able to locate the exact tools needed for the work you are doing.

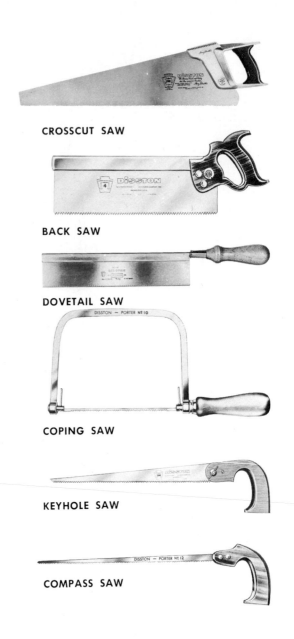

CROSSCUT SAW

BACK SAW

DOVETAIL SAW

COPING SAW

KEYHOLE SAW

COMPASS SAW

Saws courtesy of Disston Division, H. K. Porter Co.

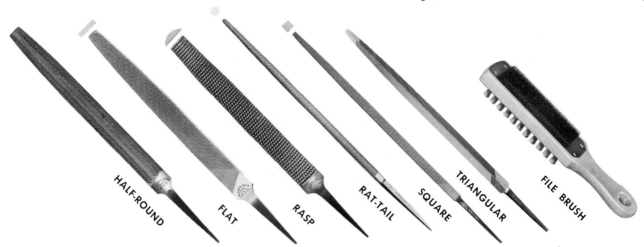

HALF-ROUND   FLAT   RASP   RAT-TAIL   SQUARE   TRIANGULAR   FILE BRUSH

Files courtesy of Nicholson File Company

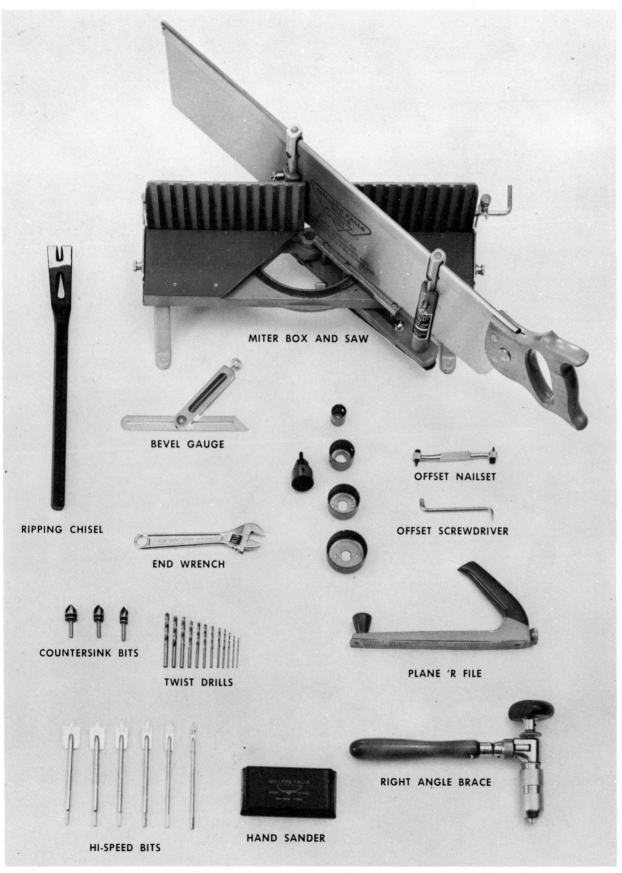

MITER BOX AND SAW

RIPPING CHISEL

BEVEL GAUGE

END WRENCH

OFFSET NAILSET

OFFSET SCREWDRIVER

COUNTERSINK BITS

TWIST DRILLS

PLANE 'R FILE

HI-SPEED BITS

HAND SANDER

RIGHT ANGLE BRACE

Hand tools courtesy of Millers Falls Company

HAND TOOLS

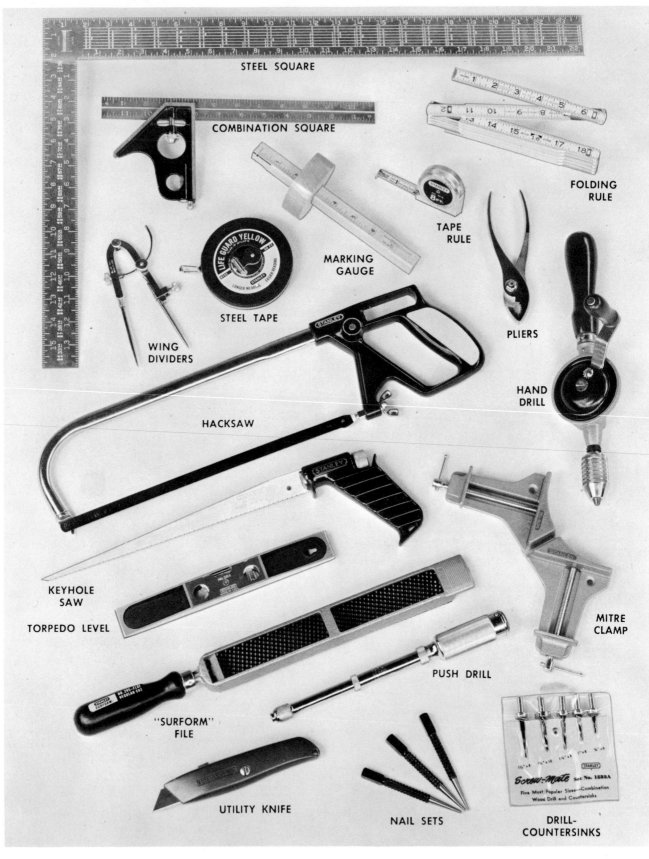

STEEL SQUARE

COMBINATION SQUARE

FOLDING RULE

TAPE RULE

MARKING GAUGE

STEEL TAPE

WING DIVIDERS

PLIERS

HAND DRILL

HACKSAW

KEYHOLE SAW

TORPEDO LEVEL

MITRE CLAMP

PUSH DRILL

"SURFORM" FILE

UTILITY KNIFE

NAIL SETS

DRILL-COUNTERSINKS

Hand tools courtesy of Stanley Tools

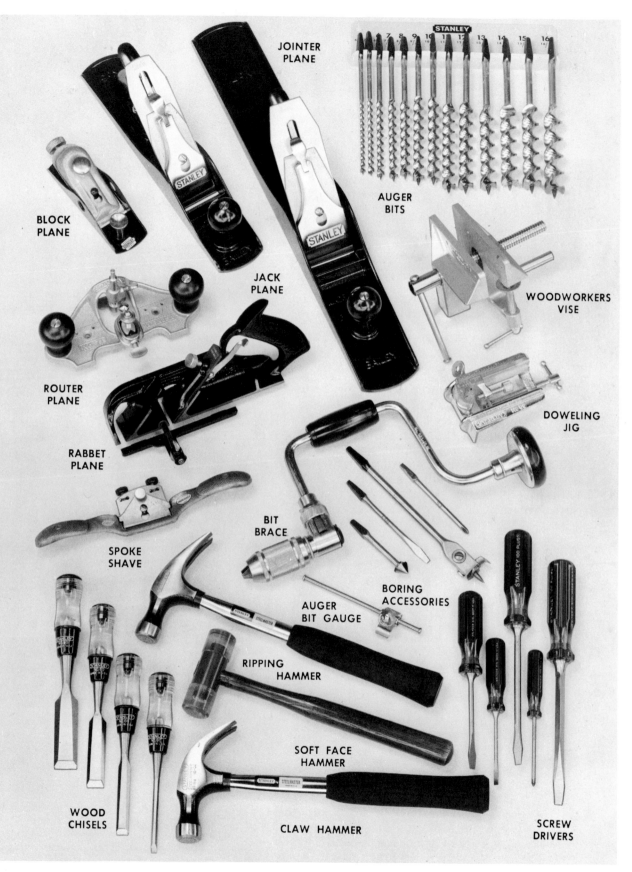

BLOCK PLANE

JOINTER PLANE

AUGER BITS

JACK PLANE

WOODWORKERS VISE

ROUTER PLANE

DOWELING JIG

RABBET PLANE

SPOKE SHAVE

BIT BRACE

BORING ACCESSORIES

AUGER BIT GAUGE

RIPPING HAMMER

SOFT FACE HAMMER

WOOD CHISELS

CLAW HAMMER

SCREW DRIVERS

Hand tools courtesy of Stanley Tools

PORTABLE POWER TOOLS

ORBITAL SANDER saves much labor when used for fine and finished sanding. Can be used with abrasives of various types and grades.

POWER UNIT is used primarily as a ⅜" drill but was designed to provide extra power for operating numerous attachments.

The portable electric power tools, shown here and on the facing page, contribute immensely to the speed and convenience of shop work. They are compact and can be carried to the job. The nine items shown are of top quality and represent the many functions of the various types and makes of portables shown in action on other pages of this book. Each power tool has its purpose—and performs it with ease and efficiency.

DRIVER-DRILL is designed to function as a power screwdriver but can be quickly converted to serve as an electric drill.

ROUTER makes fast work of dadoing, grooving and routing. With separate attachments it can be used as a shaper and power plane.

SABER SAW cuts curves and scrolls. Can be used to saw plywood parts to size and for "thrust cutting" from inside areas of plywood panel.

CIRCULAR SAW facilitates job of sawing parts to size, especially when extreme lengths of material must be ripped. Safety guard protects operator.

SUPER SAW operates with reciprocating action for heavy-duty sawing of both curved and straight work. Self-starting blade action makes it particularly useful for making inside cutouts.

BELT SANDER is almost indispensible for heavy-duty sanding, surfacing and shaping. Many types and grades of abrasive belts are available for particular job requirements.

ELECTRIC DRILL is probably the most popular and widely used tool in the average shop. This model is shockproof and provides ample power to operate variety of attachments shown on following pages.

Portable power tools courtesy of Millers Falls Company

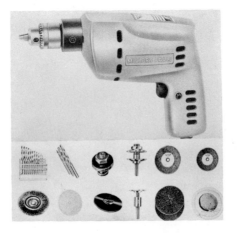

Electric Drill with standard attachments

Saber Saw

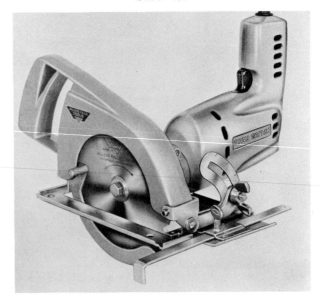

Circular Saw

Orbital Sander

THE VERSATILE ELECTRIC DRILL

Popularity of the electric drill comes not only from its fast ability at drilling holes, but because the better makes can perform a variety of other operations with their many attachments. This does not mean that the drill is designed to put the single-purpose portables out of business. Indeed, the average electric drill could not stand the strain of continuous and heavy-duty operations.

But for light-duty shop work, where a variety of power tools are needed for limited use, a good electric drill equipped with the attachments shown on these pages, can be of great service.

Be cautioned at the start, however, to pick a good standard make of drill. Unfortunately, there are inferior ones on the market—and the attachments that go with them are more of the novelty and "gadgety" sort than the high-quality tools shown here.

The shockproof electric drill illustrated on these pages is rated at 2.7 amps—enough to power its full complement of attachments. It is double-insulated against electric shock and with its shatterproof nylon housing it weighs about 20 percent less than the average drill.

But even the best electric drills should not be used for heavy sawing operations lasting for hours at a time. For such work the more highly rated power unit shown on page 32 should be used to drive these attachments. For many lighter jobs around the house, however, you will welcome this versatile tool and the many practical attachments that go with it.

Disk Sander

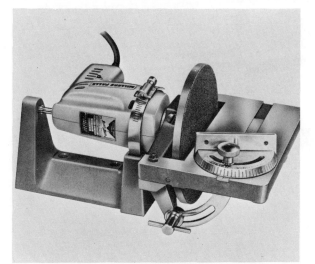

Bench Sander

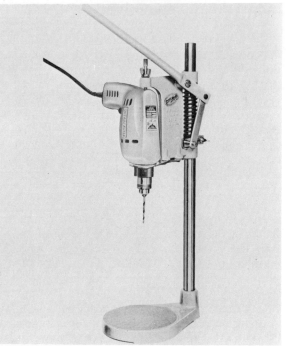

Bench Buffer

Bench Grinder

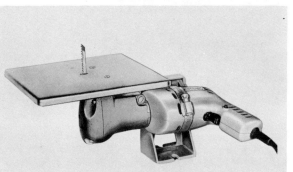

Table Jig Saw

Drill Press

Shockproof drill and attachments courtesy of Millers Falls Company

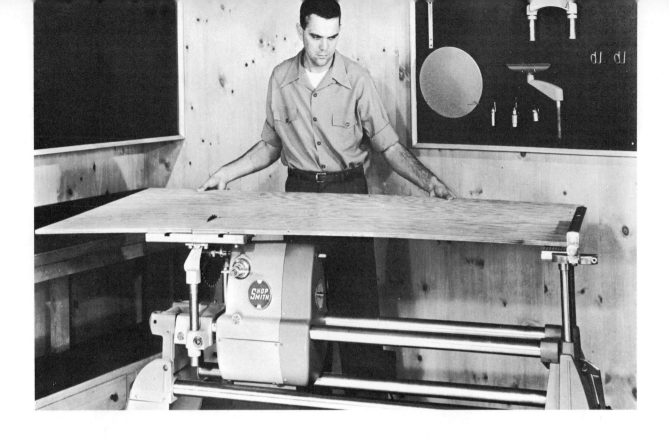

COMBINATION WOODWORKING MACHINES

Shopsmith Combination

Certainly the most versatile and efficient of the combination machines is the popular Shopsmith. This multipurpose machine is ingeniously engineered to do all manner of woodworking jobs. It functions just as efficiently for one operation as another. Moreover, its many attachments are designed for rapid change, and, as shown in the above illustration, these various attachments may be stored compactly on a wall rack or in a cabinet handy to the machine.

The manufacturers of Shopsmith are not bragging when they say their machine can be used ". . . from start to finish." For it provides complete operational facilities for crosscutting, ripping, routing, shaping, dadoing, grooving, mortising, tenoning, band sawing, jig sawing, drill pressing, drum, disk, and belt sanding, jointing and turning. It also has a compressor-sprayer attachment to take care of finishing.

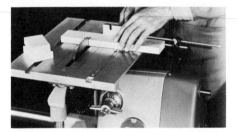

Combination of circular saw and jointer is shown above. As a 9" circular saw the blade is quickly adjusted to cut thin or heavy stock. Flexibility of table movement provides for wide variety of sawing operations.

All Shopsmith photos courtesy of Magna American Corporation

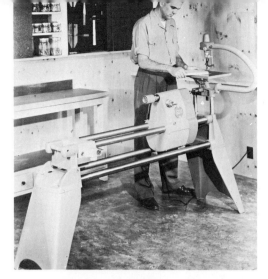

Jig saw attachment is quickly connected to power spindle with twin-tube nylon coupler.

Disk sander mounts directly to motor spindle. Table and cross-feed are adjusted for precision sanding.

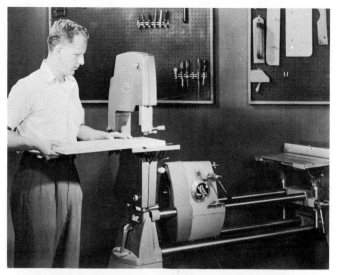

Band saw is interchangeable with other attachments. Speed of motor may be adjusted to exact cutting requirements.

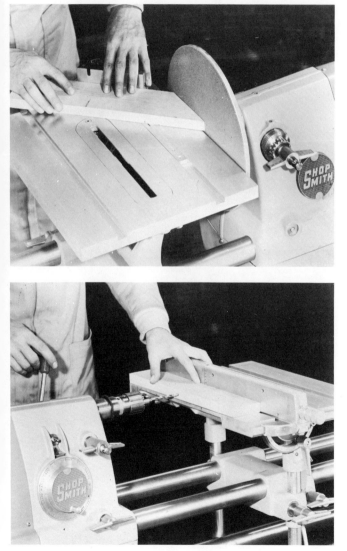

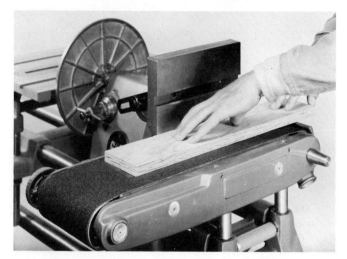

Belt sander also provides back rest to guarantee accuracy of work. Combination of disk and belt sander is possible, with attachments operating at opposite ends of power spindle.

Vertical drill press is set up by releasing headrest lock and lifting top bars. Hinged on end pivots, bars are then locked in vertical position.

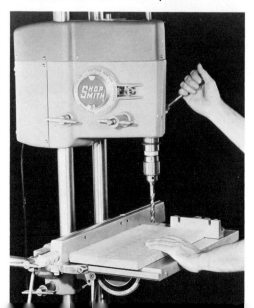

Horizontal drill press operates off power head with thrust lever. Shopsmith's selector dial is set to proper motor speed for each cutting and sanding operation.

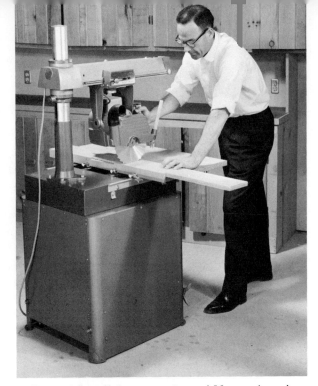

Sawsmith radial saw courtesy of Magna American Corporation

Radial Saws

Going hand in hand with Shopsmith is the Sawsmith Radial Saw illustrated above. In fact, attachments which fit Shopsmith are interchangeable with Sawsmith. And both machines feature a selector dial, which adjusts the motor to exact speed of each cutting operation.

Radial saws like the Sawsmith and the De-Walt Power Shop, shown on the facing page, are particularly well adapted to homeshop activity. The work is placed on a broad cutting counter with the blade moving into contact from above. Sawing from above—as you can observe when you use a hand saw—gives much better visual control for cutting to the line.

There are other advantages, too. With blades or cutters attached to an adjustable head, which may be elevated or lowered and moved to practically any cutting position, the choice of cuts is almost limitless. Such processes as ripping, dadoing, grooving, lapping, tenoning, mitering, beveling, routing, rabbeting, shaping, surfacing and sanding, can be performed with only a few simple adjustments of the cutter head. For many other operations such as slotting and cutting blind dados and grooves, you can lower the saw blade down upon the work.

With its many attachments for band sawing, saber sawing, grinding, turning, polishing, jointing, belt-disk-drum sanding, drilling—and even compressor finishing—a good radial saw responds to most requirements of the average shop.

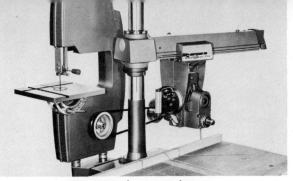

Bandsaw attachment

Belt sander attachment

Jointer attachment

Compressor-sprayer attachment

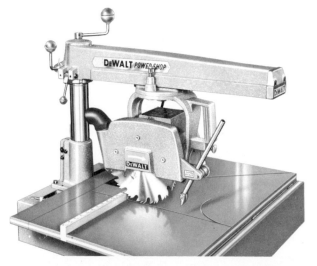

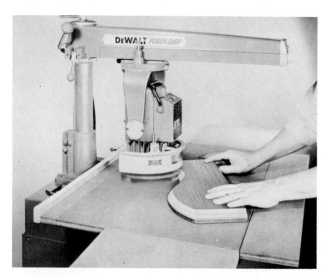

DeWalt Power Shop courtesy of DeWalt, Inc.

DeWalt radial saw comes as compact unit for mounting on bench or stand.

Shaper attachment is used for curved and straight edges. Other cutters are available for rabbeting and grooving.

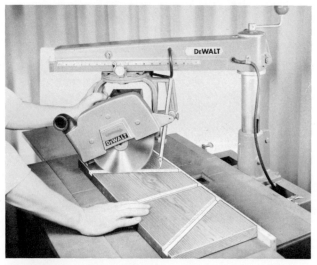

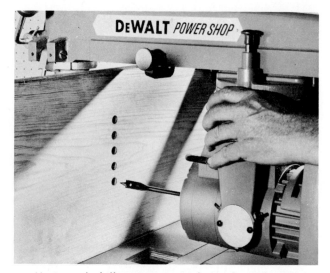

Radial saw is particularly adept at cutting square and angle dados.

Horizontal drilling is accurately performed with drill chuck attached to motor spindle.

Jig saw attachment cuts curved and circular shapes. Saw pierces work for making inside cutouts.

With radial saw blade tilted parallel to bench top, full panel of plywood slides along foot track for accurate sawing.

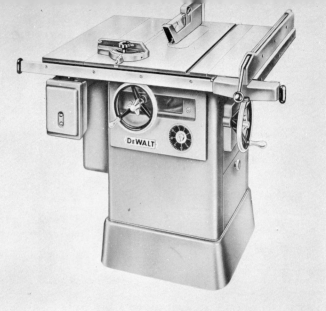

This 10" circular saw is of heavy-duty, precision manufacture. It is designed to meet the needs of experienced craftsmen engaged in extensive production building and remodeling.

The 12" band saw performs its individual chores of curved, straight, and angled sawing. It can saw solid stock or duplicate parts to a depth of 6¼". Table may be tilted to 45° for sawing miters.

SINGLE-PURPOSE WOODWORKING MACHINES

Because they stand for independent service and are constantly ready to perform their own specific operations, single-purpose power tools remain popular in many shops.

The machines illustrated represented a trend toward manufacture of lighter and more efficient power tools. While they perform with precision all the operations of their earlier counterparts, they have eliminated the massive bulk and weight which made the oldtime models suitable only for use in industrial production. These new machines are less expensive, too—and this qualifies their acceptance in both home and school shops.

In a shop that is equipped with a number of singe-purpose woodworking machines, the craftsman simply moves his work from station to station, performing each separate operation at the appropriate machine as he goes along. However, many craftsmen prefer to settle for a particular machine, or pair of machines, designed to perform the largest percentage of the woodworking operations which they are contemplating. These machines, supplemented with portable power tools, provide a practical home-shop setup.

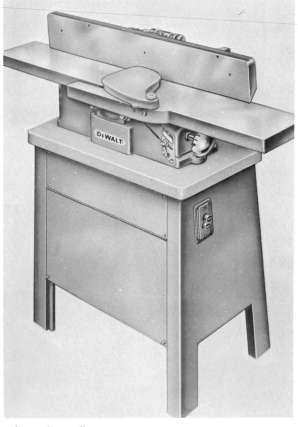

Independent 6" jointer, on its own stand, offers convenience for squaring edges of work after sawing. It can also be used for rabbeting, shaping, and beveling. Fence tilts, in both directions, to angle of 45°

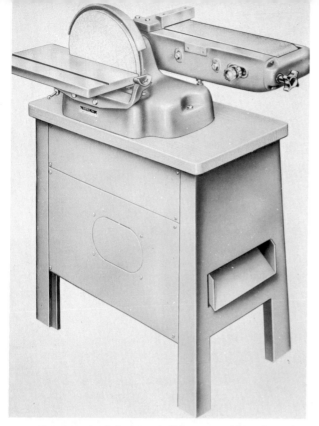

Sanders, both belt and disk, are combined on this sturdy sanding machine. This offers the advantage of complete edge and surface sanding in two consecutive operations.

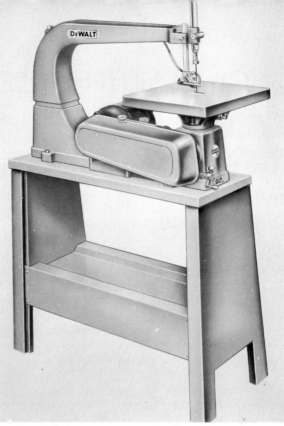

Jig saw, with throat capacity of 24", cuts to center of a plywood panel and allows plenty of scope for both inside and outside sawing of curved, scrolled, and circular sections of work.

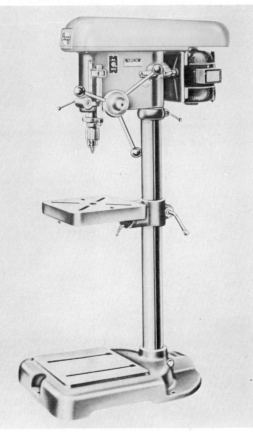

Floor model 15" drill press provides precision boring and shaping. A rugged, heavy-duty machine, this model comes with special chucks to hold sanding, buffing and polishing attachments.

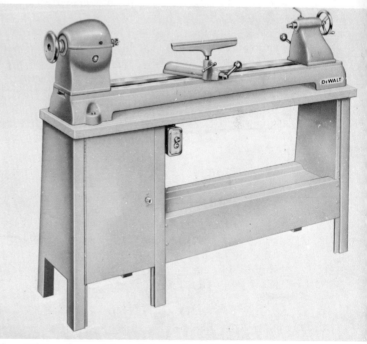

Lathe: While plywood is not too adaptable for turning, the 12" lathe may come in handy for shaping related parts of solid wood.

Photos courtesy of DeWalt, Inc.

SHOP MAINTENANCE

Like any other functional thing, the home workshop requires constant maintenance. This starts with the simple practice of keeping things picked up—with everything in its place and a place for everything. Otherwise much valuable time can be wasted searching for a lost tool which is probably hiding under the sawdust and scrap of a cluttered workbench.

Substantial assistance at clean up time can be had from a tank-type shop vacuum cleaner. It will make short work of removing sawdust and shavings from benches, tools, and machines as well as the floor areas. Furthermore it performs its job without stirring up too much dust —an important consideration when you have just finished and painted your projects.

However, despite the very best of care, tools and shop equipment are bound to become worn and damaged. The ends of screwdrivers may become chipped or misshapen, chisels broken, a saw may fall off the bench causing a cracked handle, and working parts of vises and machines may bind and balk. It is usually possible to regrind chipped points of screwdrivers and broken ends of chisels to their original shape. Loose hammer and mallet heads should be tightened promptly. A bit of oil applied regularly works wonders with balky machined parts. Tools that have become rusted may be brightened by rubbing them with steel wool, followed by wiping with anti-rust oil.

Tool Sharpening

All cutting tools should be re-sharpened from time to time. Chisels, plane blades, saws, drill and auger bits and all other types of cutters should be examined at regular intervals and their condition checked.

One of the first essentials in a well-equipped shop is a hand or power grindstone. As tools are used they are bound to become worn, nicked, and damaged. In order to recondition them, the edges must be ground.

Together with the grindstone, you should have one or more oilstones. These may be pur-

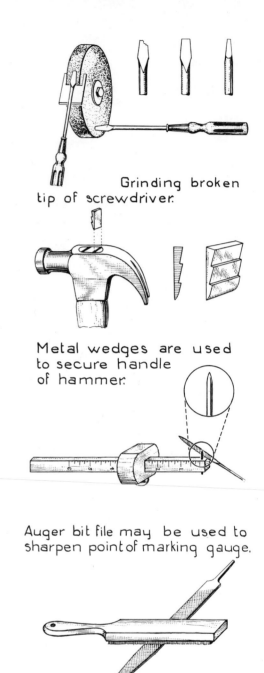

Grinding broken tip of screwdriver.

Metal wedges are used to secure handle of hammer.

Auger bit file may be used to sharpen point of marking gauge.

File should be cleaned with file card.

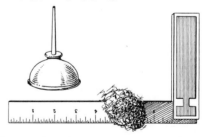

Fine steel wool and oil are used to keep tools "bright."

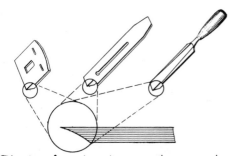

Blade of spoke shave, plane, and chisel, showing "beveled" cutting edges.

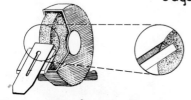

Tool rest of grinder is adjusted to proper bevel.

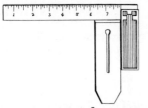

Edge is checked for squareness.

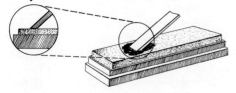

Circular motion is used to "whet" bevel on oilstone. NOTE: Blade is held on <u>exact</u> slant of bevel.

Straight edge of blade must be kept <u>flat</u> on oilstone.

Leather strop is used for final sharpening.

The grinder-hone is bench mounted for tool sharpening. This convenient combination of grindstone and revolving hone (top), with adjustable tool rests, is ideal for keeping tools in keen cutting shape. *Courtesy of DeWalt, Inc.*

chased in convenient boxes which serve as holders during the sharpening process. They are made with two surfaces: the coarser surface for sharpening and the finer for honing.

Nor does the sharpening equipment stop at this point. The skilled craftsman will insist that his cutting tools be every bit as sharp as a razor. To bring them to this degree of sharpness, he not only hones the cutting edge, but also strops it in razor fashion on a leather strop.

Common shop tools such as chisels, plane blades and spokeshave blades are all sharpened in just about the same manner. These tools have a single, beveled cutting edge and the actual sharpening is performed mostly on this edge alone. Remember always to keep the same degree of bevel along the cutting edge when the tool is being sharpened.

Unless the beveled edge of a blade is badly nicked, or rounded from too frequent rubbing on the oilstone, it may be resharpened without grinding. Spreading a few drops of thin oil on the surface of the oilstone and hold the blade on the proper slant so that it rests on its cutting bevel. Then rub backward and forward or with a circular motion on the surface of the stone. The straight (unbeveled) side of the blade is then rubbed *flat* on the surface of the stone.

However, if the cutting edge happens to be worn or damaged, it will be necessary to regrind it. Hold the blade against the revolving grindstone on the correct beveled slant and slide it back and forth against the wheel. For this operation most makes of grindstones have an adjustable tool rest which may be set at the correct bevel slant, and a flat, revolving hone wheel for finishing off the sharpening process.

How to Sharpen Drill Bits

Bits used with the various types of drills are sharpened at the cutting point. The push drill bit, which must move in reverse directions while it actually drills only on the drive stroke, is fluted on both sides. At the slightly pointed tip, each flute forms the edge of a cutter. On the other hand, the drill bit used with the hand automatic and machine drill revolves in a single direction. Its two spiraled cutting flanges form individual cutters at the slightly sloping point.

When sharpening these bits, it should be kept in mind that each type is shaped at the point with two cutters, and that each cutter is slightly slanted to provide a sharp cutting edge. Both types may be sharpened on a grinding wheel. A sharpening stone, or oilstone, may be used to improve their condition.

The sharpening of an auger bit is really not a difficult job. In fact, it only requires careful use of a small bit file in reshaping the cutting parts.

Electric drill, with grinder attachment, offers inexpensive method of keeping tools sharp. *Courtesy of Millers Falls Company.*

The cutting, or boring parts of an auger bit are the *nibs* and the *lips*. The lips consist of two cutting knives which terminate the spiral above the pointed tip, or tang, of the bit. Each lip should be filed to an even slanted cutting edge on the upper sides. The nibs which project on both sides, on the rim of the spiral, serve to cut the outside circumference of the hole. When sharpening, they should be filed from the inside. If a burr appears outside of the nibs, it should be filed off flush to the circumference of the bit.

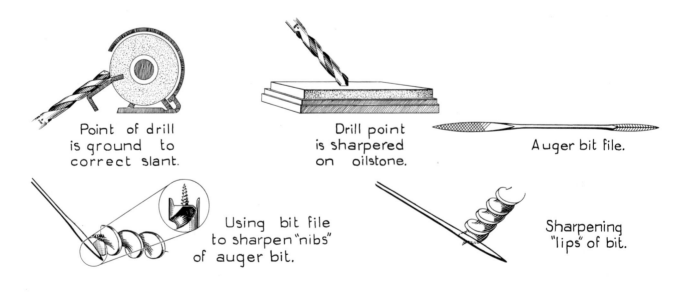

Point of drill is ground to correct slant.

Drill point is sharpered on oilstone.

Auger bit file.

Using bit file to sharpen "nibs" of auger bit.

Sharpening "lips" of bit.

3

WORKING WITH PLYWOOD — BASIC PROCESSES

PLYWOOD NOMENCLATURE

CENTERS—Inner plies running parallel to the panel face.

CHECK—A partial separation of veneer fibers, usually small and shallow, running parallel to the grain of the wood.

CORE GAPS—Rectangular or square openings, extending through or partially through a panel, which occur where the adjacent inner ply veneers have separated at an edge joint.

CORES—Inner plies running perpendicular to the panel face.

DEFECTS, OPEN—Open checks, open splits, open joints, open cracks, loose knots, and other defects interrupting the smooth continuity of the panel surface.

EDGE SPLITS—Wedge-shaped openings in the inner plies caused by splitting of the veneer during handling or pressing.

EXTERIOR TYPE—Refers to the type of plywood intended for outdoor or marine uses. This type is bonded with adhesives, affording the ultimate in water and moisture resistance. There are several grades within this type.

INTERIOR TYPE—Refers to the type of plywood intended for inside uses and for construction applications where subjected to occasional wetting or deposits of moisture.

LAP—A condition where the veneers are so misplaced that one piece overlaps the other rather than making a smooth butt joint.

PATCHES—Insertions of sound wood in veneers or panels for replacing defects. Boat patches shall be oval-shaped but sides shall taper each direction to a point or to a small rounded end; in "A" faces the rounded ends shall have a radius not exceeding $\frac{1}{8}$". Router patches shall have parallel sides and rounded ends. Sled patches shall be rectangular with feathered ends.

PLUGS—Sound wood of various shapes including, among others, circular, dog-bone, and leaf shapes, for replacing defective portions. Plugs usually are held in veneer by friction only until veneers are bonded into plywood; also synthetic plugs of fiber and resin aggregate used to fill openings and provide a smooth, level, durable surface.

SHIM—A long, narrow repair not more than $\frac{3}{16}$" wide.

SHOP-CUTTING PANEL—Panels which have been rejected as not conforming to the grade requirements of standard grades covered in this Commercial Standard. Identification of these panels shall include the notation, "For remanufacture only." Blistered panels are not considered as being within the category covered by this stamp.

SOLID CORE—Inner ply construction of solid B-Veneer pieces. No special limitation on core gaps is implied.

SPLIT—Complete separation of veneer fibers parallel to grain, caused chiefly by manufacturing process or handling.

TORN GRAIN—A marked leafing or separation on veneer surface between spring and summer wood.

TOUCH-SANDING—A sizing operation consisting of a light sanding in a standard sander. Sander skips are admissible. Where rough panels are specified to be "touch-sanded," the thickness tolerance of each piece shall be plus or minus $\frac{1}{32}$" (0.0312) of the nominal thickness specified.

VENEER—Thin sheets of wood.

WHITE POCKET—

LIGHT WHITE POCKET—Advanced beyond incipient or stain stage to point where pockets are present and plainly visible, mostly small and filled with white cellulose; generally distributed with no heavy concentrations; pockets for the most part separate and distinct; few to no holes through the veneer.

HEAVY WHITE POCKET—May contain a great number of pockets, in dense concentrations, running together and at times appearing continuous; holes may extend through the veneer but wood between pockets appears firm. At any cross section extending across the width of the affected area, sufficient wood fiber shall be present to develop not less than 40 percent of the strength of clear veneer. Brown cubicle and similar forms of decay which have caused the wood to crumble are prohibited.

60/60, 65/65, 93/93, ETC.—Such optional symbols may be used by manufacturers of overlaid plywood to indicate the weight of the overlay in pounds per 1,000 square feet.

How to Order Plywood

When ordering plywood, the first thing to consider is the exact use to which it is to be put. As already observed, while there are only two *types* of plywood, there are many *grades*. So the first consideration is whether the project you are making is to be used indoors or outdoors. Indoors, you can use interior-type plywood while outdoors you will need waterproof protection of the exterior-type.

Even for some interior construction it may be wiser in the long run to choose exterior-type plywood. For articles used in extremely damp cellars or on porch areas exposed to outdoor rain and moisture, there is obviously a margin of safety in selecting the exterior-type panel. But where work is fully protected, interior-type plywood is adequate. In fact, most interior plywoods are now bonded with moisture-resistant adhesives, which means that it takes long periods of exposure to dampness to damage them.

But the choice of a grade of plywood is not so simple. As listed and explained on pages 8-10, there are numerous grades of plywood and each grade has its own applications.

Fortunately, identification of grades of both softwood and hardwood plywoods is made easy by the use of stampings which appear on the surface and edge of standard panels. You can order what you want, with assurance you are getting exactly what you ordered, simply by checking the stamped identification marks on the panel, as illustrated at the right.

Of course, there is a wide variety of different kinds of plywood. Most of these appear in this book. All are identified and trade marked. Most dealers stock what you want or will order it for you.

It is customary to order plywood in standard 4' by 8' panels. Larger panels can be obtained on special order. But dealers would prefer not to cut into a standard size panel to sell you smaller pieces.

Economy can be effected on your plywood order by planning your work so as to make maximum use of the full panel. This is discussed and illustrated on following pages. You will observe that even if a particular project does not require a full panel, you can usually find uses for the remnants. Plywood has a habit of getting used up!

HARDWOOD PLYWOOD LABELS

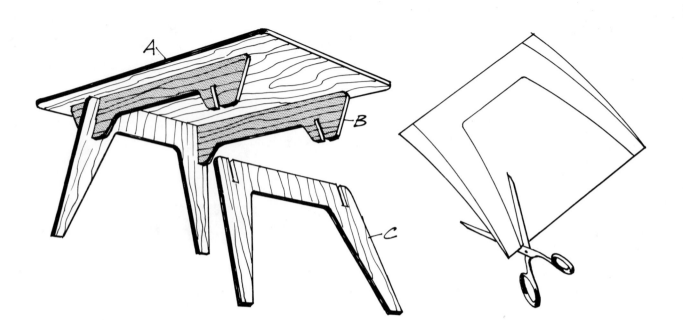

HOW TO LAY OUT
YOUR WORK

Economy should keynote the orderly procedure of laying out your work. It is easy to waste plywood if you do not establish a strategic scheme of layout.

For laying out your project parts on a full panel, place the plywood on horses such as those shown (with working drawings) on page 26. Horses of this type are yoked together with a central beam which gives mid-support to the panel. This support prevents thin panels from drooping and wiggling during laying out and sawing operations.

When many small parts must be cut from a panel it helps to make paper or cardboard patterns of the individual parts. Move these patterns about on the panel to determine the most economical cutting layout. As a rule of thumb, it is advantageous to retain as much of the length

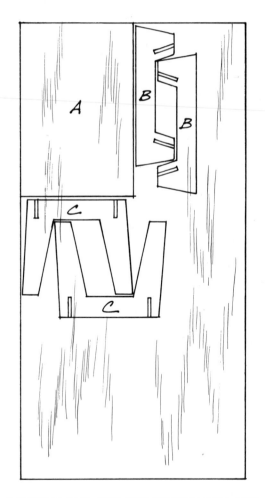

PATTERNS LAID OUT FOR ECONOMICAL CUT

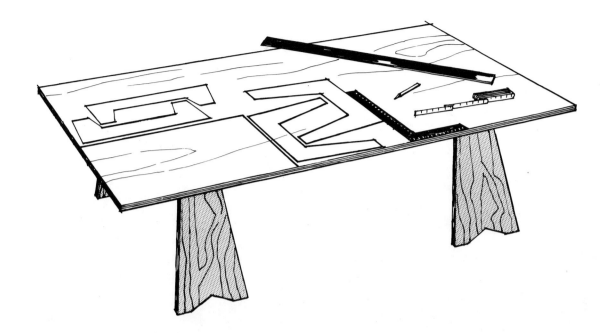

of the panel as possible. Cross-grained widths can always be edge-joined to form a section. But until somebody invents a "wood stretcher" it will remain difficult to obtain matched lengths of continuous graining.

Always allow sawing space between your marked parts. Enough edge margin should remain after sawing to allow for easy trimming and smoothing to exact size.

Go over your pattern marks with a framing square and straightedge to insure accuracy of marking. Square out sections of parts which may be roughed out in preliminary sawing operations. Obviously, it is easier to work with smaller sections of parts rather than to cut each part out, individually, from the full-size panel.

When a quantity of small, matching parts are to be cut from the panel, try to lay them out in reciprocating patterns, as illustrated at the right. After they have been roughed out, squares of sections can be stacked together for duplicate sawing.

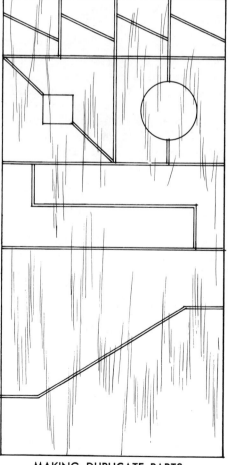

MAKING DUPLICATE PARTS

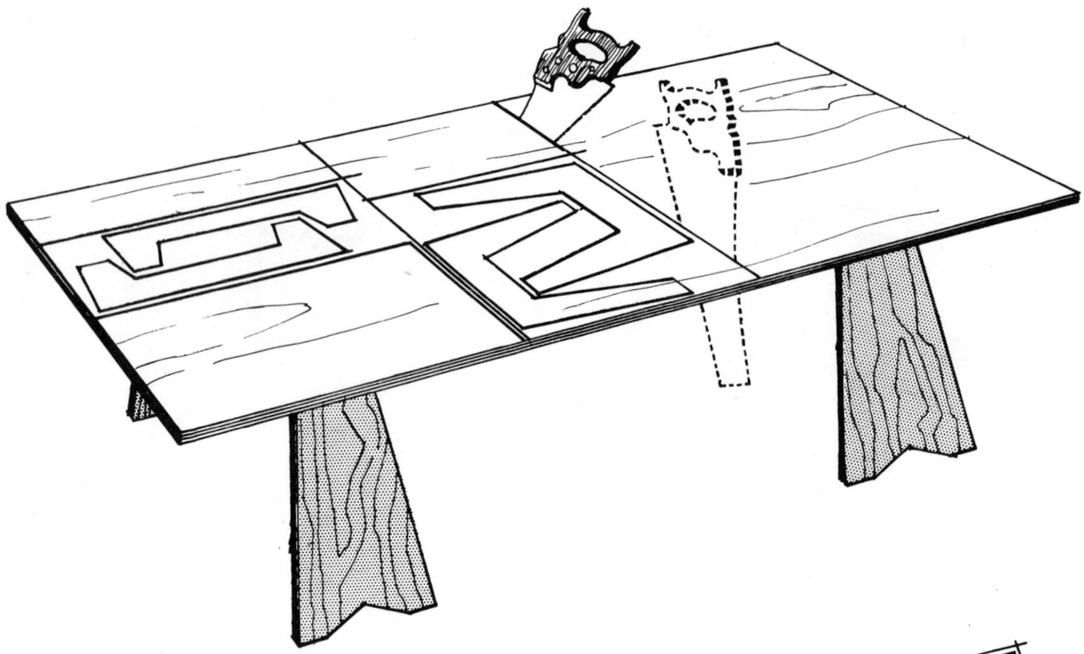

SQUARING AND
SAWING TO SIZE

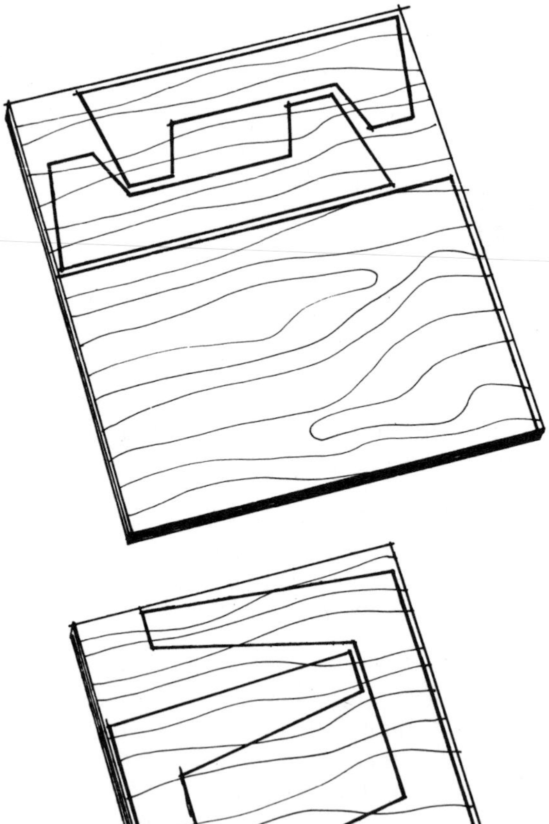

With your plywood panel resting on horses, or on a firm working surface, and with all parts marked, you are ready to go ahead with the preliminary roughing out process. As already noted, it's easier to get at your parts (especially for eventual power sawing operations) if they are first removed from the large panel in squared sections, as illustrated at right.

Use a sharp, fine-tooth crosscut saw to separate sections of parts from the panel. As illustrated above, if you are cutting off a section of plywood near the mid-area of the panel, you will find it easier to saw half way from each side. As you approach the end of the saw cut, clamp the separating edges, or support them so that the parting edges will not splinter on final saw thrust.

As illustrated on the facing page, the sawing process can be speedily performed with a number of different power tools. The one most commonly used is the portable circular saw. With a sharp crosscutting or combination blade set to proper depth of cut, the circular saw does a fast and clean job of sawing plywood. Since both circular saw and saber saw cut on the up stroke they tend to splinter edges of the top surface on which they operate. Hence, with these tools, it is a wise precaution to saw your parts from the off side (or back surface).

50

Circular saw, with table extensions, crosscuts full-size plywood panel. *Courtesy of DeWalt, Inc.*

Portable circular saw, with sharp crosscutting or combination blade, can be used to advantage for roughing out large sections of plywood. *Courtesy of American Plywood Association.*

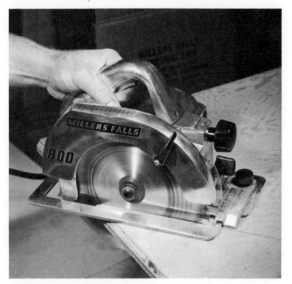

Because it is maneuverable and can saw at any angle, as illustrated above, the portable circular saw is an ideal tool for working with plywood. *Courtesy of Millers Falls Company.*

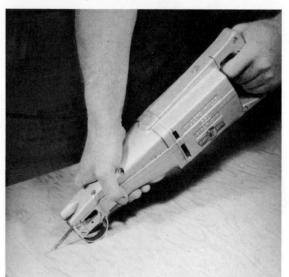

Reciprocating saw offers advantage of being able to saw curves and scrolls. It can also make "thrust cuts" to remove inside portions of panel. *Courtesy of Millers Falls Company.*

Saber saw is useful for roughing out plywood parts. It saws on up stroke and should be used from *back* surface of panel to protect veneer of facing surface. *Courtesy of Black & Decker Co.*

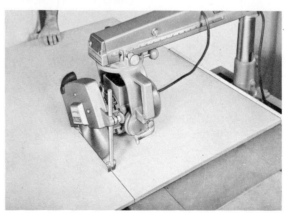

Radial saw can be adjusted to saw large sections of plywood. Broad counter surface can be extended with horses to support panel. *Courtesy of DeWalt, Inc.*

SQUARING AND SMOOTHING EDGES

When your plywood parts have been roughed out to approximate working sizes, the next job is to bring them down to exact fitting trim. You start by squaring the edges to the lines originally marked. When you do this with hand tools, be sure the work is firmly held with vise and clamps, as illustrated above.

There is one important matter which must be kept in mind when you are planing plywood. Unlike solid lumber, which has grain running only in *one* direction—and can be planed in that direction without fear of splitting—plywood has grain running in *both* directions and is vulnerable to corner splintering of *inner-plys* if planed entirely across in the direction of its surface grain.

Of course, an extremely sharp plane blade, set to shallow cut, helps to solve this problem.

But the best idea is to plane *in* from each corner rather than letting the plane travel entirely across the end.

After you have planed to the line and tested the edges for straightness and squareness, do the final smoothing with a file and sandpaper. To keep the edges sharp and square, wrap the sandpaper on a small block.

With power tools, the job of squaring and smoothing plywood edges is somewhat simplified. But caution must be observed when using a Jointer, Router or Power Plane. Again, there is that matter of alternating grain to be considered. Unless you saw the plywood part oversize, allowing an extra margin on the end to withstand splintering damage, do not run it entirely across cutters of the jointer, in one direction. Instead, as it nears the corner, lift the piece and run alternately from the opposite direction. The same procedure should be followed with the power plane and router. It is safe to work in from the corner but never across it in an out direction.

SQUARING AND SMOOTHING EDGES
WITH POWER TOOLS

Jointer squares plywood edges but requires some skill of operation to avoid wood splintering at corners. *Courtesy of DeWalt, Inc.*

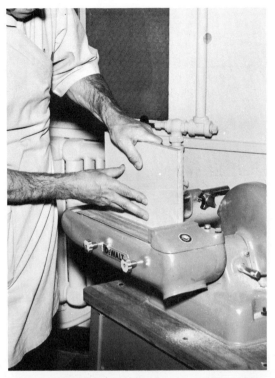

Belt sander serves ideally for smoothing edges. Backrest attachment assures accuracy. *Courtesy of DeWalt, Inc.*

Disk sander, with table set perpendicular to sanding surface, smooths and squares plywood parts. *Courtesy of DeWalt, Inc.*

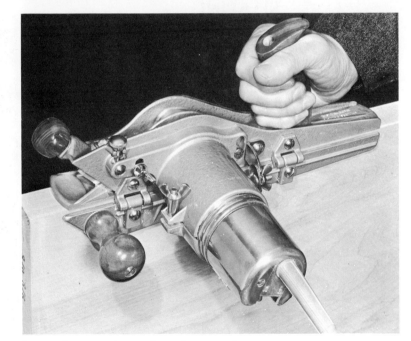

Power plane can be used to advantage for squaring edges. To avoid end splintering, cutter should not be allowed to cross corners. *Courtesy of Millers Falls Company.*

BEVEL   CHAMFER   QUARTER-ROUND   HALF-ROUND

EDGE SHAPING

Chamfering and Beveling

Often it is desirable to shape the edges of a plywood panel for functional or decorative effect. One of the most common practices is to *chamfer*, or cut away, part of the edge. Sometimes the terms chamfer and bevel are confused. The difference is that, unlike the chamfer, the bevel continues the slanted shape across the entire thickness of the edge.

In order to cut a sharp chamfer it is first necessary to mark lines with a pencil on both the surface and edge of the work. These lines indicate the margin of chamfer.

When a chamfer is being planed along a plywood edge, set the plane to a small cut and holding it on the exact angle, plane along evenly until the desired portion of the edge has been removed. The craftsman should try to keep the chamfer accurate by holding the plane firmly to avoid unevenness or rounding. It is important that the plane blade be perfectly sharp.

Block plane, with sharp blade set at shallow cut, can be used to advantage for chamfering and beveling. *Courtesy of American Plywood Association.*

54

EDGE SHAPING WITH POWER TOOLS

Unlike straight and square planing, the chamfering of plywood requires a special technique. The plane must be held in a paring position, as illustrated at left, to avoid splintering of inner plys. In order to avoid corner damage, it is well to work in from each corner rather than letting the plane cut all the way across. The small block plane is favored for chamfering, especially when a narrow plywood edge is to be planed.

Rounded Edges

Usually the edge rounding or shaping of a plywood panel is obtained by applying a shaped strip of molding along the edge. When a half-round shape is required, integral to the plywood edge, it is first necessary to mark two sets of guide lines along the edge and surface to be shaped. With these lines indicating depth and width of rounding, the edge is processed in two cutting stages.

The first set of lines mark a chamfer at *half* of the span of the final rounding. With the plane set for a very fine cut, the chamfer is shaped first. The final rounding is accomplished with a series of graduating *rounding* cuts to the second lines of marking. The edge, which is now roughly rounded, is further smoothed with a wood file and then sanded to the rounded shape. Obviously when a plywood edge is thus rounded it should later be painted to conceal the segments of edge grain.

As illustrated at the right, edge shaping can be readily performed with power tools. Again, however, the caution must be observed of not running power cutters across plywood corners in an off direction. Otherwise splintering damage may result. Skillfully operated, both the belt and disk sanders serve as safe edge shaping tools. They are particularly well adapted for chamfering and beveling when used with backrests and accurate cross-feeding guides.

Circular saw, with blade tilted, cuts bevel on end of plywood panel. *Courtesy of DeWalt, Inc.*

Portable router chamfers plywood edge. Care must be exercised not to run cutter over corner end-grain. *Courtesy of Millers Falls Company.*

Belt sander, with backrest tilted, chamfers and bevels plywood edges. Can also be used for edge and corner rounding. *Courtesy of DeWalt, Inc.*

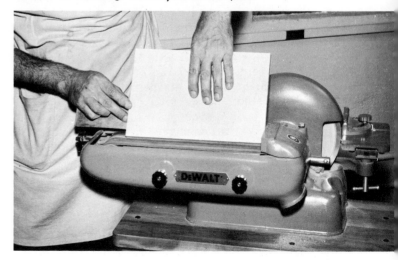

55

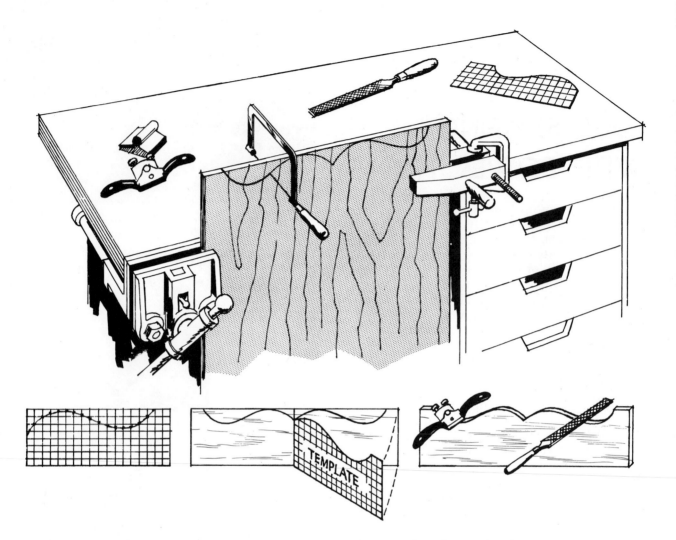

CUTTING CURVES
AND SCROLLS

Ordinarily a template, or pattern, is used to mark scrolls on plywood. When making a template, mark graphed lines on a piece of shirt cardboard or similar material, as shown in above illustration. The graphed squares should correspond to size shown on the working drawing. Exact line of the desired curve is transposed from the working drawing and spotted where it intersects lines of the graph. Spot points are then connected by a free flowing line representing the desired curve. The cardboard template is then cut to shape with a pair of scissors. From this, the curve is marked directly on the plywood.

Cutting of curves and scrolls is performed by hand with a coping saw, compass saw or keyhole saw. Because it is impossible to obtain a fine finished cut with a hand saw, an edge mar-

gin must be allowed for final smoothing to the desired shape.

When using hand tools, clamp the work in position as shown in above illustration. The saw blade must at all times cut perpendicular to the surface. If you maintain an even and uniform cutting thrust, the resulting edge should require a minimum of final trim. All sawing should be performed just outside the line of marking, thereby preventing any change of the curved pattern.

As indicated on the illustration, a file and sandpaper are required for finishing curved work. In fact, the free flow of a scrolled edge is most readily produced with skillful strokes of the file.

Curves and scrolls can be sawed with greater speed and accuracy with power tools. A variety of these are applicable, as illustrated at the right. The bandsaw is particularly useful for this purpose. Power sanders make short work of final shaping and smoothing.

CUTTING CURVES AND SCROLLS WITH POWER TOOLS

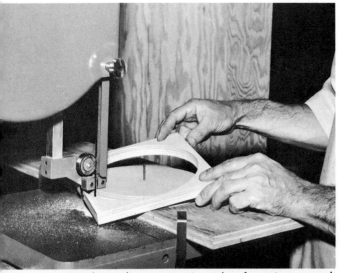

Bandsaw does a precise job of sawing curved shapes, circles and scrolls. *Courtesy of DeWalt, Inc.*

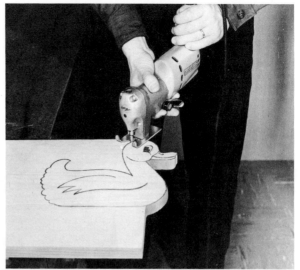

Saber saw makes easy work of cutting curved parts. Illustration above, shows saber saw attachment on electric drill. *Courtesy of Millers Falls Company.*

Portable circular saw can be used to cut mild curves in plywood panel. But straight blade is not adapted to sawing sharp bends. *Courtesy of American Plywood Association.*

Jig saw serves well for sawing intricate shapes. When used with fine-tooth blade, work requires only nominal edge smoothing. *Courtesy of DeWalt, Inc.*

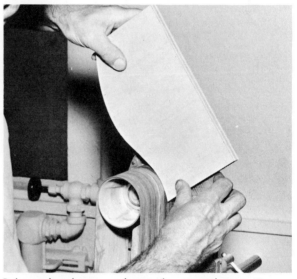

Belt sander shapes and smoothes curved parts. It offers advantage of protecting end-grain veneers against splintering. *Courtesy of DeWalt, Inc.*

Several layers of plywood can be sawed into duplicate curved parts, in one operation, with the bandsaw. *Courtesy of DeWalt, Inc.*

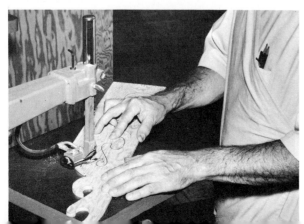

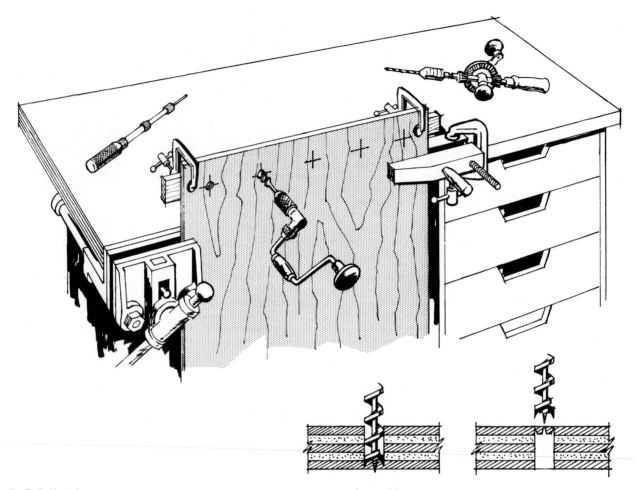

BORING HOLES

Braces and auger bits are among the most frequently used tools in the shop. The cranking action of the brace provides leverage for boring holes of large diameter, even up to 3″ with an adjustable expansive bit. But, as with most tools, there are tricks of the trade for using the brace and bit properly.

First there is the important matter of protecting your plywood against splintering when boring large holes. This is best accomplished by backing up the plywood panel with a strip of scrapwood. The scrapwood is clamped behind the area being bored as illustrated above, and prevents splintering as the bit pierces the panel.

Another way to avoid splintering is to bore from one surface until the spur of the bit comes through on the opposite surface. Then, as shown in sketch above, rebore from the opposite surface to complete the hole.

For straight boring the brace should be held so that the bit is perfectly perpendicular to the

surface. If you are unsure, use a try square to check its position.

When using an expansive bit to bore large holes, you get better leverage by making partial turns with the brace ratchet. Otherwise the resistance of the wide cutter tends to tear the wood.

For making holes of small diameters, either the hand drill or push drill is used. Good results are obtained by holding the drill steady and turning the operating crank evenly, at the same time keeping pressure on the handle.

The push drill is especially helpful when a large number of small holes must be drilled for screw fastenings. Through the simple action of pushing the handle, the drill automatically twists and drills the hole.

In the area of power tools, the electric drill makes the boring of holes a fast and simple chore. As shown on the facing page, other power tools also contribute to the ease and accuracy of boring and drilling operations.

BORING HOLES WITH POWER TOOLS

Electric hand drill, with ¼" chuck, turns twist drills of equivalent shank size and of smaller diameters. It can bore holes up to 1" with high-speed power bits. *Courtesy of John Oster Manufacturing Company.*

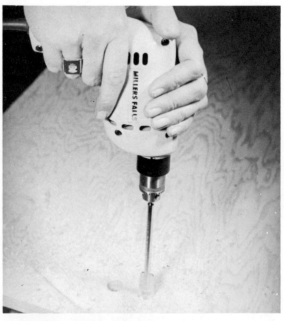

High-speed bits, used with electric drill, bore holes up to 1-½" when used with larger ⅜" chuck. *Courtesy of Millers Falls Company.*

Hole saw revolves around pilot drill; saws holes of diameters ranging from ⅝" to 2-½". Power unit turns saw at right but tool also fits hand drills. *Courtesy of Millers Falls Company.*

Drill press assures accuracy of boring; makes holes in several thicknesses of plywood in one operation. *Courtesy of DeWalt, Inc.*

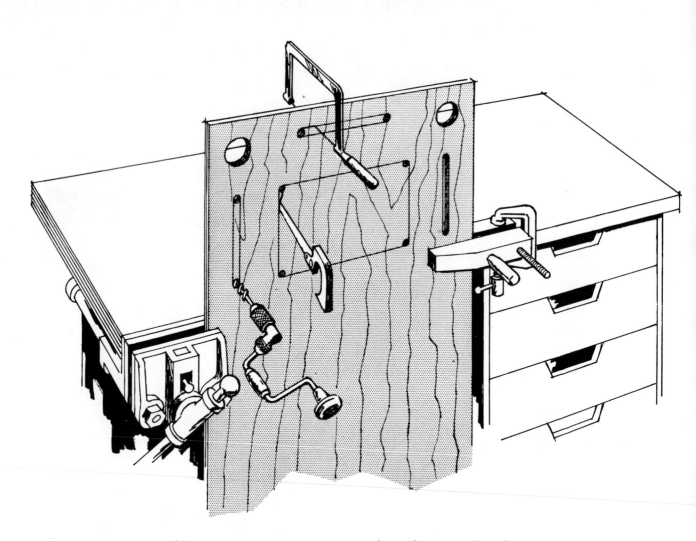

INSIDE CUTOUTS

It is often necessary to cut out slots, circles and curved shapes *inside* the edge area of a plywood panel. Handle slots and decorative inside scrollwork requires this process. One method is to bore a series of overlapping holes to slot width for removing the cutout area. The slot is then trimmed with a sharp chisel and smoothed with file and sandpaper to exact shape.

For inside scrollwork, the coping saw may be "threaded" through a hole which has been bored within the cut-out marking. The shape is then sawed from the starting hole.

Keyhole and compass saws are especially designed for inside cutting and can be used to advantage where holes and shapes must be sawed in central areas of broad panels. These, too, require a starting hole and such saws are apt to make a rough cut. But they are needed

where the span of work prevents use of the loop frame type of saw, especially for existing construction, where the tool must be brought to the work rather than the work to the tool.

Power tools can best perform your cutout assignments. They offer greater cutting accuracy and can do the job faster.

The saber saw, in particular, is not only able to saw from mid-field of a plywood panel but it is also self-starting. As shown on the facing illustrations, by tilting this tool over on its nose, so that the blade can scratch against the surface in a near-horizontal position, the saber blade scratches its own starting slot.

For duplicate inside cutting of multiple parts, the power jig saw is especially useful. It can saw several thicknesses of plywood in one operation. Other power tools make easy work for cutting and shaping both inside and outside the plywood periphery.

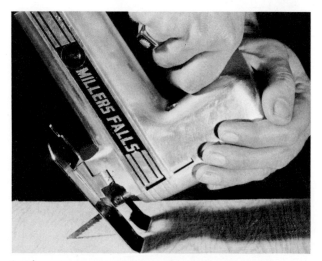

Inside cutouts are easily made with self-starting saber saw. Saw is tilted to scratch its way through panel. *Courtesy of Millers Falls Company.*

Scrolled inside shapes are cut out of panel with saber saw. This is an ideal power tool for such work. *Courtesy of Stanley Tools.*

Skilled craftsman saws letter cutouts from plywood. Note self-inserting feature of saber saw. *Courtesy of Black & Decker Company.*

Square and rectangular cutouts and slots can be sawed with the portable circular saw. Straight cuts must be trimmed at corners to remove inner portion. *Courtesy of Black & Decker Co.*

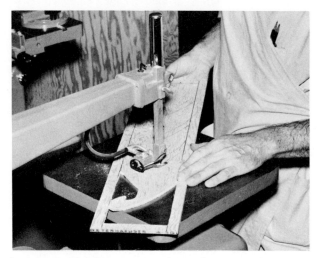

Intricate inside shapes are most easily cut on the power jig saw. Blade is threaded through starting hole which is drilled along marking of inner area. *Courtesy of DeWalt, Inc.*

Shaping of inside cutout edges is most easily accomplished with power router. Belt or spindle sander finishes the job. *Courtesy of Skil Corporation.*

Use of sanding block increases accuracy of hand sanding. It is particularly useful for rounding corners and shaping small parts. *Courtesy of Millers Falls Company.*

Surface sanding of plywood is performed best with a hand sander or with the orbital sander illustrated above. Medium to fine grades of sandpaper should be used. *Courtesy of Millers Falls Company.*

SANDING

As already indicated in this chapter and throughout the book, sanding plays a big part in the processing of plywood. To some extent this requirement has been anticipated by plywood manufacturers, who bring better grades of their product to you already sanded. However, as your work progresses, further sanding will be needed, especially for shaping and smoothing freshly cut plywood edges.

Much of the basic sanding should be taken care of even before the work has been put together. The parts are easier to get at this way. Two or more grades of sandpaper should be used; first a medium grade and then, for final sanding, a fine grade.

All sanding should be performed *with* the surface grain of the panel. To insure an even and thorough job, a sandpaper block should be used wherever possible. Edge portions must be especially well sanded, with sharp surface veneers slightly dulled along the edges to prevent splintering.

Power sanders simplify the job. As shown here and on preceding pages, there are many types of electric sanders available. Each type is desgined for specific purposes. As an example, orbital sanders go over the work lightly with a minimum amount of abrasive wear. Belt and disk sanders, on the other hand, are designed for deep abrasion and shaping of the wood. Care must be exercised when using them on plywood to avoid damage to surface veneers.

When surface is sanded with portable belt sander, caution must be observed to avoid oversanding with resulting damage to surface veneers. Use fine grade sanding belt and do not bear down on machine. *Courtesy of Millers Falls Company.*

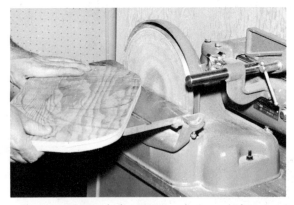

Shaping of rounded corners and convex edges can be performed accurately on stationary disk sander. *Courtesy of DeWalt, Inc.*

4

WORKING WITH PLYWOOD — JOINERY

Joinery

Nail Fastening

Screw Fastening

Construction Joints

Rabbet, Dado, and Grooved Joints

Lap and Miter Joints

Edging and Framing

Gluing and Clamping

Attaching Hinges

Hardware and Accessories

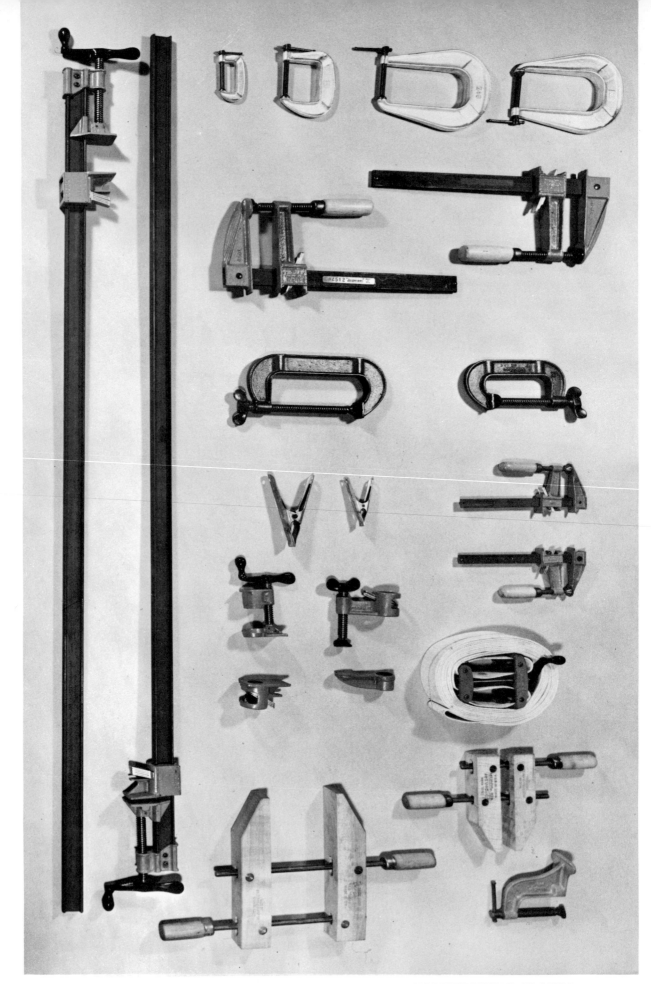

WOODWORKING CLAMPS
Courtesy of Adjustable Clamp Company

JOINERY

The projects you build of plywood can be no stronger than the joints that hold them together. There are, in fact, many different types of joints, each adapted to special construction needs. Frequently nails and screws are used. Other types of construction require joints which are especially cut and fitted to be secured with clamps and glue. Often a combination of wood fitting, metal fasteners and adhesives is required.

Some of the essential materials and equipment of Joinery are illustrated on these pages. The assorted clamps shown on the facing page are needed not only to secure joints, but to serve as holding devices for your work.

Various adhesives are illustrated at the right. These include the waterproof epoxies and waterproof resorcinol glues which hold their bond even when permanently immersed in water. Then there is the water resistant, plastic resin glue—good for anything but constant exposure to water. For protected, indoor use, casein glue and contact cements bond plywood joints securely and economically.

The common wood fasteners, sketched below, play a vital part in plywood joinery. Application of all these items is described and illustrated on following pages.

ADHESIVES
Courtesy of The Borden Company

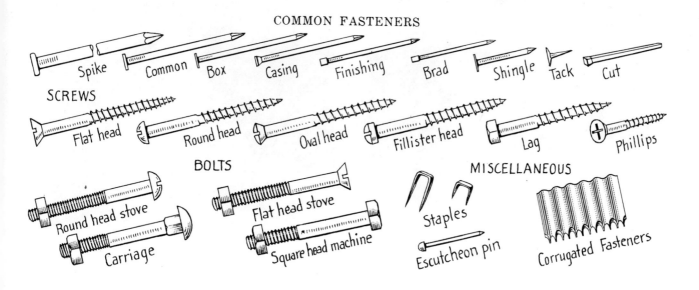

COMMON FASTENERS

Spike Common Box Casing Finishing Brad Shingle Tack Cut

SCREWS

Flat head Round head Oval head Fillister head Lag Phillips

BOLTS MISCELLANEOUS

Round head stove Flat head stove Staples

Carriage Square head machine Escutcheon pin Corrugated Fasteners

NAIL FASTENING

Obviously, the most elementary way of fastening two pieces of plywood is simply to nail them together. Nails, properly spaced and driven, can provide a strong joint. They are used most frequently for box-type, butt construction.

Finishing or casing nails are usually used with plywood. As shown in illustration at the right, the proper size of nail is determined by the thickness of the plywood being fastened. For ¼″ plywood, 2-d (1″) to 4-d (1½″) will suffice, while thicker panels require larger nails.

When making butt joints, it should be observed that nails driven at a slight slant have greater holding power. With plywood, it is not necessary to stagger the nail line to avoid splitting. But when driving nails near the ends and edges of the panel, it helps to drill a small pilot hole, sightly thinner than diameter of the nail, to prevent splintering of edge veneers.

Because the heads of finishing nails can be indented and concealed, they are often used to reinforce other glue joints. After the finishing nail has been driven, the head should be set just below the surface. This is done with a nailset of corresponding size. The indentation is then filled with plastic wood or putty. For exterior construction, rustproof nails should be used.

The right size of finishing nail is determined by thickness of plywood. Nails ranging from 2-d (1″) to 10-d (3″) are shown in above illustration.

To avoid splitting edge veneers of plywood, pilot holes for nails are drilled through the connecting piece. Holes should be slightly smaller than nails being used.

Nails are evenly spaced and driven carefully to avoid surface damage. Nailset is used to indent the heads. These indentations are filled with plastic wood or putty.

Glue and small brads secure the ¼″ bottom panel of plywood drawer. Clamp is used to draw parts together during nailing operations.
Photos courtesy of American Plywood Association.

SCREW FASTENING

Screws have greater holding power than nails. Their only disadvantage is that they cost more and require more time and effort to drive. Like nails, screws come in various types and sizes. As illustrated at the right, the proper size is determined by the thickness of the plywood being fastened.

When driving screws, it is first necessary to drill a pilot hole to receive the thread and shank. These holes should be made slightly smaller than the actual screw size.

Flat head screws should be driven flush to the surface. To do this, a countersink bit is used to chamfer the pilot hole to fit the beveled screw head. Another method is to recess the screw head slightly beneath the surface. This requires counterboring.

The accompanying sectional sketch of the Stanley Screw-Mate drill bit, shows the graduations of three sizes of holes required for proper counter-boring. In one drilling operation the Screw-Mate does the job of three separate bits.

Strong plywood joints can be made with a combination of screws and glue. When driven from outside surfaces, the screw heads should be concealed with a plastic filler. Counterbored holes can be plugged and sanded flush. Brass, bronze, stainless or galvanized screws are used for exterior construction.

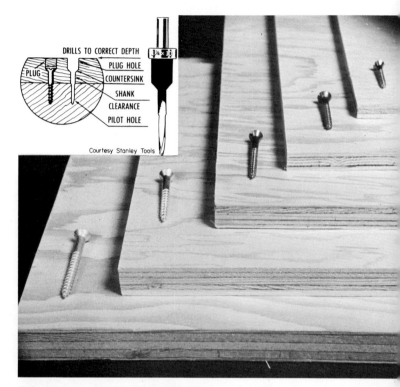

Selection of proper size screws is determined by thickness of plywood. Shown above are sizes ranging from 1″ #6 to 2″ #12. *Courtesy of American Plywood Association.*

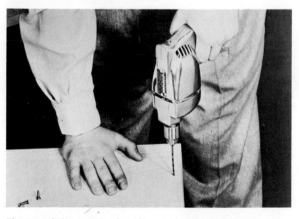

Electric drill speeds the job of drilling pilot holes for screws—especially when used with Screw-Mate bits shown in inset. *Courtesy of John Oster Mfg. Co.*

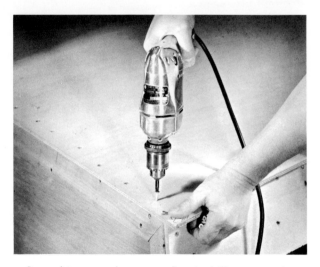

Screwdriver attachment on electric drill saves much time when many screws must be driven. *Courtesy of Black & Decker Company.*

Surface holes and indentations of screw heads are either covered with grain and dowel plugs or filled with plastic substance, as shown above. *Courtesy of American Plywood Association.*

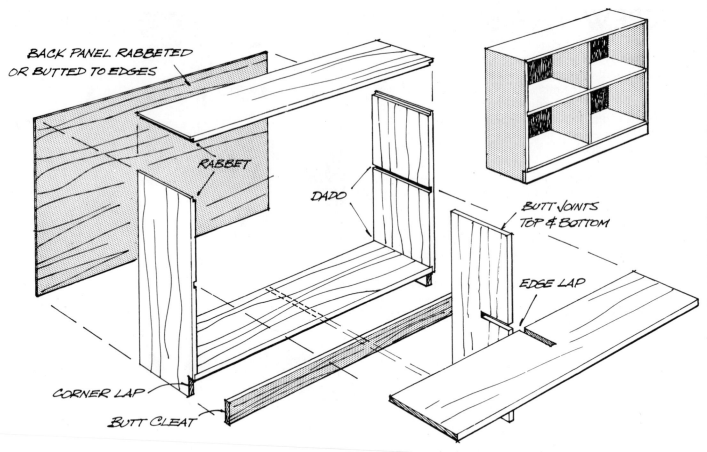

BACK PANEL RABBETED
OR BUTTED TO EDGES

RABBET

DADO

BUTT JOINTS
TOP & BOTTOM

EDGE LAP

CORNER LAP

BUTT CLEAT

Bookcase construction showing typical joinery.

CONSTRUCTION JOINERY

As illustrated above, the construction of a plywood project usually involves cutting a number of different types of joints to fasten parts together. Of the various types shown, obviously the simplest to make is the butt joint. Photographs of drawer construction, on the facing page, demonstrate the process of overlapping the ends and edges of plywood pieces and nailing them together to form butt joints.

A strong butt joint must, however, be made with a degree of accuracy. Joining parts should be cut perfectly square at the connecting edges. Such squareness is easy enough to obtain with precision power tools such as the circular and radial saw. But, if the job is done by hand, connecting ends must be planed and checked for squareness before the joint can be nailed together.

Butt joints are made much stronger when reinforced with glue. Since the edges of plywood consist of alternating layers of both end grain and side grain, glue adheres to the side grain

segments to form a strong bond. Obviously, this would not be possible with solid lumber where end grain cannot retain a glue bond.

Other typical joints, including the dado, rabbet, groove, lap and miter, are illustrated above and described on following pages. Among these, the dado and rabbet are most commonly used in plywood construction. When accurately cut and reinforced with glue, these joints provide an almost indestructible means of fastening.

Often it is necessary to splice two sections of plywood together with the surface grain running in the same direction. This calls for edge jointing which employs one of the methods illustrated at the right. With plywood, the most commonly used edge joints are the butt and rabbet types. Both types are adaptable to gluing. For thicker panels of plywood, the edges are often butted and glued and secured from the back with corrugated fasteners.

Butt joints are commonly used for corner fastening. With thin plywood, the corner can be reinforced with a strip of solid wood. Glue makes the joint much stronger.

The easiest way to build plywood boxes and drawers is simply to butt the parts together and secure them with finishing nails and glue.

Plywood drawer bottom, butt fastened with nails and glue, strengthens the assembly of front, back and sides. Most drawers are made with rabbet joints, dados and grooves.

Photos courtesy of American Plywood Association

Edge joints

Butt

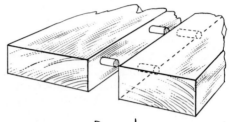

Dowel

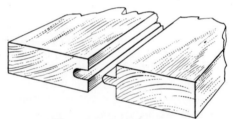

Tongue & Groove

Rabbet

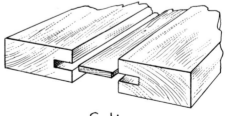

Spline

RABBET, DADO AND GROOVED JOINTS

Rabbet joints are most frequently used for end and edge fastening of plywood parts; for recessing the back panels of cabinets and for connecting the fronts and sides of drawers. They are made by removing part of the edge of one piece so that a joining part may fit flush within the cut-away area.

While short end-rabbets for drawer fronts can be cut by hand in two sawing operations, the longer edge-rabbets required for backs of cabinets should be sawed on a circular saw or made with a jointer, router or shaper.

Dado joints are cut across wood parts in the narrow direction. The cutout part forms a cross groove into which the joining part fits. As illustrated at the right, dados can be cut by hand. But photos on the facing page demonstrate that they can be made much more quickly and accurately with power tools. The circular saw or radial saw, equipped with a dado cutting head removes the cutout portion in one operation.

Grooved joints differ from dados only in that they are cut in the long direction of the part—in the direction of the surface grain. The most common wood joint made with grooves is the familiar tongue and groove cut along the edges of construction lumber. The accurate cutting of grooves virtually demands use of power tools; preferably the circular or radial saw. Shapers and routers, equipped with groove cutting heads, can also do the job.

Measuring and marking the dado.

Use of saw and straight edge for cutting dado.

Finishing dado with chisel.

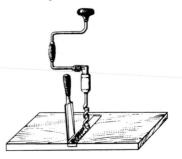

Blind dado roughly cut to size with brace and bit.

Use of router plane.

Dado joints should be cut accurately to assure snug fit of joining parts. When glued together they provide strong and lasting construction. *Courtesy of American Plywood Association.*

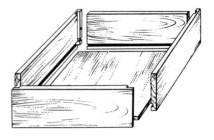

Common drawer construction showing assembly of dados, grooves, and rabbets.

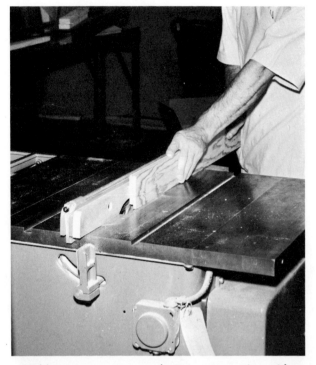

Rabbets are cut accurately in one operation with dado head on circular saw. With regular saw blade, a surface and end cut are required to remove rabbet. *Courtesy of DeWalt, Inc.*

Jointer, shaper and router can also be used to cut rabbet joints. On jointer, rabbet should be removed with a series of shallow cuts. *Courtesy of DeWalt, Inc.*

Dado joints are cut precisely with dado head cutters on circular saw. Regular blade can also be used to remove dado with series of saw cuts. *Courtesy of DeWalt, Inc.*

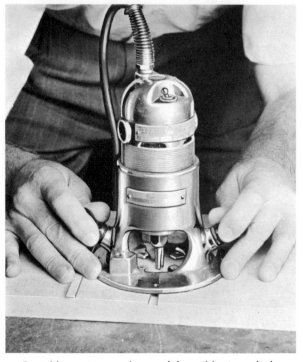

Portable router can be used for rabbeting, dadoing and grooving. Guide strip is usually clamped across work to assure accuracy of cut. *Courtesy of Stanley Tools.*

71

LAP AND MITER JOINTS

Lap joints, as illustrated below, are frequently required for structural reinforcement of plywood parts. While they can be cut with hand tools, they are made more accurately and quickly with a circular saw or radial saw.

Miter joints require a maximum of precise cutting. Even the slightest inaccuracy in cutting end bevels of joining mitered parts will show up conspicuously when the parts are fitted together. This is especially true when the miters must form an exactly square corner. For this reason, if the miter is sawed by hand, the saw must be guided in a miter box, as illustrated at the right.

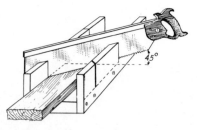

Sawing a miter with a home made miter box.

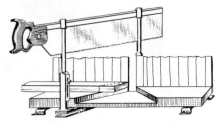

An adjustable iron miter box.

End-lap joint.   Middle-lap joint.

Securing miter joint with glue and finishing nails.

Machine sawing of miter joints assures maximum accuracy. Both circular saw and radial saw can be adjusted precisely to the exact cutting angle.

Making spline cut in miter joint.

Inserting hardwood spline.

Corner construction of plywood shows precise fitting of end bevels to form exact miter. When properly fitted, miter joints can be glued and nailed together. *Courtesy of American Plywood Association.*

Miter corner joint secured with spline.

Circular saw, equipped with dado head, performs fast and accurate job of cutting lap joints.

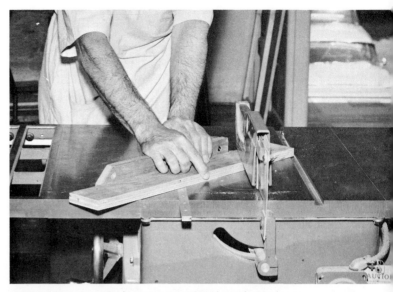

Miter joints are sawed at exact required angle on circular saw. Cross feed has micrometer adjustments for angle.

Even compound miters can be cut on radial saw with dual adjustments of arm and blade. Maneuverability of radial saw adapts it to wide variety of cutting operations.

Photos courtesy of DeWalt, Inc.

Radial saw is tilted to bevel position for accurate sawing of end miter.

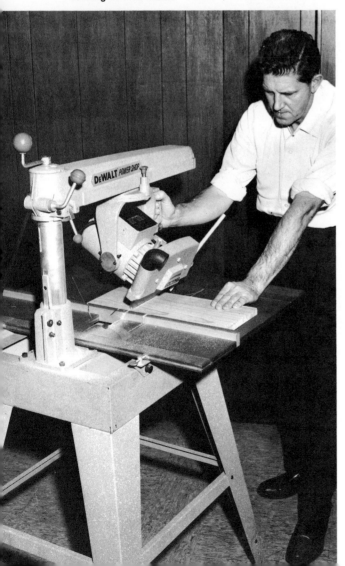

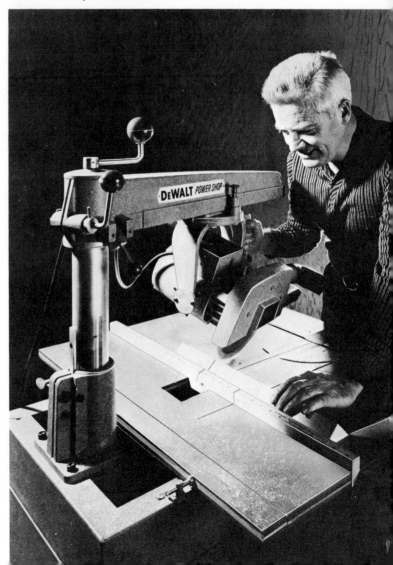

EDGING
AND FRAMING

For work that is going to be painted, plywood edges can be thoroughly sanded or shaped with integral chamfers and rounding. But when the work is to be stained and finished naturally so the grain shows through, some form of edge covering should be used to conceal the end segments of plywood.

As illustrated at the right, thin strips of weed, or shaped molding, can be nailed and glued along the edges. Special veneered edge tape, with adhesive backing, may also be used. Veneer-faced aluminum edge molding is especially made for this purpose. Several solutions are indicated in the accompanying illustrations.

When the four edges of a plywood panel require covering, the framing strips should be rabbeted or butted along the edges. As shown in the second and third sketches, corners are either butted or rabbeted.

Illustrated below are a couple of methods used for making reinforced plywood panels. This construction is suitable for strengthening cabinet doors and surface areas that are surfaced with thin sheets of plywood.

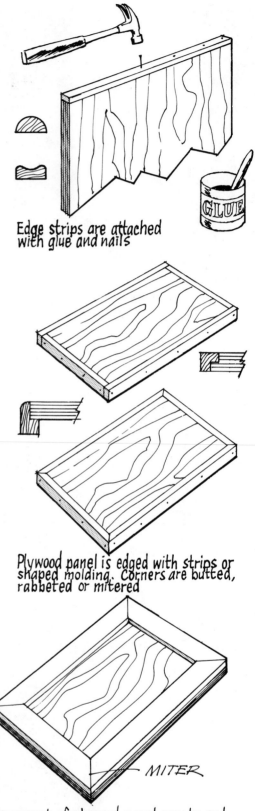

Edge strips are attached with glue and nails

Plywood panel is edged with strips or shaped molding. Corners are butted, rabbeted or mitered

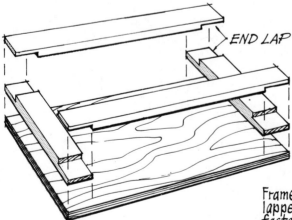

END LAP

MITER

Frame reinforcement of plywood panel may be end lapped, mitered, doweled or butted with corrugated fasteners and glue

Self-sticking veneer tape simplifies process of covering plywood edges. It should not be used, however, where work is exposed to moisture. *Courtesy of American Plywood Association.*

Thin strips of veneer can be glued over edges and trimmed flush to adjoining surfaces. Corners of veneer are mitered or butted. *Courtesy of American Plywood Association.*

Wedge strips of solid wood are inserted in bevel groove cut along plywood edge. When glued in place, this strip becomes integral to the plywood panel. *Courtesy of American Plywood Association. tion.*

Special aluminum edge fittings for corner construction, as shown below, simplify some forms of plywood construction. Other aluminum edge moldings are covered with wood veneers. *Courtesy of Reynolds Metals Company.*

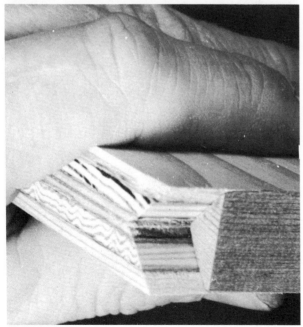

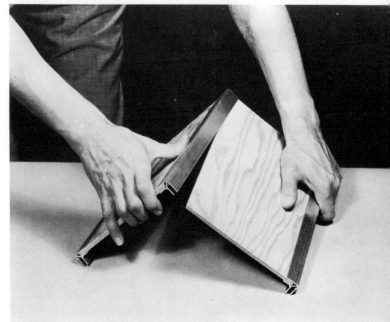

GLUING
AND CLAMPING

Since plywood is, in itself, composed of sheets of wood glued together, it has a natural affinity to glue bonding for its further construction.

There are many different kinds of glue on the market. They vary in strength and purpose. Some that are suitable for light construction cannot withstand heavy service. Others that serve well for indoor construction would soon fall apart if exposed to outdoor wet and dampness. So careful selection must be made of an exact type of glue that will best serve your working requirements.

Of the glues shown in page 65, the two most favored are the waterproof resorcinol type for exterior use and plastic resin moisture resistant glue for interior work. Both provide a strong bond. Also, for enduring exterior use and for waterproof marine applications, epoxy adhesives are excellent, especially when a strong but resilient bond is required.

While some adhesives are self-bonding and need no pressure, most glued joints do require the pressure of clamps during the drying or curing period. Clamps come in a vast assortment of types and sizes, as illustrated on page 64 and in the adjoining photographs which show their many . applications. But like the many other woodworking tools shown in this book, each type of clamp has its own special purpose.

The clamping of glue joints can become an unwieldy process if a few basic precautions are not observed. When dealing with heavy bar clamps it is wise, whenever possible, to lay the clamps on a surface and place the work in the clamp, rather than trying to juggle the heavy clamps around a light assembly of work. Also, use smooth strips of scrapwood to protect the surfaces of your work against clamp marks.

Clamping operations are assisted when a few finishing nails are started through a connecting part to tack that part in position before clamp pressure is applied. Since clamps exert pressure in the direction of their alignment, care must be taken to line them up evenly. Work should be checked with a square as the pressure is applied. Otherwise the parts will be joined out of alignment—a difficult situation to correct once the glue has set and clamp pressure released.

Glue is applied to *both* edges being joined. If work is to be finished in natural grain, excess glue should be wiped off to avoid marring of stained areas.

Glued parts are brought together preparatory to clamping. A few finishing nails, started in advance, could be used to tack parts together.

Pressure of bar clamps hold parts together while glue is drying. Work should be checked for squareness during clamping operations.
Photos courtesy of American Plywood Association

Handscrew clamps press small dadoed parts together after glue has been applied. *Courtesy of Adjustable Clamp Company.*

Combination of long and short bar clamps press glued edge joints of panel. Note clamping of reinforcement strips to prevent panel buckling. *Courtesy of Adjustable Clamp Company.*

Glued frame is pressed together with bar clamps. Clamps are also used to hold parts together while nails and screws are being driven. *Courtesy of Adjustable Clamp Company.*

Veneer press, used for surface gluing of panels, is made with press screws and sturdy bolted frame. *Courtesy of Adjustable Clamp Company.*

C-clamps, used in conjunction with triangular jig strips, press mitered plywood corners together after **glue has been applied. *Courtesy of American Plywood Association.***

After gluing, this ingenious clamping jig applies pressure of a single handscrew clamp to four mitered corner joints of frame. *Courtesy of Adjustable Clamp Company.*

ATTACHING HINGES

Among the many different kinds of hinges shown on the facing page, perhaps the most common is the standard *butt* hinge. This is used frequently in plywood construction for attaching doors, drop leaves and other folding parts.

Butt hinges come in two types, namely loose-pin and fast-pin. The loose-pin type come apart with removal of the pivot pin. Thus the parts which are connected with these hinges can be easily disassembled. This is often a convenience, particularly when projects later require removal of hinged parts for further processing and finishing.

A bit of skill is required for the proper fitting of butt hinges. As shown in the sketches at the right, the hinge leaves must be recessed slightly beneath the surfaces to which they are fastened. This calls for some accuracy in cutting out the mortised area. If the hinge is improperly aligned, the connecting parts are apt to fit unevenly. This can become especially noticeable when improperly hinged cabinet doors are in closed position.

A variation of the butt hinge is the lapping cabinet hinge shown on the top right photograph of the facing page. This hinge is particularly well suited for plywood because the screws can be driven into the connecting surfaces rather than along the sectional plywood edges.

Other surface hinges, including the H, HL and strap types, are attached flush to the outer surface of doors and connecting parts. These require no special cutting or fitting. But they must be mounted so that the pivot pin is exactly in line with the edge of the door and the connecting edge of the cabinet. If they fall out of line, the hinge will bind when the door is opened.

Most hardware and department stores stock a wide variety of hinges, including the types shown on these pages. Often the right type of hinge not only serves utilitarian purposes of the project but contributes, as well, to its decorative embellishment. So be careful to pick the right hinges and then take your time and attach them properly.

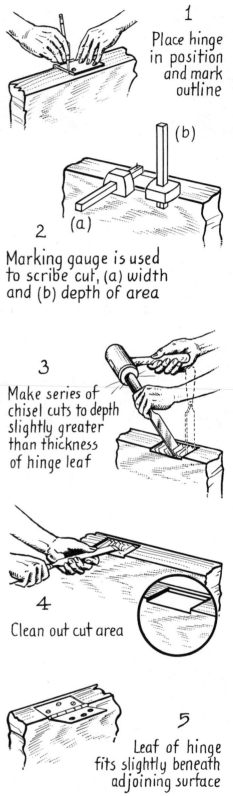

HOW TO FIT BUTT HINGES

1 Place hinge in position and mark outline

2 Marking gauge is used to scribe cut, (a) width and (b) depth of area

3 Make series of chisel cuts to depth slightly greater than thickness of hinge leaf

4 Clean out cut area

5 Leaf of hinge fits slightly beneath adjoining surface

COMMON TYPES of HINGES

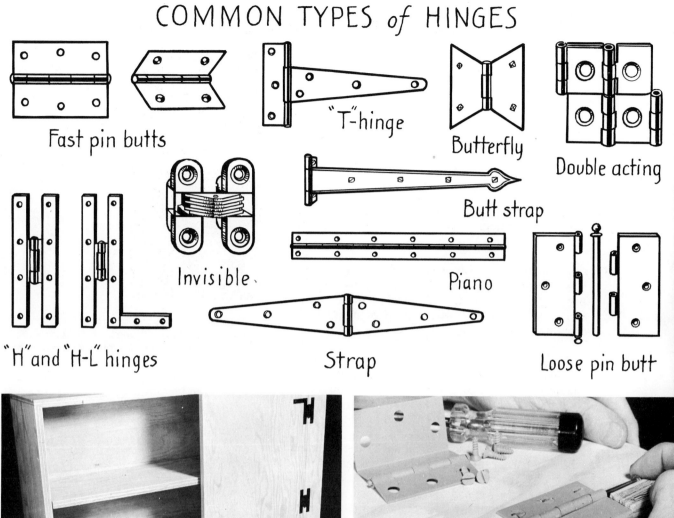

Fast pin butts

"T"-hinge

Butterfly

Double acting

Invisible

Butt strap

Piano

"H" and "H-L" hinges

Strap

Loose pin butt

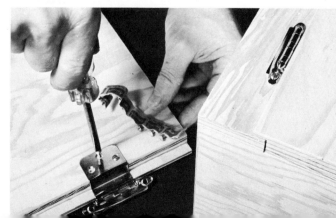

Surface hinges, such as the H and HL types shown above, are easy to attach. But pivot pins must be aligned to edge of door to avoid binding. *Courtesy of American Plywood Association.*

Semi-concealed cabinet hinges, shown above, fit rabbeted edge of door. These also offer advantage of surface fastening. *Courtesy of American Plywood Association.*

Cabinet hinges of this type work well with plywood because screws can be driven into surfaces rather than segments of plywood edge. *Courtesy of American Plywood Association.*

When many screws must be driven in process of attaching hinges, power screwdriver facilitates the job. Screwdriver bits fit various sizes of screws. *Courtesy of Millers Falls Company.*

HARDWARE AND ACCESSORIES

For final fitting and furbishing of your plywood projects, an almost limitless choice of functional and decorative hardware is available. Prefabricated chair and table legs of assorted types and sizes are sold at most hardware and department stores. Catches, drawer pulls, handles, brackets, shelf supports and numerous other items can be obtained in a variety of designs and sizes.

If you will consult your hardware dealer or check the catalogs, you will have little difficulty finding exactly what you need.

Illustrated on this page are a few of the cabinet accessories required for many of the projects presented in this book. Other items are specified on the working drawings which accompany these projects.

The final fitting of hardware and accessories is usualy regarded as the triumphant phase of the do-it-yourself program. For when you start to put on the hardware you have finally arrived at the final stage of project development.

But do not be in too great a rush! Remember, while it is permissible to fit your hardware after the project is built, you will find it advantageous to remove it again before applying the paint and final finish. Then you can put it back in the same holes and tighten up the screws for keeps!

Adjustable shelf supports are inserted in holes bored along inner panels of bookcase. Movable shelves and other flexible features can be obtained with proper hardware.

Sliding door cup pulls are tapped into prebored indentations of finished door panel. Other items shown are flush pulls, knob, and block pulls.

Various types of door catches, hinges, casters, brackets and innumerable other hardware accessories are neatly packaged and displayed at hardware and department stores. Look them over and pick your needs.

Photos courtesy of American Plywood Association.

Drawer handles come in a variety of types and designs. It is considered good practice first to fit the hardware and then remove it for the finishing process.

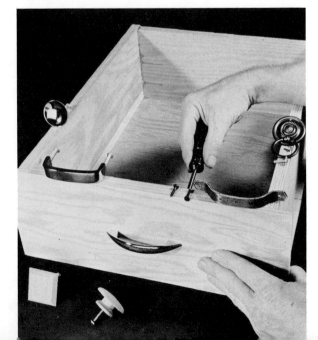

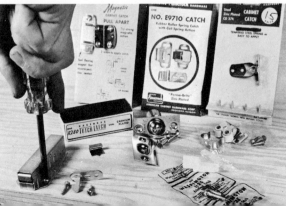

5

PLYWOOD FINISHING

Preparing the Work for Finishing

Choice of Stain

How to Apply Stain

The Shellac Finish

The Varnish Finish

The Lacquer Finish

Natural Finishes—Oil; Firzite; Exterior and

Marine (Vinyl, Acrylic, Epoxy, and

Urethane)

How to Paint

Care of Brushes and Finishing Equipment

Brushes of assorted sizes are the first requisite of a good finishing job. *Courtesy of Tip Top Brush Co.*

Preparing the Work for Finishing

Before any of the finishing steps are undertaken, the work should be carefully examined for scratches, mars, grain irregularities, dents, glue spots, and other imperfections.

Glue which has adhered at places of joining will not absorb stain and must, therefore, be carefully removed before any further steps are taken. Ordinarily, glue can be scraped or peeled off with a sharp knife, chisel, or cabinet scraper.

Dents and depressions may often be lifted by placing a wet piece of plotting paper directly over the spot and pressing it with a hot flatiron. Cracks, unless they are large ones, can ordinarily be filled with wood filler, and toned to the same color as the desired final finish. Stick shellac, wood putty and plastic fillers may be bought in colors which blend exactly with most standard tones of finished wood. These are used to fill larger cracks or openings. All other imperfections will generally be overcome by the final and thorough use of sandpaper.

Too much emphasis cannot be placed on the importance of thorough sanding. Much of the basic sanding should be taken care of even before the work has been put together. The parts are easier to get at in this way. Two grades of sandpaper should be used; first a medium grade and then, for final sanding, a fine grade.

All sanding should be performed with the grain of the wood. To insure an even and thorough job a sandpaper block should be used wherever possible.

Hand block is used for preparatory sanding and for rubbing with fine abrasive paper between finishing coats. *Courtesy of Pittsburgh Plate Glass Co.*

Plywood Finishing

Since most types of plywood are surfaced with natural wood, finishing procedures are much the same as those used for any ordinary wooden material. There are exceptions, however, particularly in the finishing of fir plywood.

While many people admire the wild and uninhibited grain of fir plywood, others do not. Hence, rather than finish it naturally, as one would other less ostentatious wood graining, many prefer to use special stains and paints to subdue or conceal the fir grain patterns.

There is also a difference between methods of finishing plywood for interior and exterior exposure. Plywood furniture and other household items used indoors do not require special protection. But for use outdoors, plywood must the thoroughly sealed with one or two coats of a special plywood primer. (Firzite or similar sealer) This acts as a protective base for further finishing coats. It penetrates the plywood grain and safeguards the surface against checking when exposed to outdoor moisture.

Choice of Stain

Choosing the right stain provides the first point of discussion in the art of wood finishing. There are many different types of stain and each type has its own appeal. Many insist that the richer woods are better off without any stain, but most people do have occasion to use wood stains and it will be well to discuss a few of the more common types.

Water Stains

Water stains are extremely popular because they are easily mixed and do not fade very readily. Pure aniline colors are mixed in hot water and are applied directly and permitted to penetrate and dry on the wood. Water stains are not rubbed. The only objection to stains of this type is that they are apt to raise the grain of the wood, *after* application. This fault, however, can be overcome by sponging the plywood with water and permitting it to dry. The grain, which has been raised during this initial sponging, is then carefully sanded with fine sandpaper, thus providing a protected surface for the water stain.

Spirit Stains

Spirit stains, like water stains are mixed with pure aniline colors. However, the liquid agent is alcohol. Spirit stains must be applied carefully because they dry very quickly. When they are applied with a brush, a degree of skill is necessary in order to avoid streaks where brush strokes overlap. In large furniture factories, stains of this kind are generally applied with an air brush.

Oil Stains

Oil stains are favored by many people because they are very easy to apply, and because they enable the worker to develop many interesting effects of tone and color, which would be difficult to attain with stains of other types. The oil stain is mixed from aniline colors compounded in oil and turpentine. Sometimes a small amount of linseed oil is added to give additional body to the stain. Stains of this type which are sold already mixed may contain benzol, benzine, or naphtha as their mixing ingredient.

The oil stain is a common favorite because it does not dry quickly and may be worked over with a rubbing rag after it has been applied. Moreover, it can be worked for tones and contrasts which cannot be obtained with any of the other varieties.

Use of Wood Filler

In order to obtain an effective finish on plywood, it is necessary not only to color it, but, in the case of open-grained woods, to fill those portions which are to be finished. Close-grained woods, on the other hand, do not require a filler because the texture of the wood is not porous or open, and for this reason the ordinary finishing agents will provide whatever filling may be necessary.

Wood filler can be purchased in paste form. It consists of silica, a white powder, mixed in linseed oil, turpentine, and japan. The so-called transparent finish is cream-colored and may be tinted to any desired tone or shade through the introduction of oil colors.

Filler should be thoroughly mixed and diluted with turpentine until it is of the consistency of heavy cream. Generally speaking, it is good practice to stain the work first and then apply the filler with a stiff brush. It dries and hardens in a relatively short time, and for this reason large projects should be handled in portions, with the filler brushed on in separate applications. After each portion has been treated and allowed to dry for a few minutes, it is rubbed vigorously across the grain with a coarse rag or piece of burlap. The idea is to work the paste well into the open and porous grain. After the initial cross-grain rubbing has been performed, the filled portions are again rubbed with the grain, this time with a finer piece of cloth.

If the filler adheres and hardens in places on the surface of the work, it should be carefully removed with a rag moistened with turpentine. Excess filler should be removed at intersections and places of joining, with a sharpened stick or knife blade covered with a rag.

While it is not always necessary sometimes re-staining the article after the filler has been applied is a worthwhile practice. Frequently this operation improves the appearance of the finished product. Naturally, it is rather difficult to color the wood filler to the exact desired shade, and thus when the work is re-stained, the color may have to be adjusted and brought to the shade desired.

Wood filler should be given at least twenty-four hours to dry and harden before you continue with further steps of finishing.

How to Apply Stain

The application of water or spirit stains is relatively simple, as both of these types of stain are merely brushed on the well-sanded wood and permitted to penetrate the surface. Sometimes it is necessary to remove carefully with a rag any excess stain from portions of the wood, especially on the end grain. The idea is to let the stain penetrate and dye the wood.

However, in the application of oil stains, especially where a special effect is desired, the technique is somewhat different. For example, let us say that a small table is being stained. The stain is first brushed freely and quickly on the four legs and the underneath structure. While it remains wet on these portions, it is rubbed carefully with a rag until the grain and surface characteristics of the wood show through. Moreover, in the rubbing process, it is possible to tone out certain portions of the wood to obtain either uniform or contrasting effects. Light rubbing with very fine steel wool will help in this process.

For certain types of close-grained veneers, notably birch and maple, there is a definite advantage in mixing the oil stain to a fairly heavy consistency. The heavy oil stain permits extra rubbing with cloth or fine steel wool and is excellent for obtaining tone effects. It allows the worker a greater margin of control in obtaining the desired tones and uniformity of color.

The Shellac Finish

Shellac, as it is prepared commercially, is usually composed of 4 lbs. of shellac gum mixed in 1 gallon of alcohol. This mixture is referred to as a 4-lb. cut. However, it is not wise to apply the shellac directly to the work in this consistency. It should be diluted.

Before proceeding with any of the steps of shellacking, you should be sure that the article to be covered is thoroughly dry and clean, that no dust or dirt is adhering to the surfaces, and that it is altogether ready for the final finishing steps.

For the first coat, the regular commercial

Stains should be carefully mixed before applying. Pigment settles at bottom of can and requires thorough stirring.

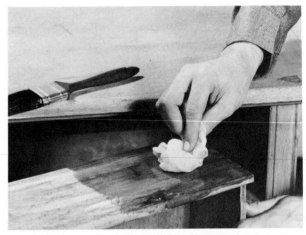

Brush is used to apply stain to sections of work. Stained area is then rubbed with a lint-free rag to bring out natural graining of wood.

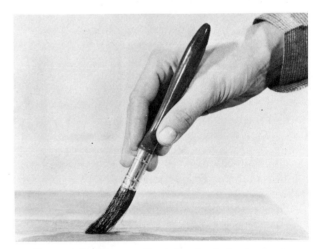

Best angle for smoothest brush stroke is demonstrated here. Careful brushing contributes to good finishing results.

shellac should be cut with alcohol in any amount varying from one-third to one-half. It should be almost water thin. Since shellac dries quickly when it is being applied, you should proceed briskly and evenly, working with the grain of the wood to avoid excessive brushing. The first thin coat is absorbed into the wood and provides a base for further coats.

After each coat of shellac, the work should be carefully rubbed with fine garnet paper (wet or dry) or steel wool. Ordinarily, three or four coats of shellac will provide an excellent finish. The final coat may be sprinkled with fine pumice stone and rubbed with an oil-soaked felt pad to obtain perfect smoothness. Afterward the work should be thoroughly waxed, both to protect the finish and to bring it to a beautiful luster.

It is generally agreed that the shellac finish should not be applied over a stain that has been mixed in alcohol, or for that matter, over any other type of spirit stain. The alcohol in the shellac is apt to cut and fade stains of this type.

The Varnish Finish

Varnish has many advantages over other types of finishing agents in that it may be applied more easily and provides an excellent luster. However, it is by no means impervious to damage and, unless a specially fine quality of varnish is used, it will, in time, crack and check, and require refinishing.

One of the first requisites in varnishing is to find a dust-free work room. The very fact that varnish dries slowly, makes it vulnerable to any dust or dirt which may come in contact with it during the drying period.

However, after the varnish has been suitably cut with turpentine, you will delight in the fine free fashion in which it flows from the brush. Indeed, as the work is being brushed, ample time can be taken to smooth out the brush strokes, pick up drips, and examine and re-touch all parts of the article.

Although there are a number of quick-drying varnishes on the market, most of them excellent, still you should allow ample time for each coat of varnish to become thoroughly dry. When this time arrives, each coat in turn is carefully rubbed and smoothed with fine garnet paper

After the third coat of shellac or varnish, work should be wet-rubbed with fine, waterproof abrasive paper. Pumice powder or rottenstone also produce glass-smooth surface.

Photos courtesy of E. I. DuPont De Nemours & Co.

85

before the next coat is applied. This provides an even binding surface for the succeeding coat.

Three good coats of varnish generally suffice. The final coat, which should be rubbed to a smooth luster, is polished thoroughly with a mixture of fine pumice stone and rottenstone, or with rottenstone alone. The rubbing is performed with an oil-soaked felt pad. After all parts have been carefull polished, the finished article may be waxed, both for extra luster and to protect the finish.

The Lacquer Finish

A product bearing this name has been used in the Orient since the beginning of civilization. Because of its many excellent qualities it has been greeted with much enthusiasm and is used to a great extent by the furniture industry.

Lacquer provides an exceptionally durable finish. It does not crack or mar very readily and it resists the action of liquids, as well as changing climatic conditions. Moreover, it dries quickly and with the proper equipment is not difficult to apply.

Although lacquer may be obtained in various shades and colors, we are concerned at present with its use in clear form, that is, like shellac and varnish. The ingredients of lacquer (it contains a high percentage of lead acetate, or "banana oil") cause it to be injurious to a stained surface. For this reason, it is wise to first cover the stain with one or more sealing coats of shellac, before any lacquer is applied.

Because it is extremely quick in drying, the most satisfactory way of applying lacquer is with an air brush. When skillfully sprayed on the work it dries uniformly and evenly. However, if it is properly diluted with its exclusive thinner (lacquer thinner) it may be brushed on, providing, of course, that you proceed with due caution and take care not to repeat brush strokes.

There are two schools of thought regarding the treatment of lacquer after it has been applied. Some assert that each coat should be sanded or steel-wooled in the manner of varnish and shellac, while others maintain that the dull even luster of the untouched lacquer should provide the final finish. However, if the final coat is carefully rubbed with either fine steel wool or pumice, no harm will result and, indeed, the beauty of the surface may be enhanced.

Natural Finishes

Oil Finish

For bringing out the inherent characteristics of wood, for the beautification of fine graining, and for the development of a lovely natural luster, no type of finish can surpass that which is obtained with boiled linseed oil. The luxurious, rich tones which oil produces in natural walnut, gumwood, teak, mahogany, and similar hardwoods causes this type of finish to be especially desirable. Moreover, the surface which is treated with oil is amply protected against ordinary damage, and it may be freshened up at any time with new applications of oil.

To produce this finish, it is first necessary to thin the boiled linseed oil with an equal quantity of turpentine. The mixture is applied with a brush, excess oil being removed with an absorbent rag. Successive coats of oil are applied, up to three or four, allowing each coat to dry before applying the next. The final coat is carefully rubbed with a clean cloth until a warm luster has been produced. The oil penetrates the wood, and once it has hardened, there is little likelihood of it coming off and soiling covers or clothing.

Firzite Finish

The advantages of endurance and appearance obtained with a linseed oil finish are approximated, with much less work, with the Firzite finish.

The finishing agent, called Weldwood Deep Finish Firzite acts primarily as a plywood sealer. But when hand rubbed with a cloth it imparts a durable oil-type finish, heretofore possible only with numerous coats of linseed oil. Penetrating deep below the plywood surface it fills the grain and protects it against scratches and water marks. Moreover, after two or more applications its penetration into the wood pores smooths the surface to a dull luster and subdues show-through of wild grain.

Firzite is applied to the sanded plywood with a brush or cloth. After five to ten minutes it is wiped with a lint-free cloth and let dry overnight. It is then lightly sanded with a fine grade of garnet paper and thoroughly dusted off before a second coat is applied. Two well rubbed coats are generally sufficient but absorbent woods may require additional applications. When the final coat is dry, buff with OO steel wool. If desired, luster may be increased by waxing.

Exterior and Marine Plywood Finishes (Vinyl, Acrylic, Epoxy, and Urethane Finishes)

The numerous new "wonder paints" which chemical science has produced during recent years come as a boon to users of exterior grade plywood, and to boatmen in particular. For these finishes not only provide a waterproof coating to safeguard surface veneers of plywood against checking damage but also, in many instances, they furnish enduring armorplate protection against damage to the surface itself.

Vinyl exterior finishes, which come in color as well as clear liquid, form a film of plastic which adheres to the surface and increases in thickness and durability with each additional coat. This flexible film, tightly bonded to the wood, stretches and contracts—an important consideration in the finishing of boats, where the wood is constantly "working" while under way. It dries quickly; with most types of vinyl paints successive coats may be applied after one hour of setting. The only disadvantage of vinyl is that it loses its elasticity with age. Hence, additional coats must be applied, as required, a year or so after the original application.

Acrylic paints are compounded from alkyd modified with acrylic resin. Acrylic resin is closely related to Plexiglas and acrylic-based paints have many of the same qualities. This coating furnishes a hard, glass-smooth surface, impervious to moisture, acids, alkalis, gasoline, oil and most chemicals.

An advantage of acrylic is its almost instant drying quality. Complete finishing of three or four coats may be performed as a continuous operation with no drying period or sanding required between coats. However, this advantage becomes a disadvantage under certain circumstances. For the acrylic finish is somewhat thicker and more difficult to apply by brush than vinyl. Better results are obtained by spraying. Thus the liquid penetrates readily into seams and crevices to provide good sealing and waterproofing. For convenience on small projects, acrylic finishes are now available in spray cans in clear or colors.

Spray finishes, in cans, are handy for small projects or for touch-up of finished parts. *Courtesy of Pittsburgh Plate Glass Co.*

Epoxy paints are the new miracle workers of the finishing field. For unlike other types of finishes which depend on evaporation and air-curing in order to dry, epoxy cures and hardens by catalytic action. This is accomplished by combining two separate chemical compounds. When these two parts are mixed together the "cure" commences and hardening starts.

Thus epoxy paints and clear finishes are marketed in a package containing two separate cans. One contains the resin and the other the curing agent. Because curing action commences as soon as these two compounds are mixed together, there is a limit to the usable life of the resulting epoxy mixture. The period of usability, called the "pot life," lasts from eight to forty-eight hours (according to directions on containers of various manufacturers); it depends, too, on the temperature of the place where the mixture is used. Incidentally, it is impractical to apply epoxy at temperatures below 50° Fahrenheit because a colder temperature protracts the cure and allows atmospheric deterioration. Conversely, heat accelerates the cure. For this reason, the pot life of the epoxy mixture may be prolonged by keeping it under refrigeration.

While epoxy is a bit sticky to apply by brush, it is often put on in this way. When large areas are to be covered, a paint roller or spraying equipment can be used to advantage.

87

Most of the epoxy manufacturers offer this finish in colors as well as clear liquid. Like epoxy adhesive, it forms a permanent bond to the plywood surface. Besides adhering perfectly it makes a hard yet resilient coating of high abrasive resistance and is impervious to damage of most chemicals and liquids. Moreover, it goes on "for keeps," providing a finish which is virtually maintenance-free.

Urethane finishes may be called the first cousins of epoxy since they possess the same general characteristics. However, polyurethane offers the advantage of being a one-container—one-compound type of finish. There is no mixing and waiting. The curing time (pot life) of urethane is somewhat longer than that of epoxy and temperature restrictions are not quite so critical. It is generally available as a clear liquid.

How to Paint

The same basic rules carry through in painting that apply in preparing work for a natural finish. However, painting is not quite as precise an operation as shellacking or varnishing. In most cases, paint will serve to conceal many of the blemishes which might mar or damage the appearance of work which is finished naturally. But it is a good idea to prepare the surface on which paint is to be applied.

Surfaces should be well sanded and free of grease spots, dirt, cracks, or nail holes. Nail holes and cracks can be filled with putty or similar filling substance. Porous, open-grained woods should be carefully filled.

It is always wise to give plywood a clear priming coat before proceeding with additional coats of paint. The priming coat is absorbed by the wood and provides a base for the coats which follow. Where several successive coats are to be applied, each coat, in turn, should be lightly sanded. The final coat is then evenly applied and permitted to remain unsanded.

One or more priming coats should also be applied as a base for enamel. At least two coats of enamel should be used.

Care of Brushes and Finishing Equipment

It goes without saying that paints, shellacs, varnishes, stains, and so forth, should always be kept in air-tight containers when they are not in actual use. White shellac is subject to damage

Spraying equipment can be used to advantage for finishing most projects. Skillful spraying produces professional results. *Courtesy of Burgess Vibro-crafters, Inc.*

Paint rollers save time when finishing large areas. They can be used to advantage for painting full-size panels. *Courtesy of Pittsburgh Plate Glass Co.*

if it is kept in the light. For this reason it should be kept in an earthenware light-proof container. It will corrode the ordinary metal can and leak away if kept over an extended period.

A sealed metal container should be kept handy for storing steel wool, rags, pumice stone, and other materials.

It is a good idea to wash brushes out in a brush-cleaning solution (various brands are available in hardware stores) after they have been used. Special solvents are required for the "wonder paints," as noted on their labels. In this way the bristles are kept clean and soft. After cleaning, brushes may be left in water to which a small amount of the cleaning powder has been added, but they should never be permitted to rest on their bristles. This causes the bristles to bend, and in time renders the brush worthless. To avoid such damage, it is a good idea to hammer a tack in the mid part of the brush handle and suspend the brush on the rim of the can so that its bristles, while they are immersed in the liquid, do not rest on the bottom of the can.

6

UPHOLSTERING
AND COVERING
PLYWOOD

1 Here is everything the job requires. The ¾″ strip in the middle is used as a braceboard.

HOW TO COVER A PLYWOOD COUNTER

If you need a good, serviceable ¾″ counter on your plywood cabinet, here is how to make one. Use the flexible, vinyl covering material called Counter Corlon. First take top measurements of your cabinet allowing proper overlap. Add 4⅛″ to cutting dimensions of the width —this is sawed off to form a 4″ backboard. Shape a ⅜″ quarter-round along one edge of the counter and backboard. Then proceed with construction as shown in the following step-by-step photo sequence.

2 Brush contact cement on the plywood surface and on back of the vinyl covering.

3 Apply vinyl covering allowing overlap along edges. The 4″ backboard rests flush to edge of counter, ready to be bent perpendicular after adhesive sets.

4 Backboard is bent up at right angle to plywood surface and bracing strip is glued and nailed along back edges.

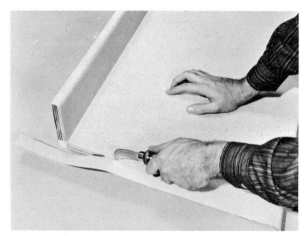

5 Overlapping edges of covering are trimmed with linoleum knife. End edges can be covered with same material.

Photo sequence courtesy of Armstrong Cork Company

HOW TO UPHOLSTER
A PLYWOOD HEADBOARD

Here is an easy upholstering job based on nominal corner shaping of a ½" plywood panel. Start by cutting your plywood to the end-width of a box-spring cot, and about 20" high. Cut the top corners to the curved shape shown in the photos. Attach two 1" by 2" mounting strips about 3" in from each end of the panel. After the headboard is upholstered, these strips are fastened with screws to base of the cot. Using 2" foam rubber, proceed with upholstering as shown in the following step-by-step photo sequence.

1 Mark shape of headboard on 2" foam rubber with chalk or crayon. Allow ½" margin along all edges.

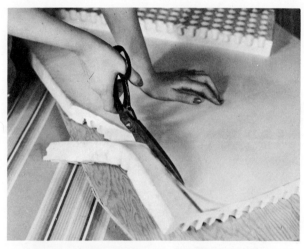

2 Cut foam rubber to marking of headboard. Sharp scissors are best for cutting.

3 Bevel the foam edges on the perforated side. Glue overlapping 4" tape along all edges of the smooth side.

4 Draw tape over edges of plywood and after applying adhesive, tack neatly along edges of back surface.

5 Finally, cover the foam padding with fabric of your choice.

Photo sequence courtesy of Natural Rubber Bureau

HOW TO UPHOLSTER A PLYWOOD CHAIR CUSHION

1 Foam rubber upholstery materials may be purchased by the yard at department stores. Select 2″ thickness.

2 Make a pattern of chair seat and cut ½″ plywood bottom to shape.

3 Transfer pattern to foam rubber allowing ½″ margin along all edges. Cut foam pad with sharp scissors.

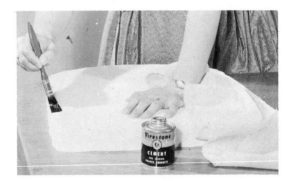

4 Apply rubber cement 1″ in from all edges of pad. Attach edge strips of tacking tape with adhesive.

5 Edge tape is cemented around perimeter of top surface and is drawn over edges of foam rubber.

6 Tape is drawn snug over cushion edges and tacked or stapled along edge surface of plywood backing.

7 Upholstered base is then inserted into seat cover which is also tacked along edges to under surface of plywood.

8 The result: A comfortable and enduring chair cushion.

Photo sequence courtesy of Firestone Tire & Rubber Co.

HOW TO MAKE AND UPHOLSTER A PLYWOOD "SKIDAROUND"

1 Start with a foam rubber square, measuring 24" by 24" by 4".

2 Make cushion cover slightly smaller—23" by 23" by 3-½"—for compression of foam filling.

3 Construct ½" plywood base consisting of 24" by 24" bottom panel; two 2" by 24" sides and two 2" by 23" ends.

4 Assemble base with nails and glue. Inside corner braces can be used to reinforce sides and ends.

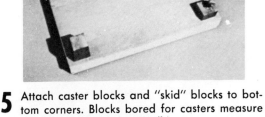

5 Attach caster blocks and "skid" blocks to bottom corners. Blocks bored for casters measure 2" by 2" by 1-½". Skids are 3" long.

6 Paint inside of base box. Attach fabric outside, tacking edges at bottom and along inner surfaces of sides.

7 Foam cushion is tucked snugly inside the edges of base. Casters allow mobility with touch of toe.

8 Upholstered "Skidaround" makes fine floor perch.

Photo sequence courtesy of U. S. Rubber Co.

CUSHION CONSTRUCTION

Perhaps you built a plywood bench, chair, or stool, and you are pretty proud of your handiwork. Then your wife comes along with a comment which shatters your enchantment: "It's nice. But isn't it awfully hard to sit on?"

That does it. For from there on in you become upholstery conscious—and the softer the padding the better. In fact, as demonstrated on preceding pages, here is an area where your wife can lend a hand.

About the softest upholstering possible is obtained either with foam rubber or a combination of polyurethane foam wrapped in Dacron fiberfill batting, as illustrated on this page. The wrapping of Dacron batting over foam provides the very ultimate of softness and at the same time produces a cushion that keeps its shape.

While at the time of writing, DuPont Fiberfill was not too readily available at retail stores, this situation will undoubtedly change. If you have difficulty purchasing this material, you should write directly to the manufacturer to find out where it may be obtained.

Dacron Fiberfill is made in a range of widths, from 19" to 62".

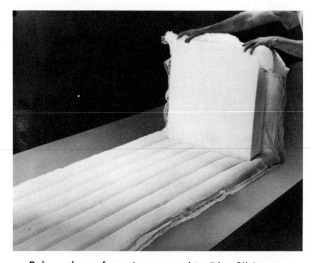

Polyurethane foam is wrapped in Fiberfill batting.

Edges of batting are sewn snugly around the foam core.

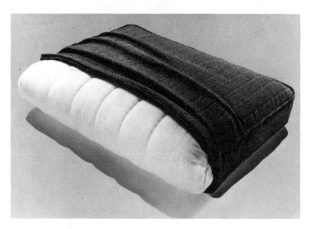

Cushion cover is tailored slightly smaller than dimensions of fill to assure snug fit.

Photos courtesy of E. I. DuPont De Nemours & Co.

7

PLYWOOD PROJECTS FOR INDOOR LIVING

Music Bench

Planter Table

Sectional Wall Storage

Magazine Rack

Wood Storage for Fireplace

Storage Hassock

Photo-Projector Cabinet

Darkroom Cabinet

Fishing Tackle Cabinet

Cleaning Stool

Desk

Rolling Shoe Cart

Storage Divider

Storage Headboard

Sewing Cabinet

Shoe Shine Kit

All projects courtesy American Plywood Association

MUSIC BENCH

A record collection can have the tendency to sprawl out of control in a teenager's room. Wouldn't it be nice to have a cabinet for all your records? Plus a bench where you could sit and listen to all your favorite music?

Indeed you can—and it's yours for very little if you make it yourself. By far the easiest way to do it is to take the materials list to your lumber dealer. You can buy those prefinished legs at most hardware or department stores, or make them of dowels.

MATERIALS

PLYWOOD

    1 panel ¾" x 4'-0" x 5'-0" INT-DFPA. A-A
    1 panel ½" x 1'-4" x 2'-0" INT-DFPA. A-D
    1 panel ¼" x 1'-4" x 1'-4" INT-DFPA. A-D

Code	No. Req'd	Part Size	Use
A	1	13" x 16"	Cabinet top
B	1	11½" x 16"	Cabinet bottom
C	2	14¾" x 16"	Cabinet sides
D	1	14" x 16"	Cabinet divider
E	1	4⅝" x 13⅞"	Front, record rack
F	1	13⅞" x 15¼"	Side, record rack
G	1	4⅛" x 15¼"	Bottom, record rack
H	1	13" x 15½"	Cabinet back
I	1	16½" x 58½"	Bench seat

MISCELLANEOUS:

    3 · 1" and 8 · ½" No. 8 flathead screws
    ½ lb. 6d finished nails
    1 box 1" No. 18 brads
    Small bottle of glue and sandpaper
    1 pt. white semi-gloss enamel and undercoater
    ¼ pt. trim enamel in your choice of color

CUTTING DIAGRAMS

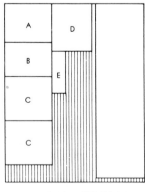

¾" x 4'-0" x 5'-0" INT-DFPA·A-A

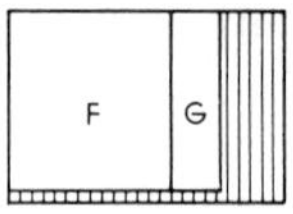

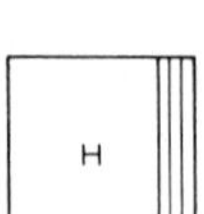

¼" x 1'-4" x 1'x4" INT-DFPA·A-D

½" x 1'-4" x 2'-0" INT-DFPA·A-D

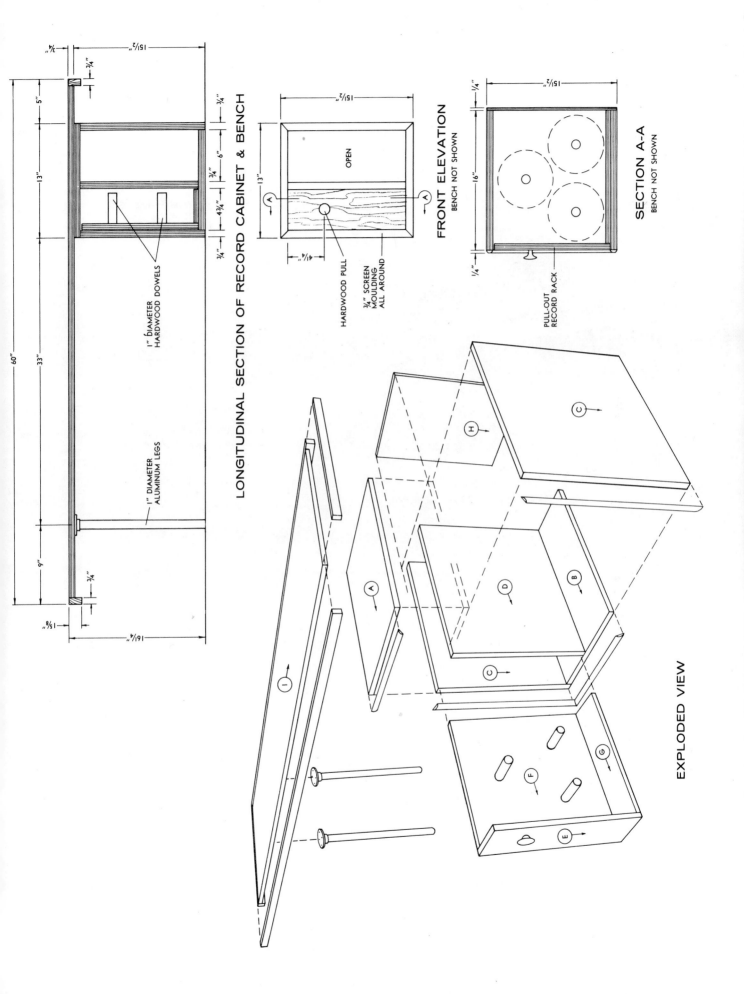

LONGITUDINAL SECTION OF RECORD CABINET & BENCH

15½"
¾"
5"
13"
33"
60"
9"
1⅝"
16¼"
¾"

1" DIAMETER HARDWOOD DOWELS

1" DIAMETER ALUMINUM LEGS

¾"
¾"
6"
4¾"
¾"

FRONT ELEVATION
BENCH NOT SHOWN

15½"
13"
4¼"
OPEN

A — A

HARDWOOD PULL

¾" SCREEN MOULDING ALL AROUND

SECTION A-A
BENCH NOT SHOWN

¼"
15½"
16"
¼"

PULL-OUT RECORD RACK

EXPLODED VIEW

PLANTER TABLE

A variety of uses may be found for this attractive planter table. It can serve as a desk for your home office in your den or attic; as a vanity table in your bedroom, or just as a place to set your household plants in the living room.

This table may be constructed having the back fastened to the wall with only two legs supporting the front; or it may be built as a free-standing unit with four legs.

MATERIALS

PLYWOOD

1 panel ¾" x 4'-0" x 8'-0" INT-DFPA.A-A

LUMBER AND MISCELLANEOUS

No.	Size	Item	Use
12 lin. ft.	⅜" x ⅜"	Fir, pine	Drawer cleats
8 lin. ft.	¼" x ¾"	Hardwood	Drawer guides
*6 lin. ft.	¾" x 2"	Fir or pine	Wall fastening cleat
2 or 4 ea.	¾" diam.	Aluminum pipe	Legs with flanges
2 ea.	1" diam.	Wood pulls	Drawer pulls

F.h. wood screws, finish nails, glue and finishing materials as required.

* For 2 legged unit only, with back fastened to wall.

CUTTING DIAGRAM

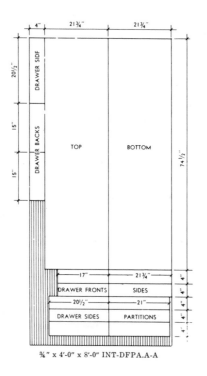

¾" x 4'-0" x 8'-0" INT-DFPA.A-A

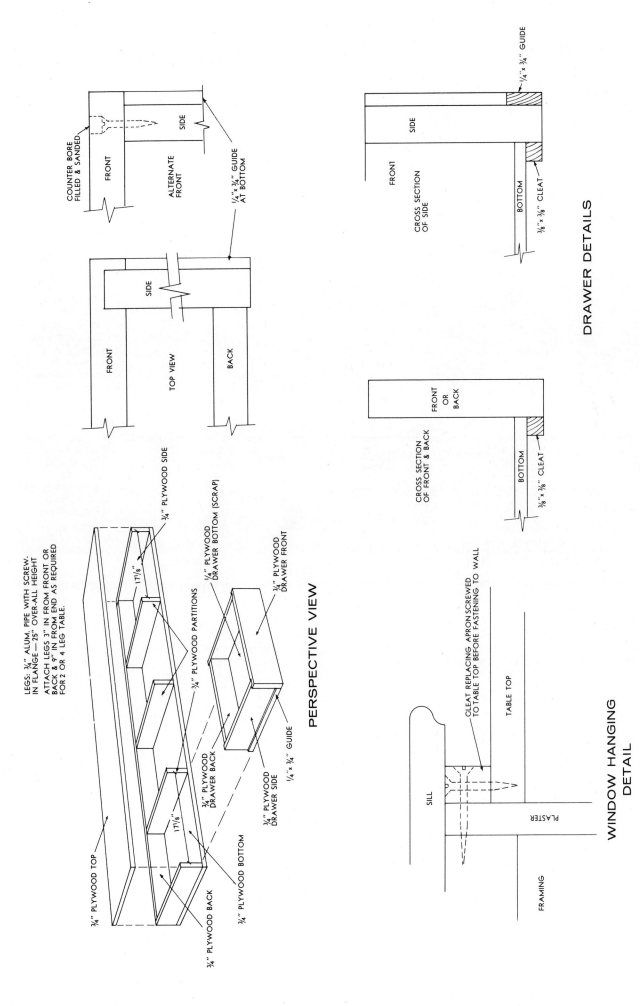

LEGS: ¾" ALUM. PIPE WITH SCREW-
IN FLANGE — 25" OVER-ALL HEIGHT

ATTACH LEGS 3" IN FROM FRONT OR
BACK & 9" IN FROM END AS REQUIRED
FOR 2 OR 4 LEG TABLE.

¾" PLYWOOD TOP

17⅛"

17⅛"

¾" PLYWOOD BACK

¾" PLYWOOD BOTTOM

¾" PLYWOOD SIDE

¼" PLYWOOD PARTITIONS

¼" PLYWOOD DRAWER BOTTOM (SCRAP)

¾" PLYWOOD DRAWER FRONT

¾" PLYWOOD DRAWER BACK

¾" PLYWOOD DRAWER SIDE

¼" x ¾" GUIDE

PERSPECTIVE VIEW

COUNTER BORE FILLED & SANDED

FRONT

SIDE

ALTERNATE FRONT

¼" x ¾" GUIDE AT BOTTOM

FRONT

SIDE

TOP VIEW

BACK

¼" x ¾" GUIDE

FRONT

SIDE

CROSS SECTION OF SIDE

BOTTOM

⅜" x ⅜" CLEAT

FRONT OR BACK

CROSS SECTION OF FRONT & BACK

BOTTOM

⅜" x ⅜" CLEAT

DRAWER DETAILS

SILL

CLEAT REPLACING APRON SCREWED TO TABLE TOP BEFORE FASTENING TO WALL

TABLE TOP

PLASTER

FRAMING

WINDOW HANGING DETAIL

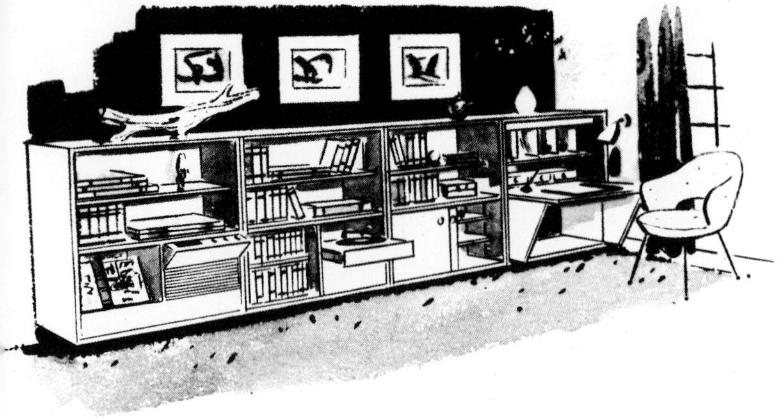

SECTIONAL WALL STORAGE

A smart yet inexpensive living-room furnishing, this ultra-modern built-in holds everything from hi-fi equipment to stationery; it can be built over a single weekend. You can easily adapt the arrangement shown, adding or omitting sections, to suit available wall space. Why not take the materials list to your lumber dealer for an estimate?

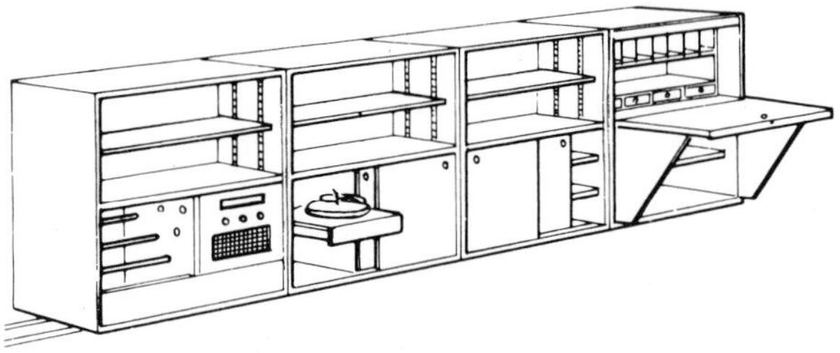

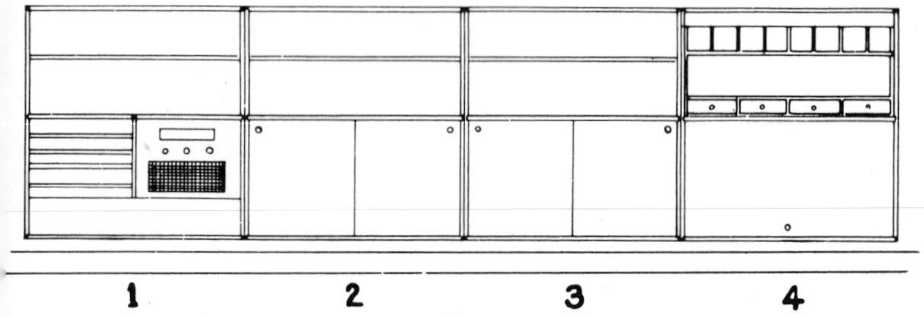
1
2
3
4

MATERIALS

FIR PLYWOOD

No.	*Size*	*Grade*	*Where Used*
2 panels	4′ x 8′ x ¾″	INT-DFPA. A-A	End, tops, top shelves, desk door, desk supports, magazine rack front
1 piece	4′ x 4′ x ¾″	INT-DFPA. A-A	
5 panels	4′ x 8′ x ¾″	INT-DFPA. A-D	Counter, bottoms, sliding doors, sides, lower shelves, backs, record player platform and front, speaker front, cabinet
1 panel	4′ x 8′ x ½″	INT-DFPA. A-D	partition Drawer fronts, backs and sides. Drawer and letter file framework. Light trough, record storage. Record
1 piece	4′ x 4′ x ½″	INT-DFPA. A-A	storage partitions and drawer bottoms

LUMBER

Size	*Quantity*	*Where Used.*
2″ x 3″	32″	Wall cleats
¾″ dowels	6 ft.	Magazine rack
1″ x 2″	40 ft.	Miscellaneous

HARDWARE AND MISCELLANEOUS

Description	*Quantity*	*Where Used*
Adjustable shelf standards, 21¼″ long	12	Shelves
Sliding door hardware	2 sets	Doors
⅝″ piano hinge	4 ft.	Desk
Bullet catches	3	Desk
Flush pulls	9	Doors
2′ fluorescent light fixture	1	Desk
2″ x 2″ butt hinge	1 pair	Cabinet No. 1
Spring catches	1 pair	Cabinet No. 1
Fingerpulls	5	Sliding doors, desk tops
Finishing materials	4	Radio face
Thumb screws	As needed	Speaker
Fabric		
Screws, finish nails & glue		

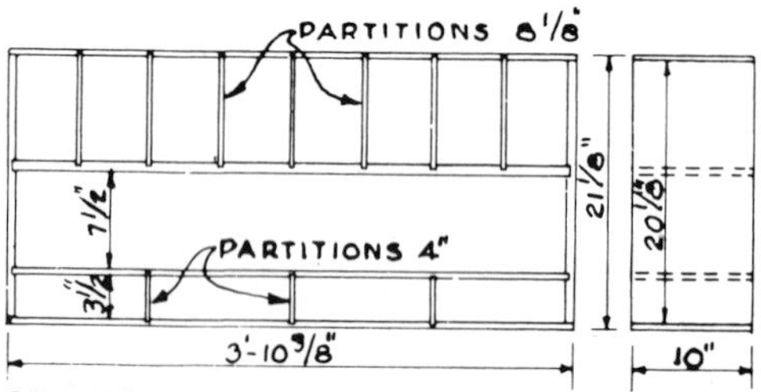
PARTITIONS 8 1/8
PARTITIONS 4"
7 1/2
3 1/2
21 1/8"
20 1/8
3'-10 3/8"
10"

DRAWER AND LETTER FILE FRAMEWORK — TOP AND BOTTOM 1/2" PLYWOOD – PARTITIONS 1/4" PLYWOOD

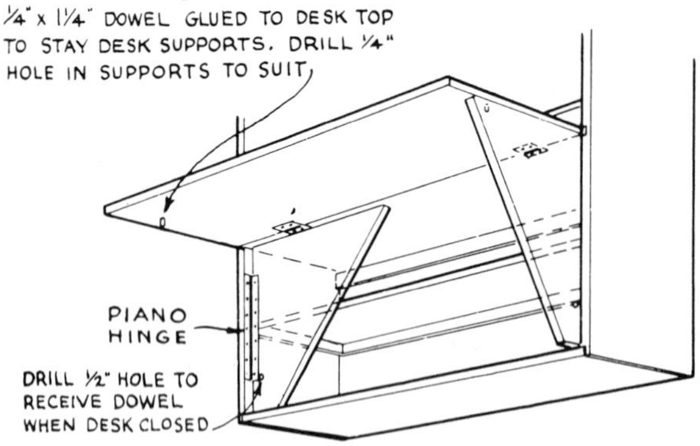
1/4" x 1 1/4" DOWEL GLUED TO DESK TOP TO STAY DESK SUPPORTS. DRILL 1/4" HOLE IN SUPPORTS TO SUIT
PIANO HINGE
DRILL 1/2" HOLE TO RECEIVE DOWEL WHEN DESK CLOSED

VIEW OF UNDERSIDE OF DESK SHOWING SUPPORTS.

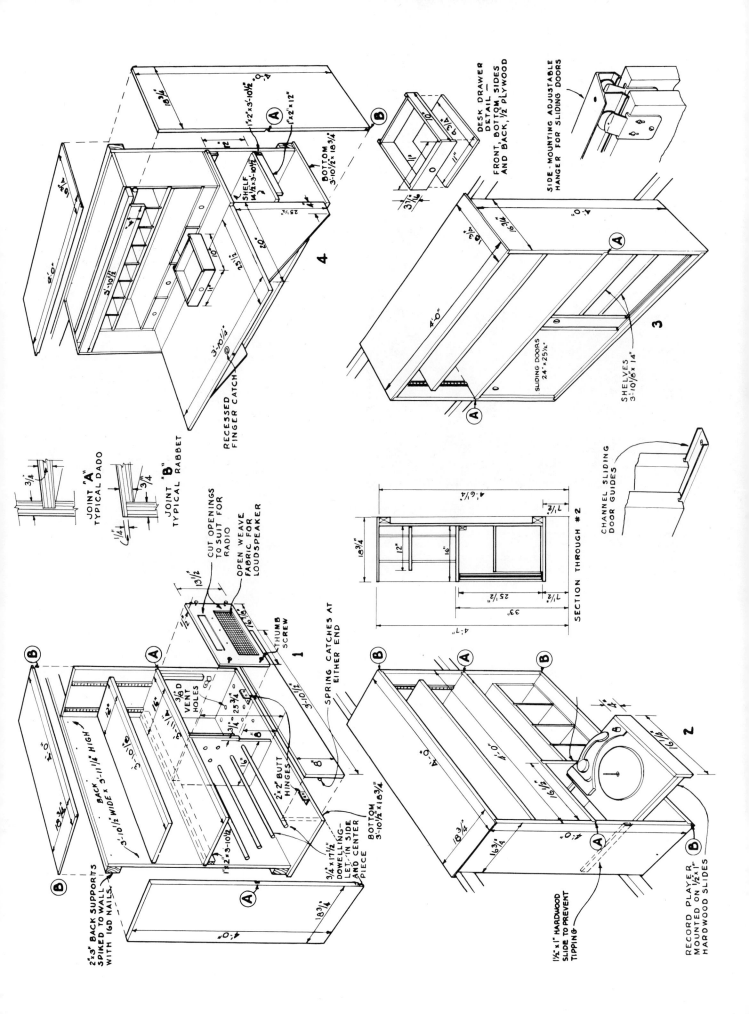

MAGAZINE RACK

Don't let the idea of making special iron legs stop you from building this useful accessory. You can make a plywood base instead, if you choose, simply by butting two pieces of plywood together to the dimensions shown on plan.

Cut spacers and ½" fir plywood partitions to size, sand edges and round top corners slightly. Fasten both spacers to edge of center partition with glue and 8d nails driven through from each side. Then cover nails by attaching front and back partition to spacers with glue and 6d finish nails. Set heads slightly, fill, sand, and finish as recommended to contrast with color of legs.

MATERIALS

Code	No. Req'd	Size	Part Identification
A	1	8½" x 23½"	Front partition
B	1	11" x 23½"	Center partition
C	1	14" x 23½"	Back partition
	4 lin. ft.	2" x 2"	Spacers
	1 only	½" Diam.	Wrought iron stand

MISCELLANEOUS

6d and 8d finish nails and glue
1⅞" No. 8 r.h. screws as required

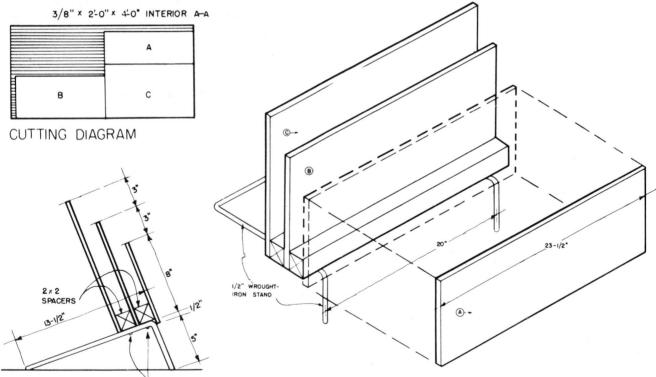

3/8" x 2'-0" x 4'-0" INTERIOR A-A

A

B   C

CUTTING DIAGRAM

3"
3"
8"
1/2"
5"
2 x 2 SPACERS
13-1/2"
1-7/8" R.H. NO.8 WOOD SCREWS

©
®
Ⓐ
1/2" WROUGHT-IRON STAND
20"
23-1/2"

WOOD STORAGE
FOR FIREPLACE

If you ever struggled to keep an unruly stack of wood tidy, you will glory in the convenience of this easy-to-build fireplace rack.

Unless you have welding equipment available, make base wedges of wood. Paint flat black, white, or a color to harmonize with room decorations.

Attach back to the end of the bottom panel you beveled to 00°, using glue and 8d finish nails, and sand flush. Fill and sand all edges, finish as recommended and attach frame. Select a tough finish and avoid light colors to prevent scuffing by logs. Many hardware and lumber dealers have rubber "crutch tips" you can put on legs to keep from marring floors.

MATERIALS

Code	No. Req'd	Size	Part Identification
A	1	24" x 31¼"	Bottom
B	1	16" x 24"	Back
	1 only	½" diam.	Wrought iron frame

MISCELLANEOUS

6d finish nails and glue
1" No. 8 r.h. screws as required

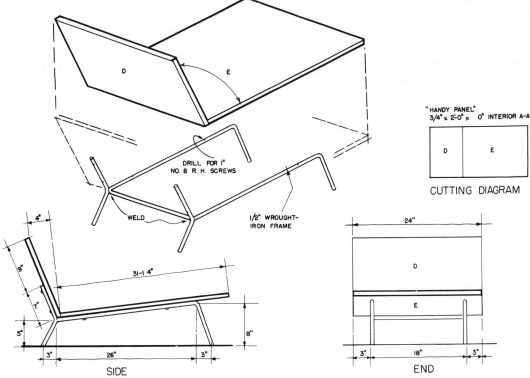

"HANDY PANEL"
3/4" x 2'-0" x 0" INTERIOR A-A

CUTTING DIAGRAM

DRILL FOR 1"
NO. 8 R. H. SCREWS

WELD

1/2" WROUGHT-IRON FRAME

SIDE

END

STORAGE HASSOCK

This storage hassock can be a handy, useful, yet an inexpensive addition to any room's furnishings. Simple details make this an excellent project for beginners in woodworking. In addition, fine experience is provided in layout, measurement, and fitting of parts.

Use of interior-type fir plywood will insure sturdy construction. Only an evening or two will be required to build this handsome well-designed hassock.

MATERIALS

Code	No. Req'd	Size	Part Identification
A	4	15" x 17¼"	Sides
B	1	12½" x 12½"	Bottom
C	1	16¼" x 16¼"	Underside of lid
D	1	17¾" x 17¾"	Lid
	1 pc.	17¾" x 17¾"	1" foam rubber
	1 pc.	3' x 5'	Vinyl fabric
	5 lin. ft.	1" x 1"	Ledger strip
	8 ea.	—	Clip angles
	1 pr.	—	Semi-Concealed hinges

MISCELLANEOUS

4d finish nails, staples and glue

CUTTING DIAGRAM

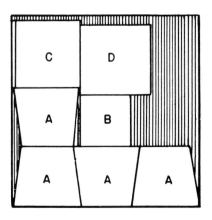

½ " x 4'-0" x 4'-0" INT-DFPA A-D

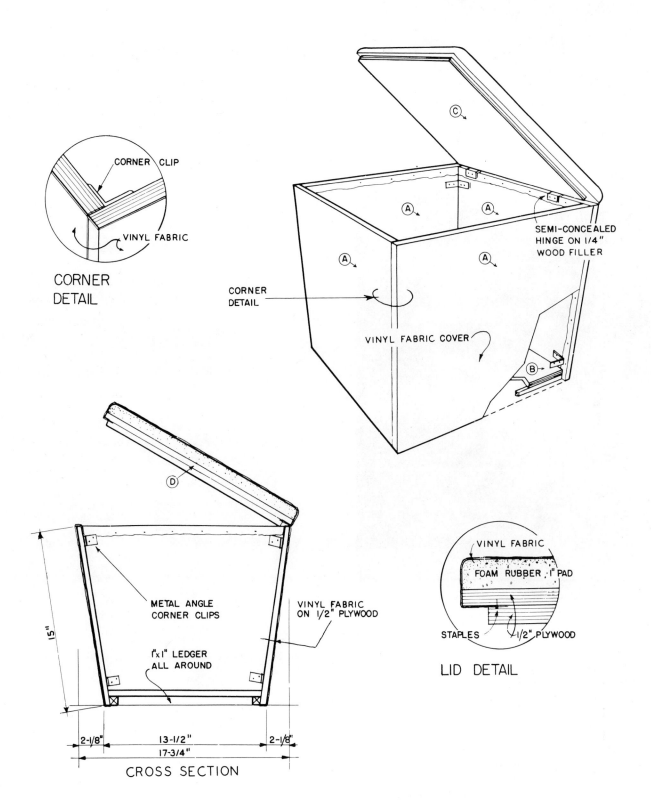

CORNER CLIP

VINYL FABRIC

CORNER
DETAIL

C

A   A

A   A

SEMI-CONCEALED
HINGE ON 1/4"
WOOD FILLER

CORNER
DETAIL

VINYL FABRIC COVER

B

D

METAL ANGLE
CORNER CLIPS

VINYL FABRIC
ON 1/2" PLYWOOD

15"

1"x1" LEDGER
ALL AROUND

2-1/8"   13-1/2"   2-1/8"
17-3/4"

CROSS SECTION

VINYL FABRIC

FOAM RUBBER, 1" PAD

STAPLES   1/2" PLYWOOD

LID DETAIL

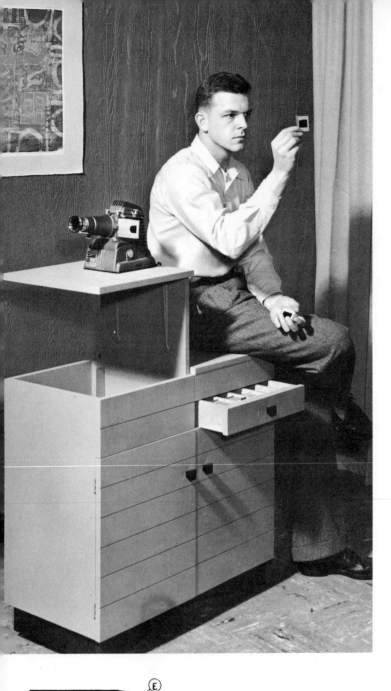

PHOTO-PROJECTOR CABINET

Protection for films, slides, and equipment eliminates possible damage and loss when this projector cabinet is put into use. And instead of the disorder and confusion that so often handicap home film showings you have convenience and a smooth performance.

MATERIALS

Code	No. Req'd	Size	Part Identification
A	1	25¼" x 32"	Front of unit
B	1	25¼" x 32"	Back of unit
C	2	14½" x 25¼"	Side of unit
D	2	14½" x 30½"	Bottom and shelf
E	2	16" x 16"	Projector top and lid
F	2	14½" x 18"	Fixed and sliding standard
G	1	13⅜" x 14½"	Drawer bottom
H	2	3" x 14½"	Drawer side
I	2	2½" x 13⅜"	Drawer front and back
J	5	2½" x 12½"	Drawer dividers
K	9	8" x 8"	Reel dividers
L	1	14½" x 14½"	Bottom of compartment
M	4	3" x 12"	Skirt Board
N	2	3" x 14½"	Skirt Board
	5 lin. ft.	¾" x ¾"	Drawer guides
	2½ lin. ft.	2" x 3"	Caster blocks
	1 ea.	2" x 2" x ¾"	Spring bolt block
	4½ lin. ft.	1" x 2"	Slide track
	2 ea.	7" x 9"	Metal shelf brackets
	1 only	No. 1697	Window spring bolt
	4 ea.	—	Rubber wheel casters
	2 ea.	—	Door pulls
	1 ea.	—	Drawer pull
	2 pr.	—	Pin hinges

MISCELLANEOUS

4d and 6d finish nails and glue

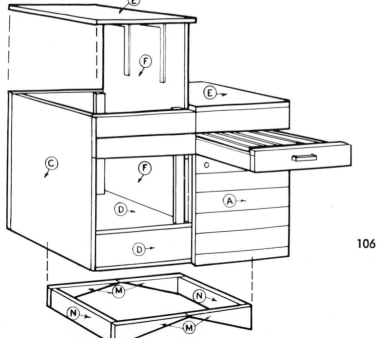

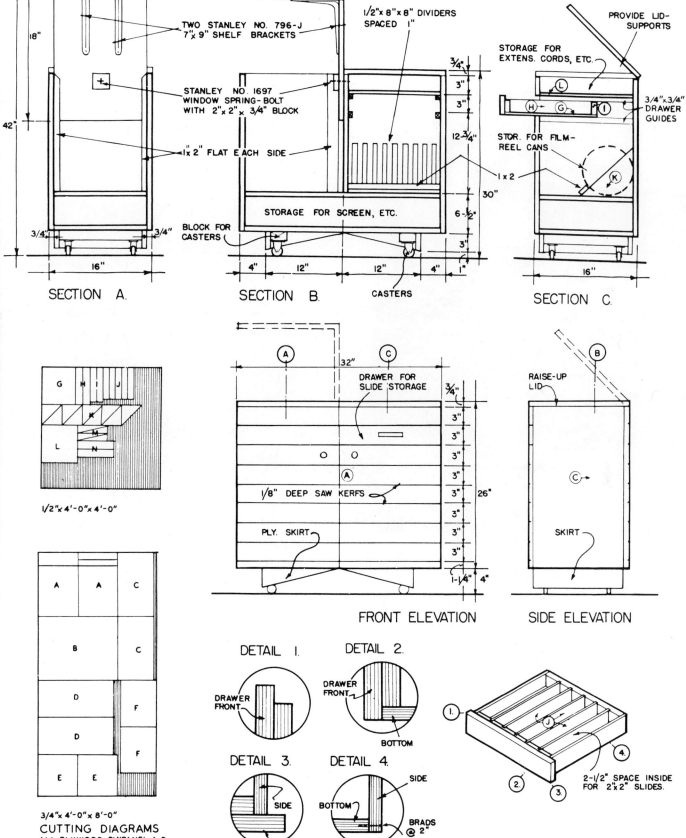

NOTE— PROJECTOR TOP IS
RAISED BY HAND TO 42" WHERE
SPRING BOLT SNAPS INTO PLACE
(PULL OUT TO RELEASE)

TWO STANLEY NO. 796-J
7"x 9" SHELF BRACKETS

1/2"x 8"x 8" DIVIDERS
SPACED 1"

PROVIDE LID-
SUPPORTS

STORAGE FOR
EXTENS. CORDS, ETC.

18"

STANLEY NO. 1697
WINDOW SPRING-BOLT
WITH 2"x 2"x 3/4" BLOCK

3/4"
3"
3"

3/4"x 3/4"
DRAWER
GUIDES

42"

1"x 2" FLAT EACH SIDE

STOR. FOR FILM-
REEL CANS

12-3/4"

1 x 2

STORAGE FOR SCREEN, ETC.

30"

3/4"
3/4"

BLOCK FOR
CASTERS

6-1/2"

3"

16"

4"   12"   12"   4"   1"

16"

CASTERS

SECTION A.

SECTION B.

SECTION C.

G H I J

K

M

N

L

1/2"x 4'-0"x 4'-0"

32"

A   C

DRAWER FOR
SLIDE STORAGE

3/4"
3"
3"
3"
3"
3"
3"
3"
3"

RAISE-UP
LID

26"

A

1/8" DEEP SAW KERFS

C

PLY. SKIRT

SKIRT

1-1/4" 4"

A   A   C

C

B

D   F

D   F

E   E

3/4"x 4'-0"x 8'-0"

CUTTING DIAGRAMS
ALL PLYWOOD PLYPANEL A-D

FRONT ELEVATION

SIDE ELEVATION

DETAIL 1.

DRAWER
FRONT

DETAIL 2.

DRAWER
FRONT

BOTTOM

1.

J

2.   3.

4.

2-1/2" SPACE INSIDE
FOR 2"x 2" SLIDES.

DETAIL 3.

SIDE

DETAIL 4.

SIDE

BOTTOM

FRONT

BRADS
@ 2"

DARKROOM CABINET

When time for a hobby is limited, organization of working space, equipment, and materials is most important. Any photographer building this darkroom cabinet will be well repaid in added convenience and efficiency.

If necessary, adjust any dimensions to your space, then cut parts specified in the diagrams and material list. Nail and glue all joints.

MATERIALS

Code	No. Req'd	Size	Part Identification
A	2	16" x 29¼"	Ends
B	1	15¾" x 34½"	Bottom
C	3	12" x 48"	Shelf
D	2	3¾" x 17-3/16"	Drawer front
E	1	16" x 36"	Top
F	1	3½" x 36"	Base
G	4	3¾" x 14⅝"	Drawer sides
H	2	3" x 16"	Drawer back
I	1	11¼" x 12½"	Door, paper cabinet
J	1	11¼" x 11½"	Side, paper cabinet
K	1	11½" x 11½"	Top, paper cabinet
L	1	10¾" x 11½"	Back, paper cabinet
M	6	¾" x 15¼"	Drawer guides
N	2	17⅝" x 20⅞"	Door
O	2	11" x 12"	Shelf, paper cabinet
P	1	25¾" x 35¼"	Back
Q	2	14⅝" x 16"	Drawer bottom
R	1	11¼" x 12"	Side, paper cabinet
	14 lin. ft.	1" x 2"	Framing
	1 pr.	For ½" plywood	Semi-concealed hinges
	4 lin. ft.	—	Felt strip and qtr. round
*	6 lin. ft.	—	Adjustable shelf standard
	6 ea.	—	Shelf brackets, 12"
	6 lin. ft.	1" x 1"	Drawer stop and nailer

MISCELLANEOUS

4d and 6d finish nails; waterproof glue

*Optional—use fixed brackets if desired

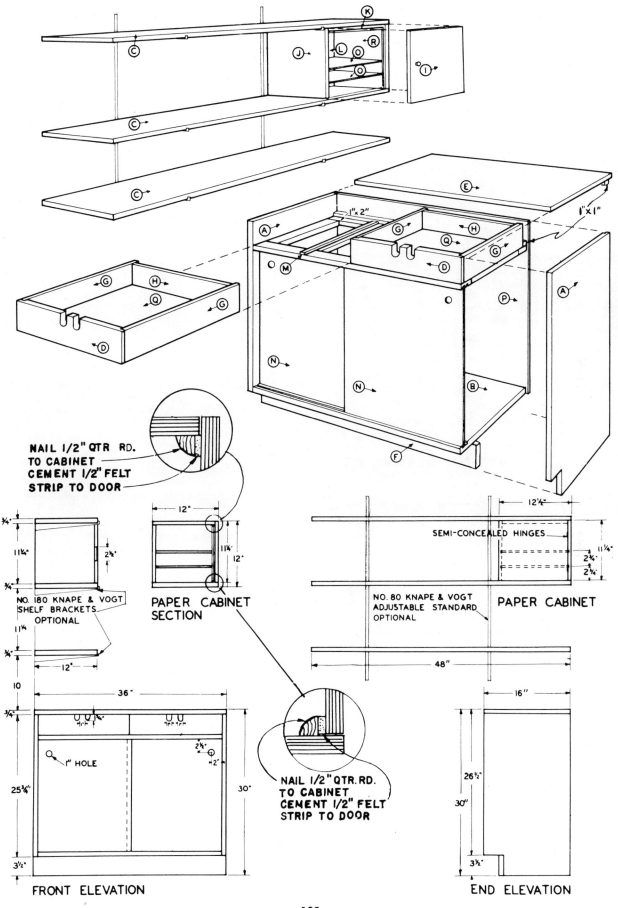

NAIL 1/2" QTR RD.
TO CABINET
CEMENT 1/2" FELT
STRIP TO DOOR

NAIL 1/2" QTR.RD.
TO CABINET
CEMENT 1/2" FELT
STRIP TO DOOR

12"

11¼"

12"

PAPER CABINET
SECTION

3/4"

11¼"

2½"

3/4"

NO. 180 KNAPE & VOGT
SHELF BRACKETS
OPTIONAL

11¼"

3/4"

12"

12½"

SEMI-CONCEALED HINGES

11¼"

2¾"

2¾"

NO. 80 KNAPE & VOGT
ADJUSTABLE STANDARD
OPTIONAL

PAPER CABINET

48"

10

3/4"

36"

1" HOLE

2½"

2"

25¾"

30"

FRONT ELEVATION

3½"

16"

26½"

30"

3½"

END ELEVATION

109

FISHING TACKLE CABINET

As soon as you have built this custom cabinet for your collection of fishing gear, declare exclusive ownership in a loud, clear voice. Otherwise, the other members of the family will naturally want to store other items in it which will disrupt the well organized storage designed into this cabinet. Be firm; there is nothing like having your fishing gear all in one place and in good condition, ready for use.

MATERIALS

Code	No. Req'd	Size	Part Identification
A	2	17" x 84"	Side
B	1	11¾" x 22½"	Drawer shelf
C	3	12½" x 22½	Shelf
D	2	4½" x 11¼"	Drawer front
E	1	24" x 80½"	Door
F	1	17" x 23¼"	Top
G	2	3¼" x 77¼"	Door side frame
H	3	3" x 20½"	Door shelf
I	1	3¼" x 20½"	Door top frame
J	1	3½" x 22½"	Base
K	1	23¼" x 80⅛"	Back
L	2	3" x 11"	Drawer back
M	4	3¾" x 12⅛"	Drawer side
N	2	10¾" x 12⅛"	Drawer bottom
P	1	7" x 20½"	Door shelf facia
Q	2	2" x 20½"	Door shelf facia
U	1	4¾" x 10"	Dowel board
V	1	12½" x 22"	Standard
W	2	11¾" x 12½"	Shelf
X	1	16¾" x 22½"	Bottom shelf

MISCELLANEOUS

1 door bolt; 4 pin hinges; 2½" diam. 8¾" long hardwood dowels; 1 pc. ¼" x 20½" x 55" cork backing; 1 metal clothes hanger. 4d and 6d finish nails and glue; clips as required.

CUTTING DIAGRAMS

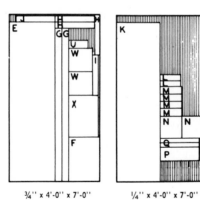

¾" x 4'-0" x 7'-0"   ¼" x 4'-0" x 7'-0"

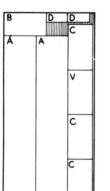

110

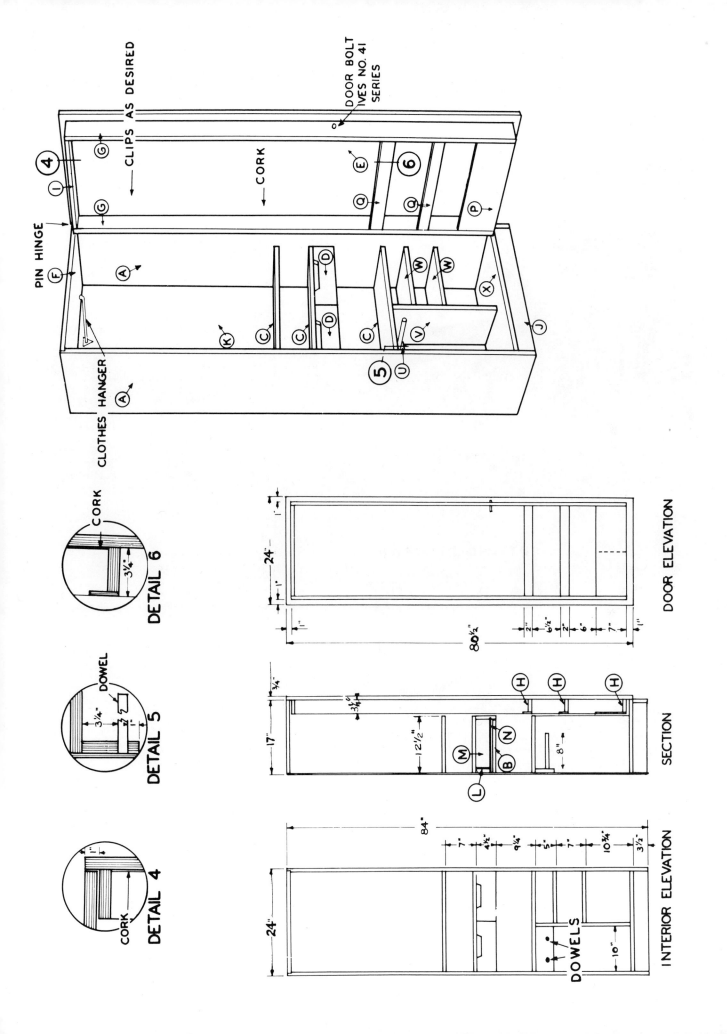

DOOR BOLT
IVES NO. 41
SERIES

CLIPS AS DESIRED

CORK

PIN HINGE

CLOTHES HANGER

CORK

DETAIL 6

DOWEL

DETAIL 5

DETAIL 4

CORK

DOOR ELEVATION

SECTION

INTERIOR ELEVATION

DOWELS

CLEANING STOOL

This simple, stylish little storage stool is a real convenience. If you are sitting at your work counter, all your cleaning supplies are within arms' reach. If you are down on all fours, the stool is a handy carry-all, which you can roll around with you while you do your cleaning.

Construction of this handy stool can be completed in an evening or two. If you wish to conceal your clearing products, hinge a plywood panel over the front.

MATERIALS

PLYWOOD

    1 panel ¾" x 4' -0" x 4' -0" INT. A-A

Code	No. Req'd	Part Size	Use
A	2	See drawings	Legs
B	2	See drawings	Legs
C	2	13⅜" x 16"	Sides
D	2	3" x 15½"	Seat support
E	1	8½" x 12½"	Top shelf
F	1	12½" x 16"	Bottom shelf
G	1	8⅞" x 9¾"	Center shelf
H	1	16" x 16"	Seat
I	1	11⅞" x 15½"	Partition

HARDWOOD

    1 pc. 1" x 2" x 6'

MISCELLANEOUS

    ⅜" scrap plywood for lamination of legs.
    Pad to suit 16" x 16" plywood seat.
    4d & 6d finish nails.
    8 - 1¼" No. 6 f. h. wood screws.
    Glue and finishing materials.

CUTTING DIAGRAM

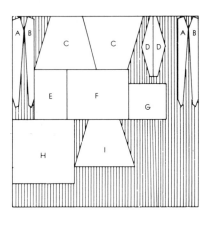

¾"x 4'- 0"x 4'- 0" DFPA INTERIOR A-A

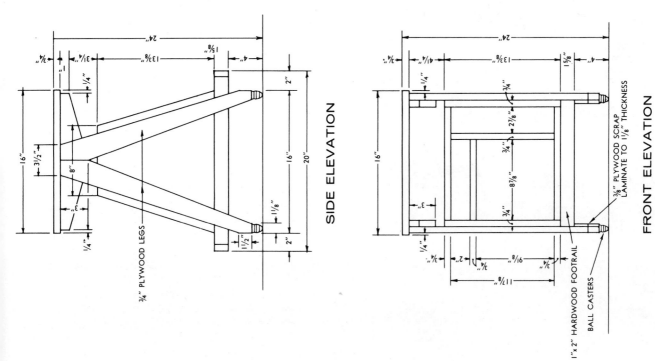

SIDE ELEVATION

¾" PLYWOOD LEGS

FRONT ELEVATION

1"x 2" HARDWOOD FOOTRAIL

BALL CASTERS

⅜" PLYWOOD SCRAP
LAMINATE TO 1⅛" THICKNESS

ALL PLYWOOD — ¾" INTERIOR A-A

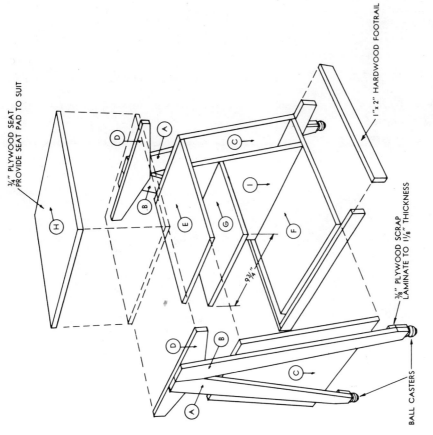

DESIGNED BY NORMAN CHERNER & ASSOCIATES

¾" PLYWOOD SEAT
PROVIDE SEAT PAD TO SUIT

1"x 2" HARDWOOD FOOTRAIL

⅜" PLYWOOD SCRAP
LAMINATE TO 1⅛" THICKNESS

BALL CASTERS

EXPLODED VIEW

DESK

Construction of this desk is simple, straightforward and sturdy, so it should serve well for years, as the writing surface height can change from 24″ up to 29″.

Select joint details to be followed from alternates given. Cut parts as required for rabbeted or butt joint construction. Check cabinet parts to insure fit before assembling. All joints should be glued and nailed.

Join sides with top and bottom shelf after recessing for hinge, then nail back in place. Nail through bottom and back into drawer divider "G" after attaching drawer supports at lower edge as shown. Nail through upper shelves "I" into partitions "N" and install with partition "J" and intermediate shelf.

Check fit of drawer parts in place and assemble as shown to meet in center, hiding drawer divider panel. Drawer fronts project past bottoms for finger pull.

Drill six holes in sides at heights given, spaced according to bolt holes in steel frame. These can be made by practically any welding or metalworking shop.

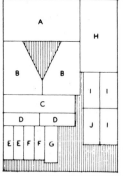

3/4″ x 4′-0″ x 6′-0″
CUTTING DIAGRAMS
ALL PLYWOOD INTERIOR A-A

1/2″ x 4′-0″ x 4′-0″

DRAWERS DETAILED SO THEY CAN BE MADE WITH HAND TOOLS (NO RABBETS, ETC.)

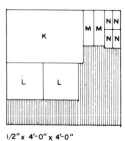

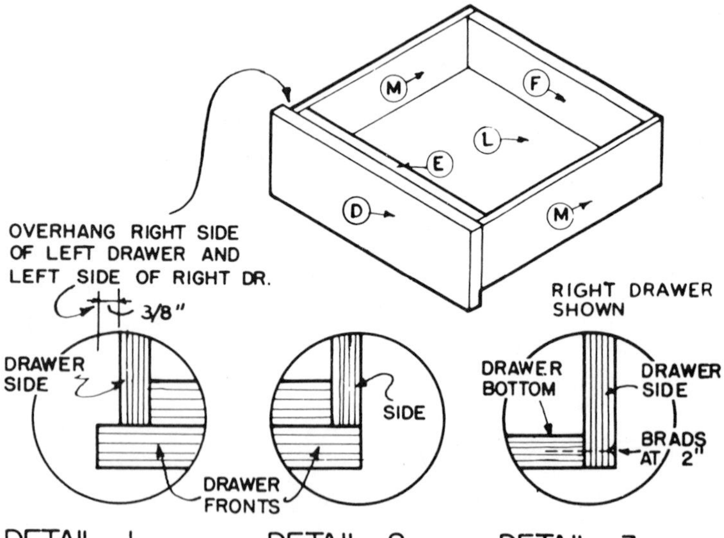

RIGHT DRAWER SHOWN

OVERHANG RIGHT SIDE OF LEFT DRAWER AND LEFT SIDE OF RIGHT DR.
3/8″

DRAWER SIDE

DRAWER FRONTS

SIDE

DRAWER BOTTOM

DRAWER SIDE

BRADS AT 2″

DETAIL 1.   DETAIL 2.   DETAIL 3.

MATERIALS

Code	No. Req'd	Size	Part Indentification
A	1	17¾″ x 32″	Desk lid
B	2	16″ x 22″	Side
C	1	7½″ x 30½″	Top
D	2	5¼″ x 15¼″	Drawer front
E	2	4⅜″ x 13¾″	Inside drawer front
F	2	4⅜″ x 13¾″	Drawer back
G	1	5¼″ x 14¾″	Divider between drawers
H	1	15½″ x 30½″	Bottom shelf
I	3	7½″ x 14⅞″	Shelf
J	1	7½″ x 15¼″	Vertical divider
K	1	22″ x 30½″	Back of unit
L	2	13¾″ x 13¾″	Drawer bottom
M	4	4⅜″ x 15¼″	Drawer side
	9 lin. ft.	¾″ x ¾″	Drawer supports
	1 only	See drawings	Wrought iron frame
	1 pc.	32″ long	Piano hinge
	1 only	As required	Chain or lid-support

MISCELLANEOUS

6d finish nails and glue; 3/16″ machine bolts as required

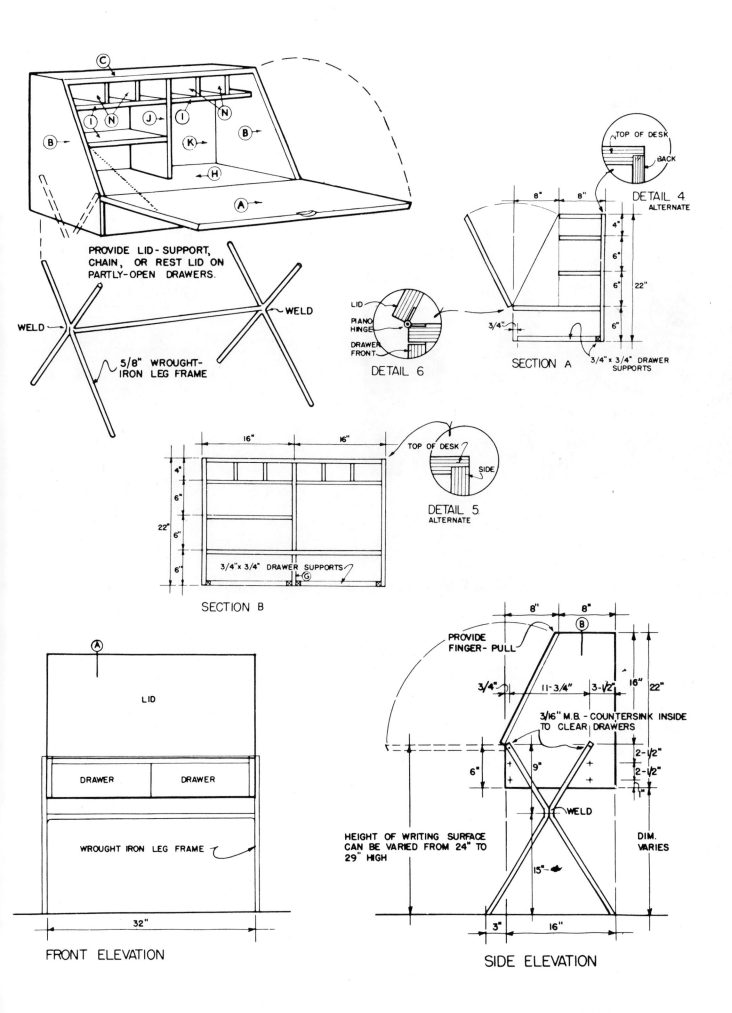

PROVIDE LID-SUPPORT,
CHAIN, OR REST LID ON
PARTLY-OPEN DRAWERS.

WELD

WELD

WELD

5/8" WROUGHT-
IRON LEG FRAME

DETAIL 4
ALTERNATE

TOP OF DESK

BACK

LID

PIANO HINGE

DRAWER FRONT

DETAIL 6

8"   8"   4"   6"   6"   22"   6"

3/4"

SECTION A

3/4" x 3/4" DRAWER SUPPORTS

16"   16"

TOP OF DESK

SIDE

DETAIL 5.
ALTERNATE

4"   6"   22"   6"   6"

3/4" x 3/4" DRAWER SUPPORTS

SECTION B

LID

DRAWER   DRAWER

WROUGHT IRON LEG FRAME

32"

FRONT ELEVATION

PROVIDE
FINGER-PULL

8"   8"

3/4"   11-3/4"   3-1/2"   16"   22"

3/16" M.B.- COUNTERSINK INSIDE
TO CLEAR DRAWERS

6"   9"   2-1/2"   2-1/2"   1"

WELD

HEIGHT OF WRITING SURFACE
CAN BE VARIED FROM 24" TO
29" HIGH

15"

3"   16"

DIM.
VARIES

SIDE ELEVATION

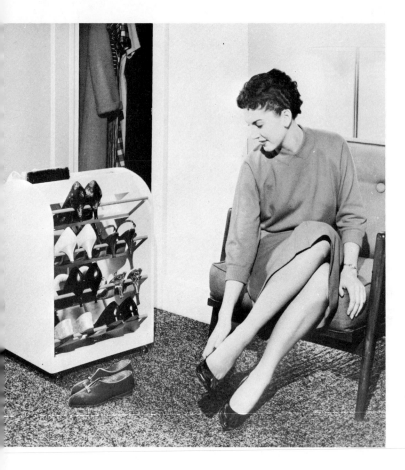

ROLLING SHOE CART

It is always difficult to find a particular pair of shoes if you have to search through a jumbled pile of footwear on the floor of your closet. Here is how to get your shoes off the floor to keep them cleaner and prevent scuffing to prolong their life.

This attractive shoe cart rolls on casters to make selection of shoes or slippers an easy task. A tray in the top of the chart provides handy access to polish, rags and brushes.

MATERIALS

PLYWOOD

1 panel ½" x 4' -0" INT-DFPA. A-D.

Code	No. Req'd	Part Size	Use
A	2	16" x 26"	Ends
B	1	16" x 17½"	Bottom
C	4	5" x 17½"	Shelves & tray bottom
D	2	2¾" x 17½"	Tray sides
E	2	1½" x 17½"	Bottom facia

MISCELLANEOUS

6d finish nails and glue
Finishing materials
½" diam. hardwood dowels
½" diam. wheel swivel casters

CUTTING DIAGRAM

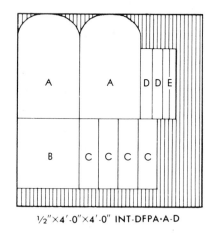

½"×4'-0"×4'-0" INT-DFPA·A-D

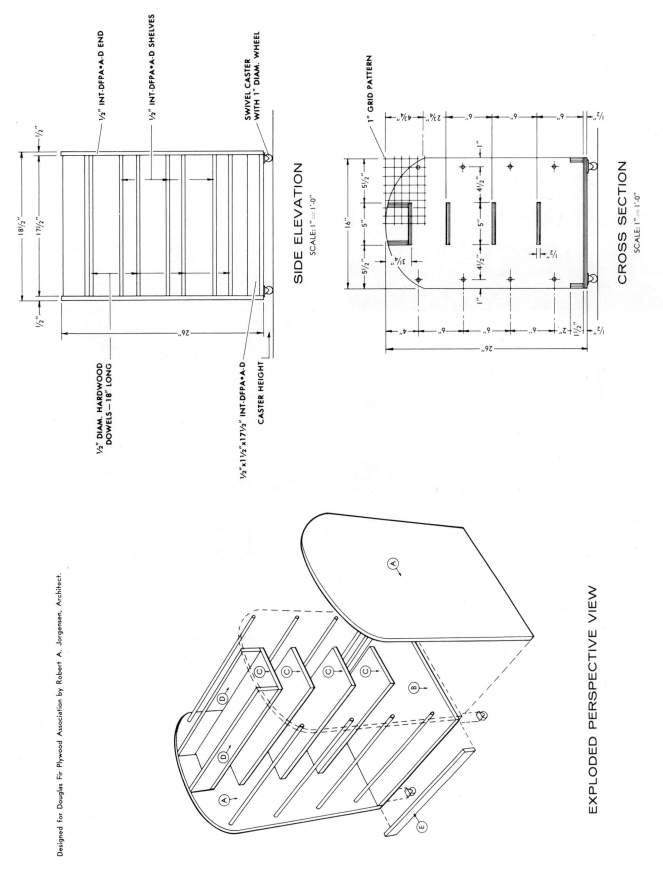

½" INT-DFPA•A-D END

½" INT-DFPA•A-D SHELVES

SWIVEL CASTER
WITH 1" DIAM. WHEEL

½" DIAM. HARDWOOD
DOWELS—18" LONG

18½"

17½"

½"

½"

26"

½"x1½"x17½" INT-DFPA•A-D

CASTER HEIGHT

SIDE ELEVATION
SCALE: 1" = 1'-0"

1" GRID PATTERN

16"

5½"

5½"

5"

3½"

4½"

5"

4½"

1"

½"

½"

2¾"

4¾"

6"

6"

6"

½"

26"

4"

6"

6"

6"

2"

1½"

½"

½"

CROSS SECTION
SCALE: 1" = 1'-0"

Designed for Douglas Fir Plywood Association by Robert A. Jorgensen, Architect.

A

D

D

C

C

C

C

B

A

E

EXPLODED PERSPECTIVE VIEW

117

STORAGE DIVIDER

This two-faced room divider will solve many storage problems. The front face has a handy drop-leaf desk, space for TV, HI-FI equipment and records; also, storage drawers which may be reached from both sides.

The rear face has cupboards for china or glassware. Decorative accessories show on both sides on open shelves. Gaily painted sliding doors have curved edges instead of finger pulls —an unusual innovation giving a contemporary look to this unit.

MATERIALS

Fir Plywood

4 panels ¾″ x 4′-0″ x 8′-0″ INT. A-A
1 panel ¾″ x 4′-0″ x 6′-0″ INT. A-A
1 panel ½″ x 4′-0″ x 4′-0″ INT. A-D
1 panel ⅜″ x 2′-0″ x 4′-0″ INT. A-D
1 panel ¼″ x 4′-0″ x 4′-0″ INT. A-A
1 panel ¼″ x 4′-0″ x 8′-0″ INT. A-D
4 panels ½″ x 4′-0″ x 6′-0″ INT. A-A

Code	No. Req'd	Part Size	Use
A	2	18″ x 95¾″	Top & bottom
B	2	4⅞″ x 95¼″	Base
C	2	18″ x 72″	End
D	11	18″ x 23¾″	Shelves
D′	1	17¼″ x 23¾″	Shelf

MATERIALS (Continued)

Code	No. Req'd	Part Size	Use
E	3	18″ x 66⅛″	Partitions
F	8	6″ x 23⅛″	Drawer front
G	1	17½″ x 23¼″	Partition
H	1	10¾″ x 23¼″	Panel
H′	1	18¼″ x 23¼″	Desk front
I	1	9¾″ x 23¼″	Panel
J	3	2½″ x 10⅞″	Drawer front
K	1	7⅛″ x 7½″	Side, desk
L	2	7⅛″ x 18½″	Top and bottom desk
M	1	7⅛″ x 8″	Partition, desk
N	1	7⅛″ x 8½″	Side, desk
O	8	6″ x 17″	Drawer side
P	6	2½″ x 6⅛″	Drawer side
Q	3	2″ x 10½″	Drawer back
R	1	7⅛″ x 8″	Partition desk
S	7	3⅛″ x 18″ (approx.)	Bottom, record storage
T	6	14″ x 18″	Partitions, record storage
U	4	17″ x 21⅝″	Drawer bottom
V	3	6⅞″ x 10½″	Drawer bottom
W	4	13″ x 17⅞″ high	Small sliding doors
X	2	13″ x 11¼″ high	Small sliding doors
Y	4	1⅞″ x 96″	Door fascia
Z	8	24″ x 66½″	Sliding doors

Lumber and Hardware

No.	Size	Item	Use
80 lin ft.	½″	Qtr. round	Caning
8	½″ x 2⅛″ x 16½″	Slides	Drawers
8	¼″ x ⅝″ x 18″	Guides	Drawers
4	¼″ x ¼″ x 7⅛″	Slides	Drawers
2	¾″ x 5½″ x 8′-0¾″	Support	Sliding doors
2	1¼″ x 1⅞″ x 8′-0¾″	Support	Sliding doors
6	⅞″ x 23¼″ long	Metal truck	Sliding doors (Small)
8 prs.	As required	Hangers and track	Sliding doors (Large)
2	As required	Lid support	Desk front
16	¾″ round	Finger pulls	Sliding doors

Miscellaneous

5 doz. No. 6—1¼″ f.h. wood screws.
6d finish nails.
24″ x 9′-6″ caning
Finishing materials

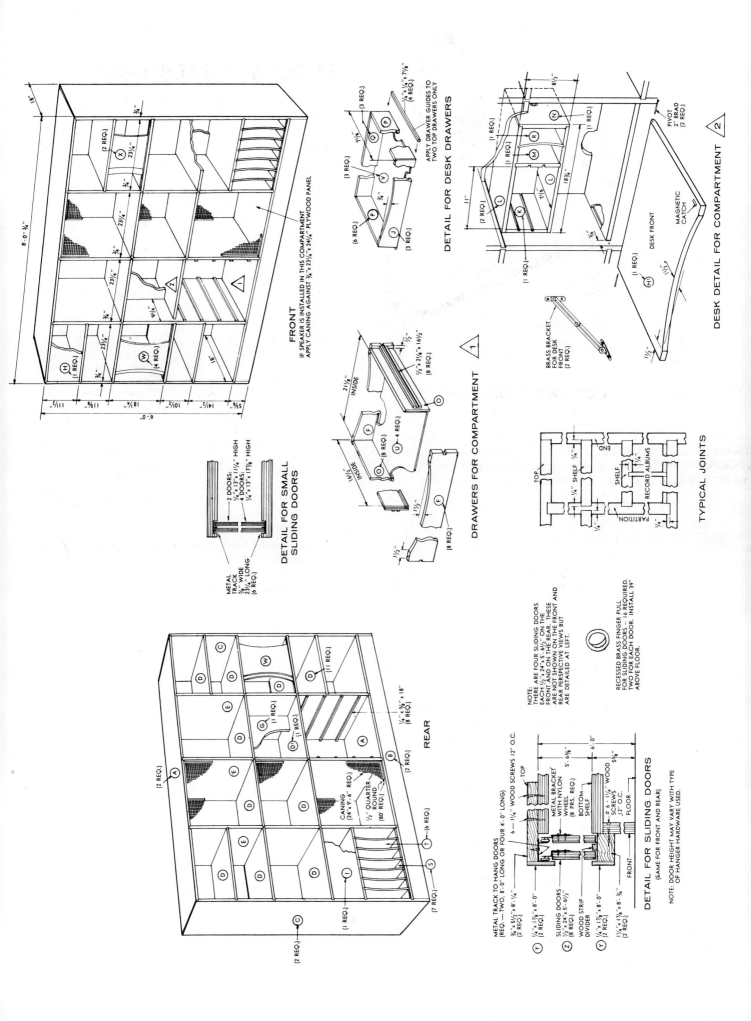

STORAGE HEADBOARD

Here is a plan for a modern all-in-one headboard that can be built in a few evenings from easy-to-work panels of plywood. The practical design provides storage space for pillows and blankets. Sections at either end serve as night tables, with shelves for a clock, radio, books or what-have-you. The sloped front makes a comfortable backrest for reading in bed.

MATERIALS

Code	No. Req'd	Size	Part Identification
A	1	8" x 83"	Top, headboard
B	1	13 1/8" x 81 1/2"	Lower shelf
C	2	10" x 12"	Upper shelf, ends
D	1	11" x 56"	Upper shelf, center
E	2	15 1/2" x 27 29/32"	Lower doors
F	2	See diagram	End standards
G	1	28 3/4" x 82 1/4"	Back, Headboard
H	2	See diagram	Intermediate dividers
I	1	See diagram	Upper divider, center
J	4	13 3/8" x 13 15/16"	Upper doors, center
K	2	13 3/8" x 11 7/8"	Upper doors, ends
L	1	10 1/8" x 15"	Lower divider, center
	10 lin. ft.	1" x 2"	Fir or pine lumber for door stops
	2 ft.	3/4"	Piano hinge
	7 pr.		Semi-concealed cabinet door hinges
	8		Friction catches

MISCELLANEOUS

4d and 6d finish nails; waterproof glue; finishing materials

CUTTING DIAGRAMS

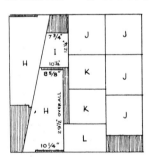

3/4" x 4'-0" x 8'-0" INT-DFPA A-A   1/4" x 4'-0" x 8'-0" INT-DFPA A-D

3/4" x 4'-0" x 4'-0" INT-DFPA A-A

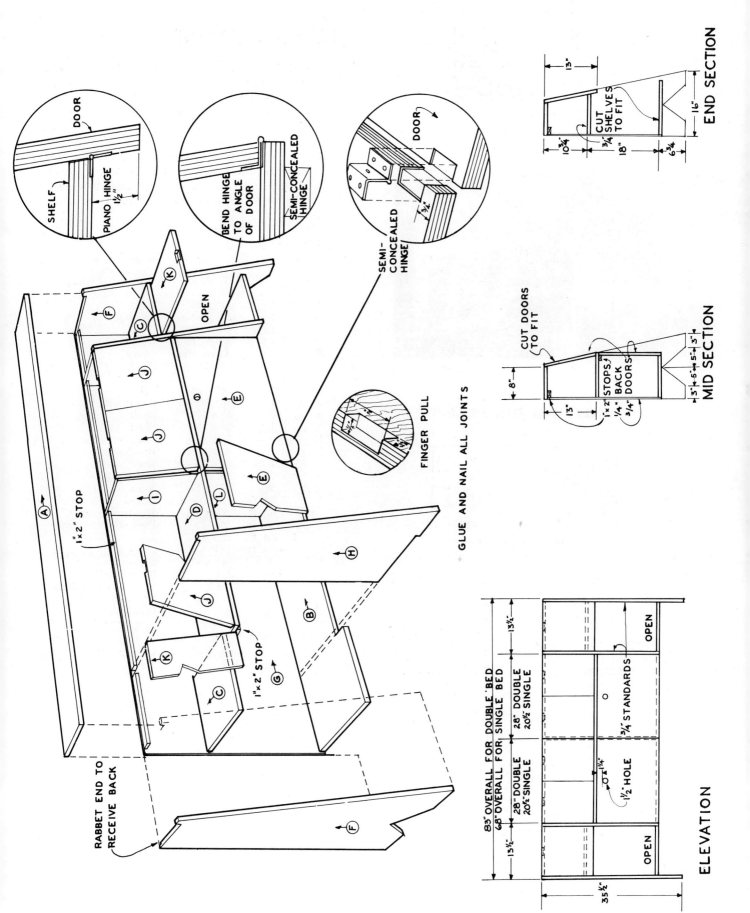

DOOR

SHELF

PIANO HINGE

1½"

BEND HINGE TO ANGLE OF DOOR

SEMI-CONCEALED HINGE

DOOR

SEMI-CONCEALED HINGE

¾"

FINGER PULL

GLUE AND NAIL ALL JOINTS

15"

CUT SHELVES TO FIT

16"

10¾"

¾"

18"

6¾"

END SECTION

8"

CUT DOORS TO FIT

STOPS

BACK DOORS

13"

1"x 2"

¼"

¾"

3"·6"·5"·3"

MID SECTION

OPEN

K

F

C

J

J

D

E

I

E

L

A

1"x2" STOP

RABBET END TO RECEIVE BACK

H

J

K

C

G

B

1"x 2" STOP

F

OPEN

83" OVERALL FOR DOUBLE BED
68" OVERALL FOR SINGLE BED

15½"

28" DOUBLE
20½"SINGLE

28" DOUBLE
20½"SINGLE

13½"

28" DOUBLE
20½ SINGLE

15½"

OPEN

¾" STANDARDS

O 1¼"

1½ HOLE

OPEN

35½"

ELEVATION

SEWING CABINET

Every woman will love the finger-tip storage incorporated into the door of this sewing cabinet. All the little items which often become lost can be stored in full view within easy reach. Wood dowels on a sloped plywood surface hold spools of thread. Lipped shelving holds scissors, patterns, material, and many other things. The sewing machine while in use rests in a well, flush with the counter top for easier sewing. A shelf for storage of the machine is provided inside.

MATERIALS

Code	No. Req'd	Size	Part Identification
A	1	24" x 41½"	Top
B	1	23½" x 40"	Sub-top
C	1	28" x 40"	Door
D	1	As required	Bottom of well
E	1	As required	Cover
F	2	8" x 16"	Shelf
G	2	4½" x 8"	Bracket
H	2	24" x 29¼"	Side
J	1	23½" x 36"	Shelf back
K	5	5" x 17¼"	Shelf
L	1	5" x 35"	Shelf
M	2	5" x 23½"	Divider
N	1	5" x 22¾"	Divider
O	1	29¼" x 40"	Back
P	1	15" x 36"	Face frame
Q	1	10" x 17¼"	Rack
	5 lin. ft.	³⁄₁₆" Diam.	Dowel
	12 lin. ft.	½" x 1¼"	Hardwood edge
	14 lin. ft.	1" x 2"	Door stop and cleats
	1½ lin. ft.	2" x 2"	Leg
	6 lin. ft.	5/4" x 2"	Blocking
	4	¼" x 4"	Bolt and nut
	1 ea.	1¼"	Swivel caster
	1½ pr.	1½"	Semi-concealed hinges
	1 ea.		Friction catch
	1 ea.		Door pull

MISCELLANEOUS

4d and 6d finish nails, screws and glue finishing materials.

CUTTING DIAGRAMS

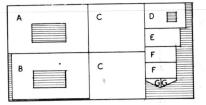

¾'' x 4'-0'' x 8'-0'' INTERIOR • DFPA • A-D

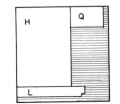

¾'' x 4'-0'' x 4'x0''
INTERIOR • DFPA • A-D

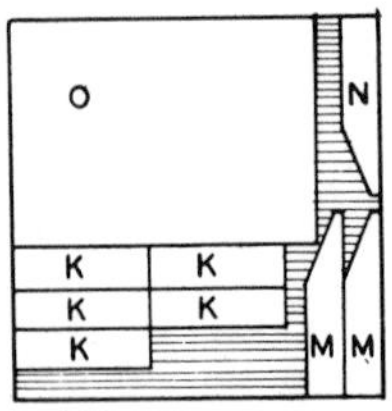

½'' x 4'-0'' x 4'-0''
INTERIOR • DFPA • A-D

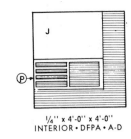

¼'' x 4'-0'' x 4'-0''
INTERIOR • DFPA • A-D

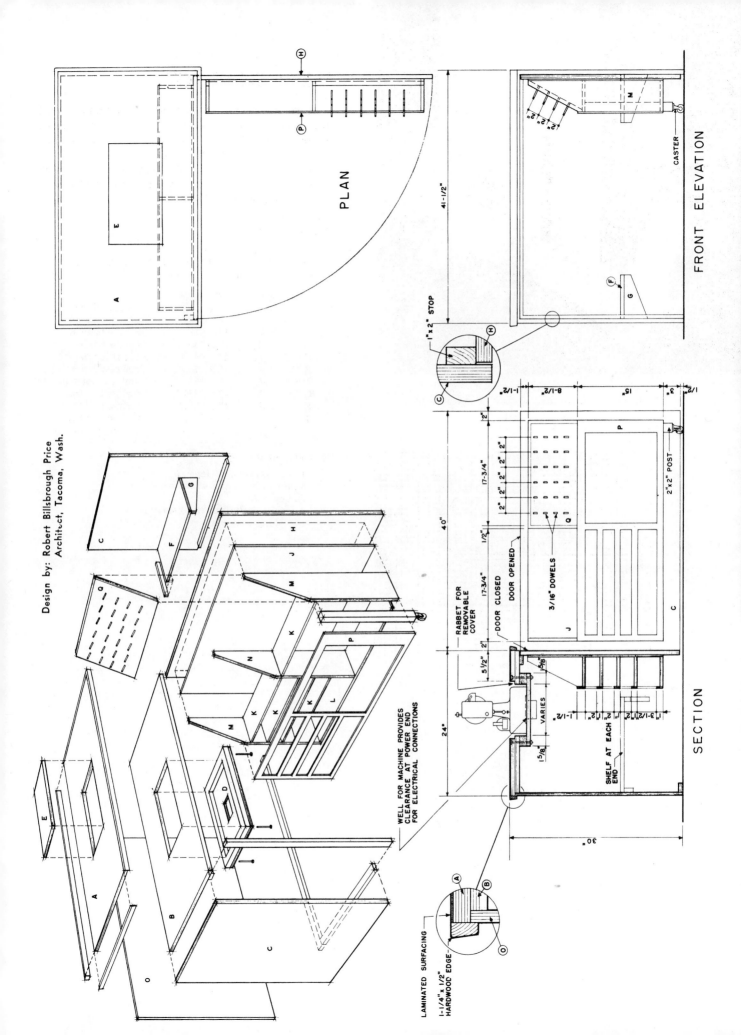

PLAN

FRONT ELEVATION

SECTION

Design by: Robert Billsbrough Price
Architect, Tacoma, Wash.

CASTER

1" x 2" STOP

RABBET FOR REMOVABLE COVER

DOOR CLOSED

DOOR OPENED

3/16" DOWELS

2" x 2" POST

WELL FOR MACHINE PROVIDES
CLEARANCE AT POWER END
FOR ELECTRICAL CONNECTIONS

SHELF AT EACH END

VARIES

LAMINATED SURFACING

1-1/4" x 1/2"
HARDWOOD EDGE

4'-1/2"

40"

24"

30"

17-3/4"

17-3/4"

5 1/2"

2"

SHOE SHINE KIT

Here is a way to get the shoeshine equipment out of that junk drawer in the kitchen and out where it will do the most good. The handy shoe shining kit pictured here goes right on the back of a closet door, keeping brushes and polish handy for the moment you discover the bloom has left your oxfords.

MATERIALS

PLYWOOD

    1 panel ½" x 4'-0" INT-DFPA. A-D

Code	No. Req'd	Part Size	Use
A	1	18" x 18"	Storage box side
B	1	18" x 18"	Storage box side
C	2	17½" x 21"	Foot rest sides
D	1	4" x 4¾"	Foot rest top
E	1	4" x 17½"	Foot rest front
F	1	4" x 19"	Foot rest bottom
G	1	4" x 13¼"	Storage box top
H	1	4" x 15¾"	Storage box front
I	1	4" x 16½"	Storage box back
J	1	4" x 14½"	Storage box bottom

MISCELLANEOUS

    1—¾" dowel 4¾" long
    4d finish nails and waterproof glue
    6d box nails
    4 each—1" Phillips head screws
    Finishing materials

CUTTING DIAGRAM - 1" GRID LINES

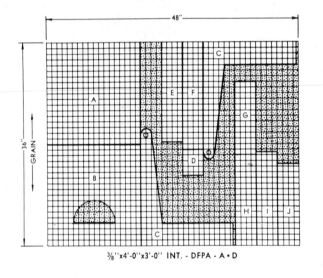

⅜''x4'-0''x3'-0'' INT. - DFPA - A • D

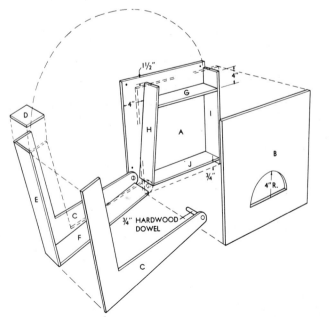

8

PLYWOOD PROJECTS FOR OUTDOOR LIVING

Patio Furniture

Outdoor Serving Wagon

Sectional Patio Tables

Sun Shelter

Sun Sled

Picnic Chest

Portable Planter Screen

Garden Caddy

Garden Lantern

Fishing Tackle Box

Portable Dog Kennel

Outdoor Fences and Screens

*All projects courtesy American
Plywood Association*

PATIO FURNITURE

Why pay fancy prices for patio furniture when it is so easy to build your own? Here is a worthwhile set which can be built from four panels of exterior-type fir plywood in a weekend or two. Table and benches can be knocked down and taken along on family picnics. The all-weather storage cabinet holds the charcoal, cooking gear and other things needed for back-yard barbecues.

MATERIALS

CABINET

Code	No. Req'd	Size	Part Identification
A	1	24" x 48"	Top
B	2	23½" x 31¼"	Sides
C	1	36" x 47"	Back
D	1	22¾" x 45½"	Bottom
E	1	20" x 30"	Shelf
F	1	23½" x 30½"	Partition
G	2	15" x 29⅝"	Doors
H	1	14¾" x 29⅝"	Door

LUMBER

10 lin. ft. 2 x 4 fir or pine
4 lin. ft. 1 x 2 fir or pine
22 lin. ft 1 x 1 fir or pine (or use plywood scraps)

HARDWARE

6 2" narrow cabinet butt hinges
3 small bullet catches

TABLE

Code	No. Req'd	Size	Part Identification
J	1	36" x 67"	Top
K	2	24" x 29"	Legs
L	1	8" x 54"	Stretcher

LUMBER

8 lin. ft. 1 x 1 fir or pine (or use plywood scraps)

HARDWARE

4 hooks and eyes

5 BENCHES

Code	No. Req'd	Size	Part Identification
M	10	16" x 16"	Legs
N	5	12" x 16"	Seats
O	10	4¾" x 16"	Stringers
P	10	4¾" x 8½"	End blocks

LUMBER

22 lin. ft. 1 x 1 fir or pine

CUTTING DIAGRAMS

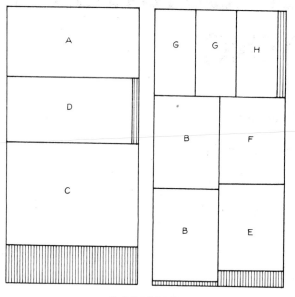

CABINET
¾"x4'-0"x8'-0" EXT-DFPA • A-C

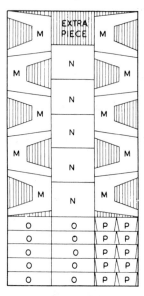

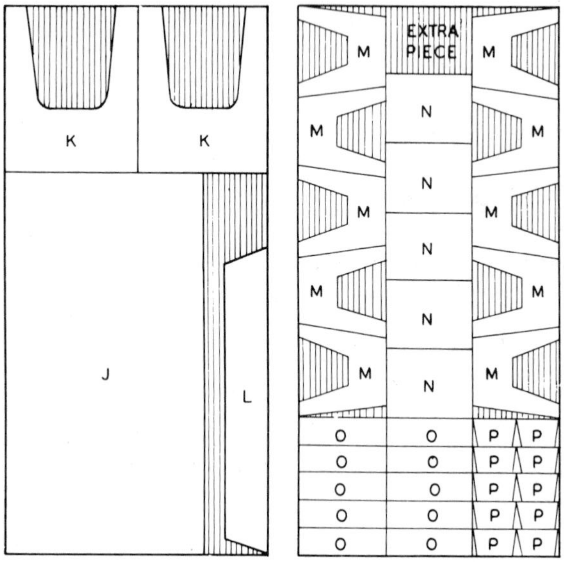

TABLE   BENCHES
¾"x4'-0"x8'-0" EXT-DFPA • A-A PLYWOOD

126

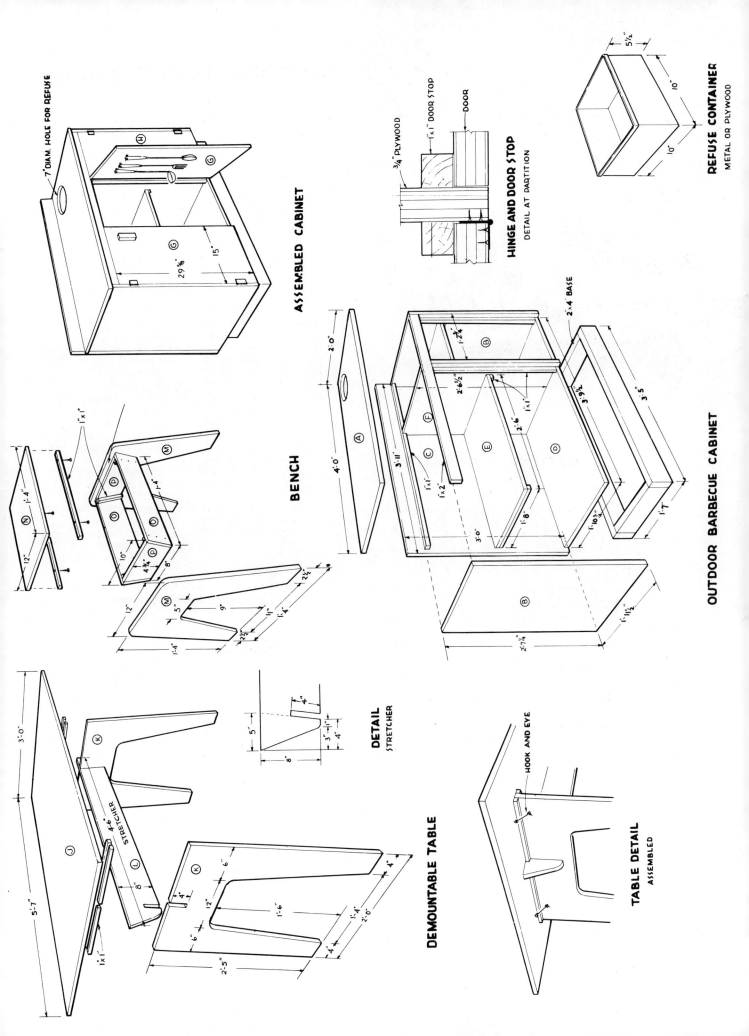

ASSEMBLED CABINET

7"DIAM. HOLE FOR REFUSE

HINGE AND DOOR STOP
DETAIL AT PARTITION

3/4" PLYWOOD
1"x1" DOOR STOP
DOOR

REFUSE CONTAINER
METAL OR PLYWOOD

BENCH

OUTDOOR BARBECUE CABINET

2"x4 BASE

DETAIL
STRETCHER

DEMOUNTABLE TABLE

STRETCHER

HOOK AND EYE

TABLE DETAIL
ASSEMBLED

OUTDOOR SERVING WAGON

Is there anything more pleasant on a warm summer evening than having a leisurely family supper outdoors on the terrace or patio? That is the thought behind this clever wagon-table, which is designed to take the work out of outdoor serving. You simply load on everything from soup to dessert, wheel it out, and enjoy yourself, forgetting those countless trips back and forth from the kitchen.

MATERIALS

Code	No. Req'd	Size	Part Identification
A	2	10" x 40"	Leg
B	2	17¼" x 22"	Flap
C	1	10" x 22½"	Top shelf
D	1	22½" x 22¾"	Bottom of compartment
E	1	22½" x 26"	Lower shelf
F	1	16½" x 22½"	Door at rear
G	1	22½" x 31¼"	Top of unit
H	2	17¼" x 25"	Side of compartment
I	1	16½" x 22½"	Door at front
J	1	11¾" x 22½"	Front face
K	1	16½" x 21"	Divider in compartment
L	1	13" x 21"	Shelf in compartment
	1 ea.	2" x 4" x 13"	Axle block
	2 ea.	1" x 2" x 20"	Pull-out support
	1 ea.	to fit wheels	Steel axle
	2 ea.	6" diam.	Rubber tire wheels
	1 ea.	⅝" round	Wrought iron handle
	2 pcs.	22" long	Piano hinges
	2 pr.	For ¾" plywood	Cabinet hinges
	2 ea.		Bullet catches

MISCELLANEOUS

6d finish nails (galvanized)
Staples, screws and washers required
Chain support for door
Metal furniture glides
Waterproof glue
Finishing materials

CUTTING DIAGRAMS

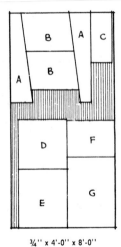

¾'' x 4'-0'' x 8'-0''
EXT-DFPA • A-C

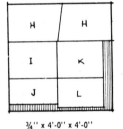

¾'' x 4'-0'' x 4'-0''
EXT-DFPA • A-C

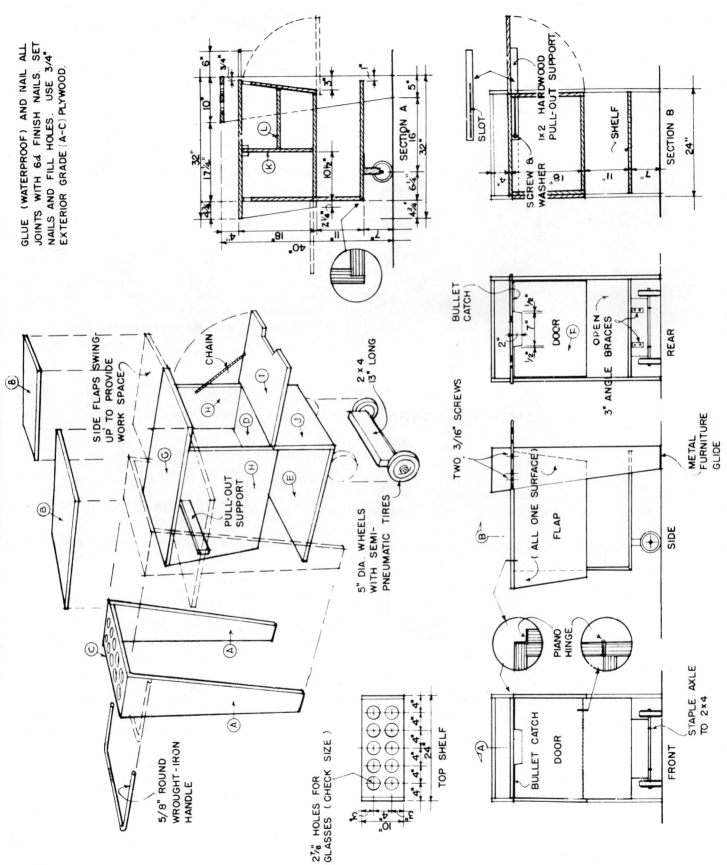

GLUE (WATERPROOF) AND NAIL ALL JOINTS WITH 6d FINISH NAILS. SET NAILS AND FILL HOLES. USE 3/4" EXTERIOR GRADE (A-C) PLYWOOD.

SECTION A

SECTION B

SLOT

1×2 HARDWOOD PULL-OUT SUPPORT

SHELF

SCREW & WASHER

BULLET CATCH

DOOR

OPEN

3" ANGLE BRACES

REAR

TWO 3/16" SCREWS

(ALL ONE SURFACE)

FLAP

METAL FURNITURE GLIDE

SIDE

PIANO HINGE

BULLET CATCH

DOOR

FRONT

STAPLE AXLE TO 2×4

SIDE FLAPS SWING UP TO PROVIDE WORK SPACE

CHAIN

PULL-OUT SUPPORT

2×4 13" LONG

5" DIA. WHEELS WITH SEMI-PNEUMATIC TIRES

5/8" ROUND WROUGHT-IRON HANDLE

2 7/8" HOLES FOR GLASSES (CHECK SIZE)

TOP SHELF

SECTIONAL PATIO TABLES

Use these colorful triangular garden tables outdoors or in. In winter they will double as smart yet practical furnishings for the children's playroom. They fit in corners, or you can group two or more together in a striking arrangement as shown in the photo. Building them is simplicity itself. Just cut tops from waterproof exterior-type fir plywood and attach inexpensive ready-made hairpin legs.

MATERIALS

Code	No. Req'd	Size	Part Identification
A	4	43″ x 43″	Top of tables
B	12	7″ x 7″	Pads for legs
	12 ea.	⅜″ diam.	Wrought iron legs

MISCELLANEOUS

Waterproof glue; screws as required

CUTTING DIAGRAMS

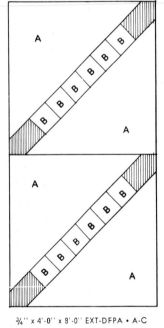

¾'' x 4'-0'' x 8'-0'' EXT-DFPA • A-C

CUTTING DIAGRAM
(4 PATIO TABLES)

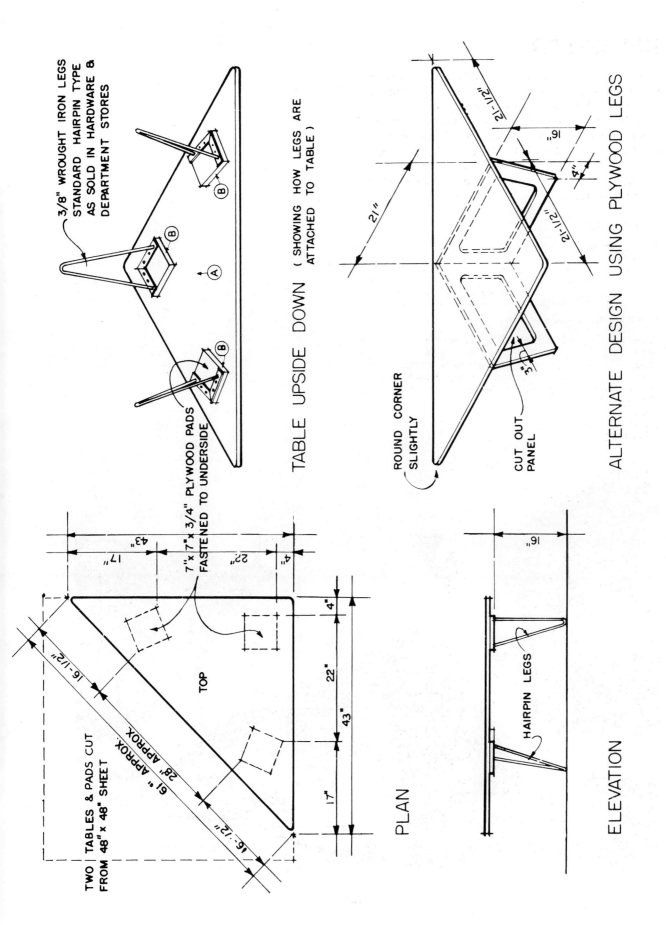

3/8" WROUGHT IRON LEGS STANDARD HAIRPIN TYPE AS SOLD IN HARDWARE & DEPARTMENT STORES

TABLE UPSIDE DOWN (SHOWING HOW LEGS ARE ATTACHED TO TABLE)

A   B

7"x 7"x 3/4" PLYWOOD PADS FASTENED TO UNDERSIDE

43"

17"   22"   4"

TOP

16-1/2" APPROX.

28" APPROX.

61" APPROX.

16-1/2"

4"   22"   43"   17"

PLAN

ROUND CORNER SLIGHTLY

21-1/2"

16"

4"

21-1/2"

21"

3"

CUT OUT PANEL

ALTERNATE DESIGN USING PLYWOOD LEGS

16"

HAIRPIN LEGS

ELEVATION

TWO TABLES & PADS CUT FROM 48"x 48" SHEET

USE 3/4" PLYWOOD EXTERIOR A-C GLUE (WATERPROOF) PLY. PADS AND NAIL WITH 6d FINISH NAILS.

SUN SHELTER

For those who enjoy sun bathing this shelter will lengthen the hours in the sun by providing needed protection against the wind.

Only two panels of exterior-type fir plywood are required to build this shelter. Panels can be easily disassembled and folded flat for storage. Painted with bright colors, one or more sun shelters can add to the charm and convenience of outdoor living.

MATERIALS

FIR PLYWOOD

No. of Panels	Size	Grade
2	¼″ x 4′ x 8′	EXT. A-A

LUMBER AND MISCELLANEOUS

1 pc.	2″ x 2″ 8′-0″ long, fir or pine
4 pcs.	1″ x 2″ 8′-0″ long, fir or pine
12 ea.	¼″ x 2½″ carriage bolts w/wing nuts
6 ea.	1″ x 2″ Galvanized steel strap hinges
24 (approx.)	1″ galvanized brads
Waterproof glue	
Finishing materials	

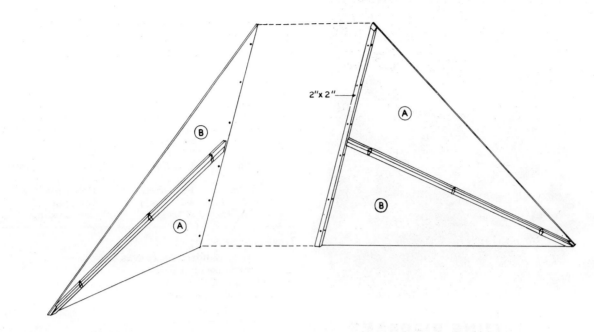

2"x 2"

Ⓑ Ⓐ Ⓐ Ⓑ

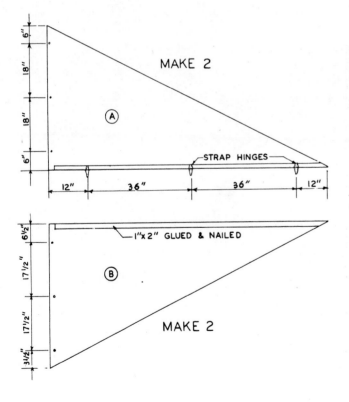

6"
18"
18"
6"

MAKE 2

Ⓐ

STRAP HINGES

12" 36" 36" 12"

6½"
17½"
17½"
3½"

1"x 2" GLUED & NAILED

Ⓑ

MAKE 2

CUTTING DIAGRAM

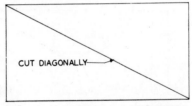

CUT DIAGONALLY

¼" x 4' x 8' EXTERIOR A-A FIR PLYWOOD

BILL of MATERIALS

FIR PLYWOOD

NO. OF PANELS	SIZE	GRADE
2	¼" x 4' x 8'	EXTERIOR A-A

LUMBER & MISCELLANEOUS

1 PC.	2"x2" 8'-0" LONG	FIR OR PINE
4 PCS.	1"x 2" 8'-0" LONG	FIR OR PINE
12 EA.	¼"x2½" CARRIAGE BOLTS W/ WING NUTS	
6 EA.	1"x 2" GALVANIZED STEEL STRAP HINGES	
24 (APPROX.)	1" GALVANIZED BRADS	

WATERPROOF GLUE
FINISHING MATERIALS

SUN SLED

This handsome unit will make a worthwhile addition to your outdoor furnishings. Ultra simplicity and rugged construction is possible with the use of exterior-type fir plywood. When complete, hours of relaxation will be yours and you will enjoy building it too.

MATERIALS

Code	No. Req'd	Size	Part Identification
A	2	See drawings	Side
B	4	7" diam.	Wheels
	6 lin. ft.	1" x 2¼" (net)	Hardwood canvas frame
	12 lin. ft.	1⅜" diam.	Hardwood dowels
	½ lin. ft.	⅜" diam.	Lock pin
	7 lin. ft.	30" width	Canvas sling

MISCELLANEOUS

Tacks as required for canvas sling
6d galvanized finish nails
Waterproof glue
Finishing materials

CUTTING DIAGRAMS

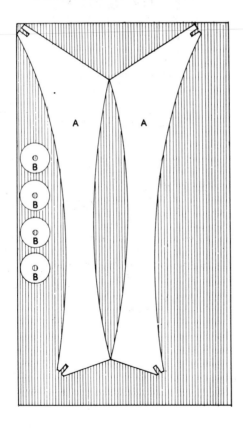

¾" x 4'-0" x 7'-0" EXT. - DFPA - A-B OR PLYSHIELD A-C

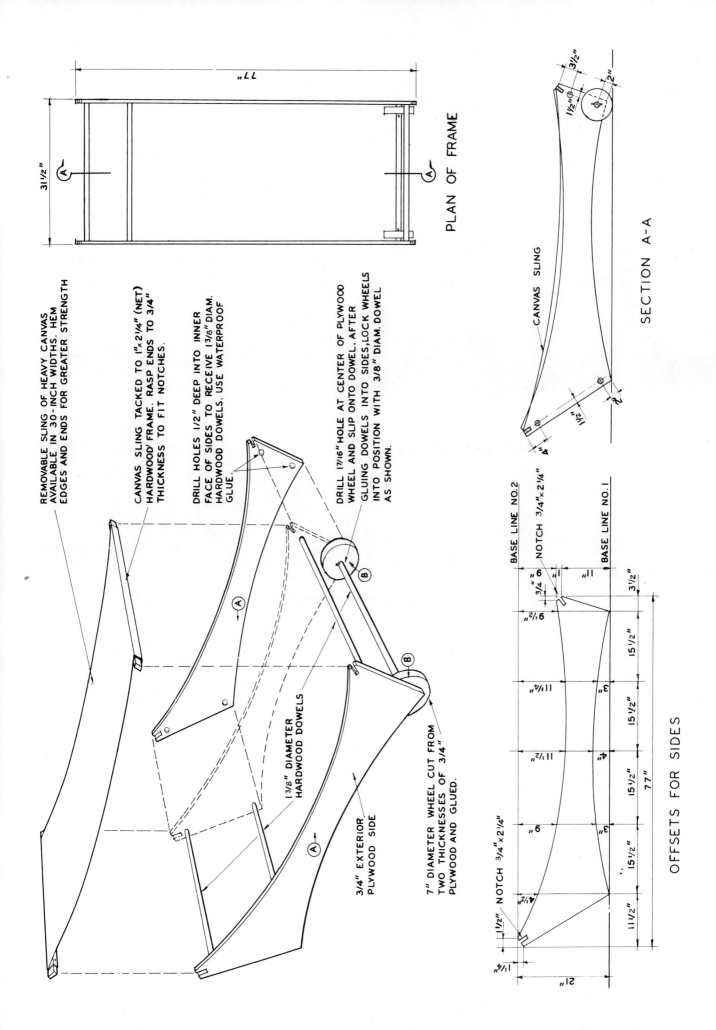

PLAN OF FRAME

SECTION A-A

31½"

77"

CANVAS SLING

3½"
2"
1½"

1½"
4"
2"

REMOVABLE SLING OF HEAVY CANVAS AVAILABLE IN 30-INCH WIDTHS. HEM EDGES AND ENDS FOR GREATER STRENGTH

CANVAS SLING TACKED TO 1"x 2¼" (NET) HARDWOOD FRAME. RASP ENDS TO 3/4" THICKNESS TO FIT NOTCHES.

DRILL HOLES 1/2" DEEP INTO INNER FACE OF SIDES TO RECEIVE 1 3/8" DIAM. HARDWOOD DOWELS. USE WATERPROOF GLUE.

DRILL 17/16" HOLE AT CENTER OF PLYWOOD WHEEL AND SLIP ONTO DOWEL. AFTER GLUING DOWELS INTO SIDES, LOCK WHEELS INTO POSITION WITH 3/8" DIAM. DOWEL AS SHOWN.

1 3/8" DIAMETER HARDWOOD DOWELS

3/4" EXTERIOR PLYWOOD SIDE

7" DIAMETER WHEEL CUT FROM TWO THICKNESSES OF 3/4" PLYWOOD AND GLUED.

OFFSETS FOR SIDES

BASE LINE NO.2

BASE LINE NO.1

NOTCH 3/4" x 2¼"

NOTCH 3/4" x 2¼"

77"

6"
9½"
3/4"
1"
11"
3½"

11¼"
15½"
3"

11½"
15½"
4"

11½"
15½"
4"

6"
15½"
3"

11½"
3"

1½"
1¼"

12"

PICNIC CHEST

This picnic chest has enough storage space for almost anything you need to take along on those outings to the country, the beach or even an over-night camping trip. There is a place for dishes and utensils with provisions for a generous supply of bottled, packaged and canned goods. The hinged front drops down to form a level surface on which outdoor meals can be prepared and served.

Build this chest with exterior-type fir plywood, which is economical and rugged yet lightweight. Factory-sanded plywood assures smooth surfaces for a fine paint finish.

MATERIALS

FIR PLYWOOD

    1 panel ¾" x 4'-0" x 8'-0" EXT-DFPA. A-A

Code	No. Req'd	Part Size	Use
A	1	23 ⅝" x 32"	Back
B	1	23 ⅝" x 32"	Hinged front
C	1	8 ⅝" x 32"	Hinged top
D	2	8 ¼" x 31 ¼"	Shelf and bottom
E	2	8 ¼" x 23 ⅝"	Ends
F	2	3" x 13 ⅝"	Cutlery tray
G	1	8 ¼" x 12 ⅝"	Divider
H	1	8 ¼" x 10 ¼"	Divider
I	1	11 ⅛" x 17 ¼"	Divider
J	1	3 ¹⁵⁄₁₆" x 11 ⅛"	Divider
K	1	3 ¹⁵⁄₁₆" x 7"	Shelf
L	1	11 ⅛" x 17 ¼"	Compartment side

HARDWARE

No.	Size	Item	Use
2 ea.	3" strap	* T-hinges	Top
1 pc.	⅝"—32" long	* Piano hinge	Front
2 ea.	1½" x 2⅛"	* Chest handle	Chest

MISCELLANEOUS

    4d finish nails and screws as required
    Waterproof glue and finishing materials

* Steel-plated brass or chrome finish

CUTTING DIAGRAM

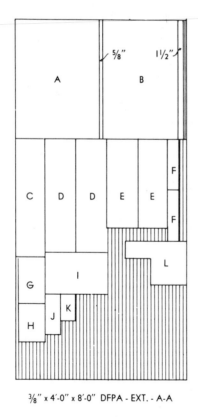

⅜" x 4'-0" x 8'-0" DFPA - EXT. - A-A

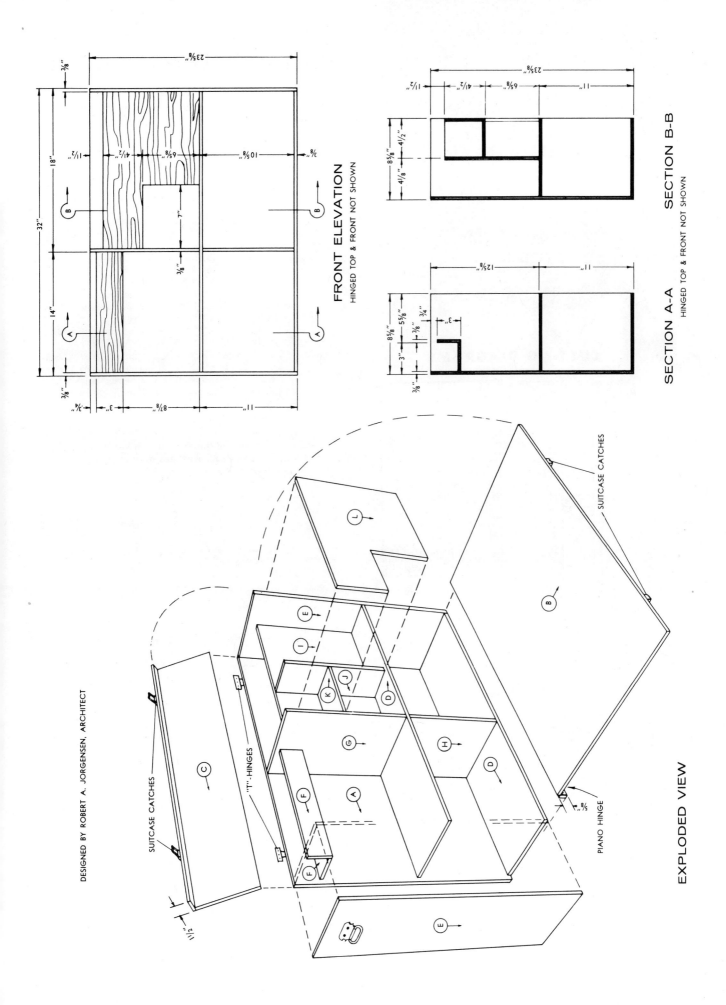

DESIGNED BY ROBERT A. JORGENSEN, ARCHITECT

FRONT ELEVATION

HINGED TOP & FRONT NOT SHOWN

SECTION A-A

HINGED TOP & FRONT NOT SHOWN

SECTION B-B

SUITCASE CATCHES

SUITCASE CATCHES

"T" HINGES

PIANO HINGE

EXPLODED VIEW

PORTABLE PLANTER SCREEN

This attractive roll-round planter screen shows off your pet sweet peas, gourds, clematis, scarlet runner beans, or what have you. Push it to any corner that needs a bright splash of color. The planter can be built in one evening, using grooved Texture 1-11 fir plywood for the box sides and plastic clothesline for the trellis.

MATERIALS

Code	No. Req'd	Size	Part Identification
A	2	12½″ x 14¾″	End
B	1	14¾″ x 40½″	Bottom
C	2	12″ x 48″	Sides
	35 lin. ft.	1″ x 2″	Framing and trellis
	3 lin. ft.	2″ x 2″	Framing
	7 lin. ft.	1″ x 4″	Blocking and trellis
	2 lin. ft.	2″ x 4″	Axle block
	2 ea.	4″ diam.	Rubber-tired wheels
	4 ea.	1″ x 3″	Angle braces
	6 ea.	³⁄₁₆″ round	Machine bolts
	54 lin. ft.	—	Plastic clothesline

MISCELLANEOUS

2 steel axles
8d common and 6d finish nails (galvanized)
Staples, screws and washers as required
Waterproof glue

CUTTING DIAGRAMS

40″

4″

4″

96″ NET

40″

4″

¾″ 12″ 3⅝″
16¼″
NET

A

A

B

A

¾″ x 2′-6″ x 4′-0″

EXT. - PLYSHIELD A-C

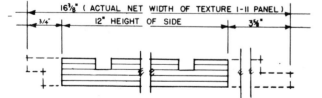

16⅜″ (ACTUAL NET WIDTH OF TEXTURE 1-11 PANEL)
¾″   12″ HEIGHT OF SIDE   3⅝″

SECTION A - A THRU TEXTURE ONE-ELEVEN PANEL
SHOWING CUTTING PROCEDURE.

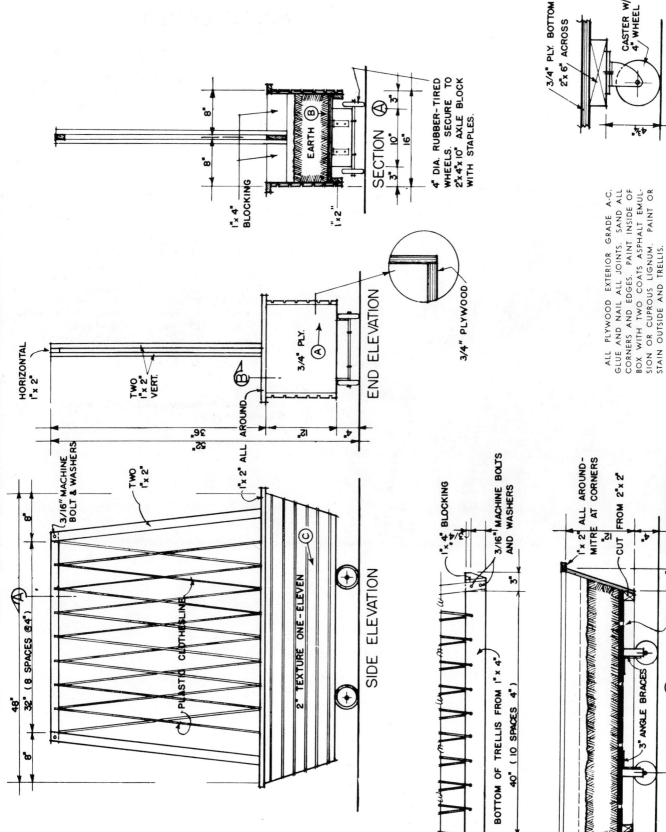
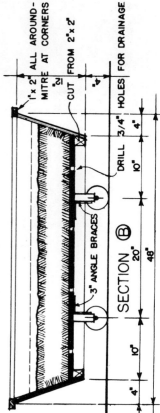

GARDEN CADDY

You can save yourself many trips between garden and tool house with this gardener's caddy to carry equipment, fertilizer, insect spray and other necessities. Roomy shelves hold flats and pots, so you also save heavy lifting.

Economical and rugged construction is achieved by the use of exterior-type fir plywood made with 100 percent waterproof glue.

MATERIALS

Code	No. Req'd	Size	Part Identification
A	2	31⅞" x 48"	Side
B	1	16" x 31⅞"	Shelf
C	1	31⅞" x 31⅞"	Bottom
	12 lin. ft.	1" x 4"	Tool brackets
	18 lin. ft.	1" x 2"	Edging
	5 lin. ft.	2" x 4"	Axle block
	4 ea.	5" diam.	Rubber-tired wheels
	2 ea.	28" long	Steel axles
	4 ea.	1" x 3"	Angle braces
	1 ea.	½" diam.	Axle bolt
	10 lin. ft.	⅜" diam.	Rope

MISCELLANEOUS

6d finish and 8d common nails (galvanized)
Waterproof glue
Screws, staples and washers as required
Finishing materials

CUTTING DIAGRAM

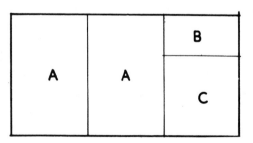

3/4" x 4'-0" x 8'-0" EXTERIOR A-C

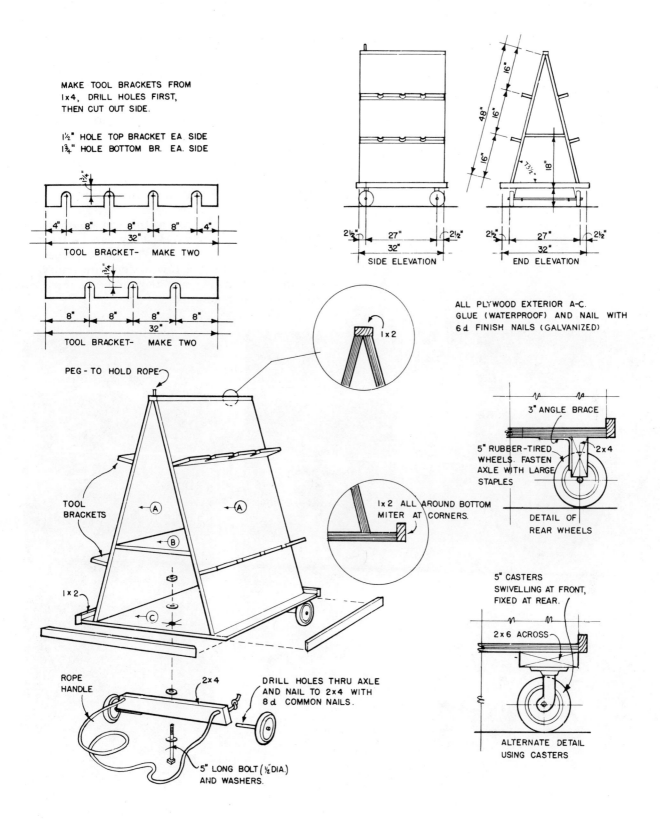

MAKE TOOL BRACKETS FROM
1x4, DRILL HOLES FIRST,
THEN CUT OUT SIDE.

1½" HOLE TOP BRACKET EA. SIDE
1¾" HOLE BOTTOM BR. EA. SIDE

TOOL BRACKET— MAKE TWO

TOOL BRACKET— MAKE TWO

PEG - TO HOLD ROPE

1 x 2

1 x 2 ALL AROUND BOTTOM
MITER AT CORNERS.

TOOL
BRACKETS

1 x 2

ROPE
HANDLE

2 x 4

DRILL HOLES THRU AXLE
AND NAIL TO 2x4 WITH
8 d COMMON NAILS.

5" LONG BOLT (½ DIA.)
AND WASHERS.

SIDE ELEVATION

END ELEVATION

ALL PLYWOOD EXTERIOR A-C.
GLUE (WATERPROOF) AND NAIL WITH
6 d FINISH NAILS (GALVANIZED)

3" ANGLE BRACE

5" RUBBER-TIRED
WHEELS. FASTEN
AXLE WITH LARGE
STAPLES

2 x 4

DETAIL OF
REAR WHEELS

5" CASTERS
SWIVELLING AT FRONT,
FIXED AT REAR.

2 x 6 ACROSS

ALTERNATE DETAIL
USING CASTERS

GARDEN LANTERN

Why restrict the enjoyment of your outdoor planting to daytime alone? A few lights, strategically planted in the shrubbery, will bring out the beauty of your garden long after the sun has set.

Illumination of grounds and gardens is, in fact, becoming a popular art. Lights are spotted among the roots, in concealed positions, or they may be brought out into the open with the rustic appeal of quaint garden lanterns.

Garden lanterns such as this are easy to make of exterior-type plywood. They can be painted in bright or varied colors to accent the greenery around them. Spot a few of them around your grounds. Then listen to the complimentary remarks of your neighbors!

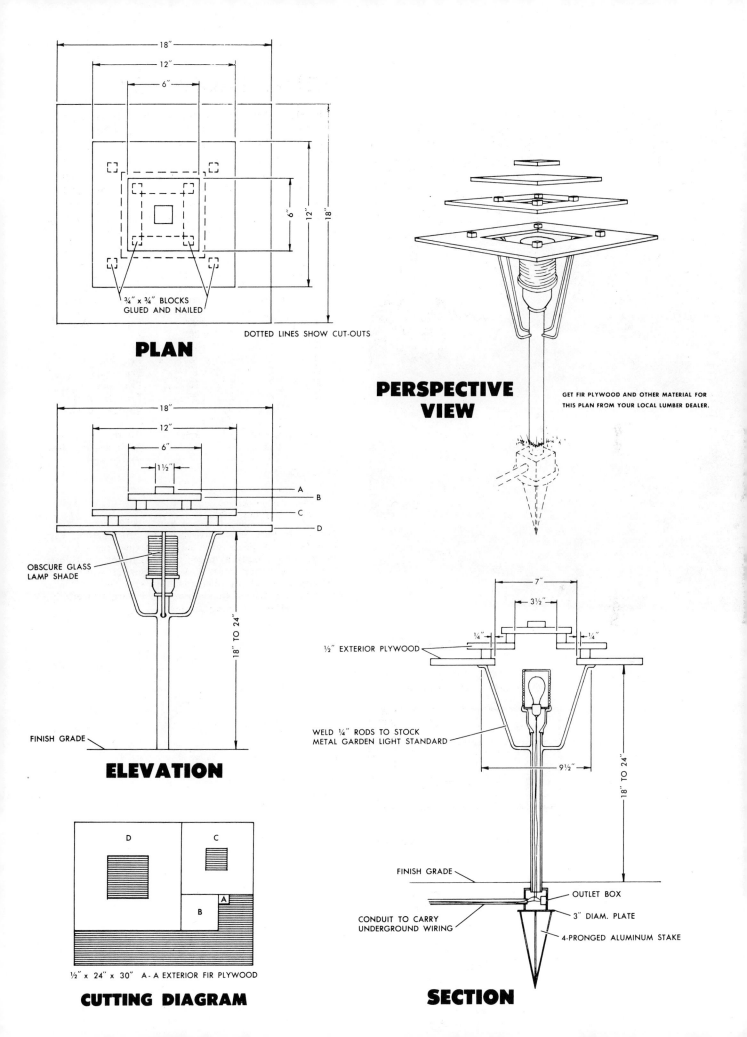

PLAN

¾" x ¾" BLOCKS
GLUED AND NAILED

DOTTED LINES SHOW CUT-OUTS

ELEVATION

A
B
C
D

OBSCURE GLASS
LAMP SHADE

FINISH GRADE

18" TO 24"

CUTTING DIAGRAM

D
C
A
B

½" x 24" x 30" A-A EXTERIOR FIR PLYWOOD

PERSPECTIVE VIEW

GET FIR PLYWOOD AND OTHER MATERIAL FOR
THIS PLAN FROM YOUR LOCAL LUMBER DEALER.

SECTION

½" EXTERIOR PLYWOOD

WELD ¼" RODS TO STOCK
METAL GARDEN LIGHT STANDARD

FINISH GRADE

CONDUIT TO CARRY
UNDERGROUND WIRING

OUTLET BOX

3" DIAM. PLATE

4-PRONGED ALUMINUM STAKE

18" TO 24"

7"
3½"
¼"
¼"
9½"

FISHING TACKLE BOX

Every fisherman is confronted with the problem of providing a suitable means of storing and transporting his necessary tackle. This lightweight plywood tackle box can take rough usage, yet keep its fine appearance. The divided plywood tray insures a convenient method of storing lures and the small items ready for immediate use. For construction use exterior-type plywood.

MATERIALS

Code	No. Req'd	Size	Part Identification
A	2	7 ½" x 20"	Top and bottom
B	2	7 ½" x 20"	Side
C	2	7 ½" x 7 ½"	End
D	1	6 ¹¹⁄₁₆" x 19 ³⁄₁₆"	Tray bottom
E	2	1 ¾" x 6 ¹¹⁄₁₆"	Tray end
F	2	1 ¾" x 19 ³⁄₁₆"	Tray side
G	8	1 ¾" x 6 ³⁄₁₆"	Tray dividers
	2 lin. ft.	¾"	Quarter round
	1 ea.	1 ½" x 2 ¾"	Chest handle
	1½ pr.	1 ¼" x 1 ½"	Hinges
	1 pr.	—	"Suitcase" catches

MISCELLANEOUS

¾" brads as required
Waterproof glue
Finishing materials

Notes: If butt joints are used in construction, vary dimensions of parts affected and follow the same sequence of assembly as noted in the instructions. Substitute ⅜" exterior type A-A fir plywood where high density overlaid plywood has been specified and cover exterior surfaces of tackle box with Fiberglas according to instructions of manufacturer.

CUTTING DIAGRAMS

DOTTED LINES SHOW CUT TO
FORM LID AFTER ASSEMBLY

B	A
B	A
C	C

⅜" x 2'-0" x 4'-0"
HIGH DENSITY OVERLAID PLYWOOD

144

D
E   E
F
G

¼" x 2'-0" x 2'-0"
EXT - DFPA - A-A

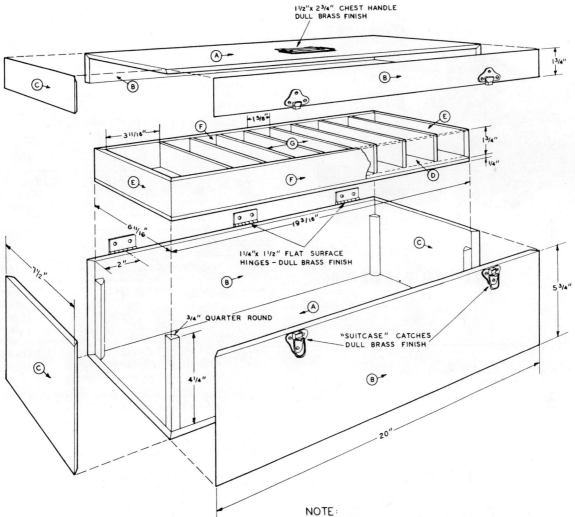

1½"x 2¾" CHEST HANDLE
DULL BRASS FINISH

Ⓐ

Ⓒ

Ⓑ

Ⓑ

1¾"

3¹¹/₁₆"

1⅝"

Ⓕ

Ⓖ

Ⓔ

1¾"

¼"

Ⓔ

Ⓕ

Ⓓ

6¹¹/₁₆"

1¼"x 1½" FLAT SURFACE
HINGES – DULL BRASS FINISH

19³/₁₆"

Ⓒ

2"

Ⓑ

5¾"

7½"

Ⓐ

¾" QUARTER ROUND

"SUITCASE" CATCHES
DULL BRASS FINISH

Ⓒ

4¼"

Ⓑ

20"

NOTE:
USE WATERPROOF GLUE AND ¾" BRADS AT ALL JOINTS.
SET BRADS AND FILL NAIL HOLES WITH COLORED WOOD
DOUGH TO MATCH HIGH DENSITY OVERLAID PLYWOOD.
FINISH PLYWOOD TRAY WITH SPAR VARNISH OR USE FLAT
UNDERCOAT FOLLOWED BY TWO COATS EXTERIOR ENAMEL.

145

PORTABLE DOG KENNEL

Whatever breed of dog you own—retriever, spaniel, setter, beagle, pointer or hound—you can use a lightweight, rugged kennel that is economical to build.

The unit is 2' wide, 3' long and 2' high. Designed for easy construction with only one panel of exterior-type fir plywood, this kennel provides a sturdy enclosure for transporting your dog out to the field or water. It fits easily into the back of a station wagon, pick-up truck or even a passenger car.

MATERIALS

Fir Plywood

    1 panel ¼" x 4'-0" x 8'-0" plyshield A-C

Code	No. Req'd	Part Size	Use
A	1	23⅞" x 23⅞"	Top
B	1	23⅞" x 23⅞"	Back
C	1	23⅞" x 35⅜"	Bottom
D	2	23⅞" x 36"	Sides

Lumber and Hardware

No.	Size	Item	Use
4 pcs.	¾" x ¾"—8'-0"	V. g. fir	Corner framing
2 pcs.	1" x 2"—8'-0"	V. g. fir	Door frames
1 pc.	12" x 48" galv.	½" x ½" wire mesh	Doors
2 pr.	1½" x 1½"	Galv. hinges	Doors
1 ea.	As required	Suitcase catch	Doors

Miscellaneous

    1" brads and waterproof glue
    Finishing materials

CUTTING DIAGRAM

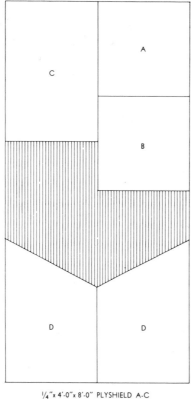

¼"x 4'-0"x 8'-0" PLYSHIELD A-C

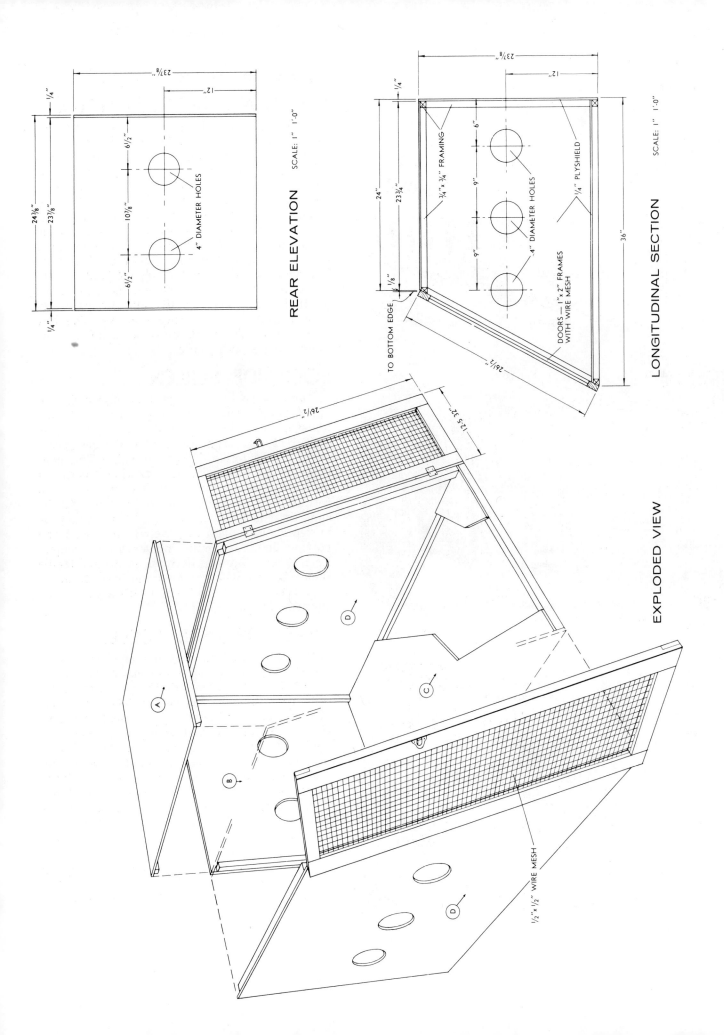

REAR ELEVATION   SCALE: 1" 1'-0"

23 7/8"
12"
1/4"
24 7/8"
23 7/8"
6 1/2"
10 7/8"
6 1/2"
1/4"
4" DIAMETER HOLES

LONGITUDINAL SECTION   SCALE: 1" 1'-0"

23 7/8"
12"
1/4"
24"
23 3/4"
6"
9"
9"
1/4"
1/8"
36"
26 1/2"
3/4" x 3/4" FRAMING
4" DIAMETER HOLES
1/4" PLYSHIELD
DOORS — 1" x 2" FRAMES WITH WIRE MESH
TO BOTTOM EDGE

EXPLODED VIEW

26 1/2"
12.5 32"
A
B
C
D
D
1/2" x 1/2" WIRE MESH

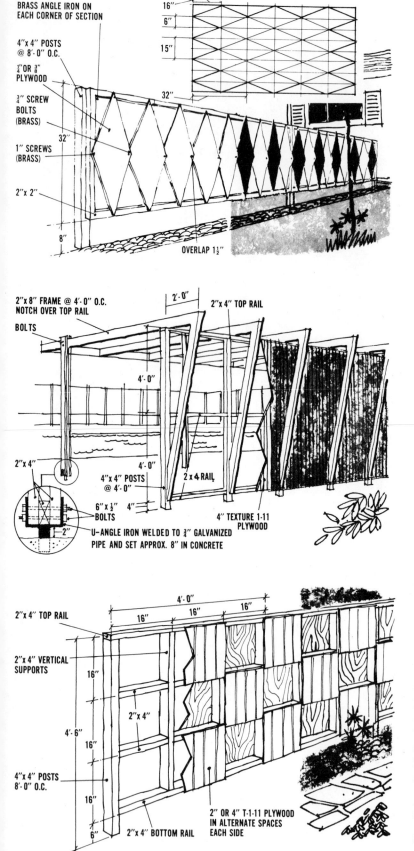

BRASS ANGLE IRON ON EACH CORNER OF SECTION

4"x 4" POSTS @ 8'-0" O.C.

¼" OR ⅜" PLYWOOD

¾" SCREW BOLTS (BRASS)

1" SCREWS (BRASS)

16"
6"
15"

32"

32"

2"x 2"

8"

OVERLAP 1½"

2"x 8" FRAME @ 4'-0" O.C. NOTCH OVER TOP RAIL

BOLTS

2'-0"

2"x 4" TOP RAIL

4'-0"

4'-0"

2"x 4"

4'-0"

4"x 4" POSTS @ 4'-0"

2 x 4 RAIL

6"x ½" BOLTS

4"

4" TEXTURE 1-11 PLYWOOD

2"

U-ANGLE IRON WELDED TO ¾" GALVANIZED PIPE AND SET APPROX. 8" IN CONCRETE

2"x 4" TOP RAIL

4'-0"
16"
16"
16"

2"x 4" VERTICAL SUPPORTS

16"

2"x 4"

16"

4'-6"

16"

4"x 4" POSTS 8'-0" O.C.

16"

6"

2"x 4" BOTTOM RAIL

2" OR 4" T-1-11 PLYWOOD IN ALTERNATE SPACES EACH SIDE

Outdoor Fences and Screens

DIAMOND PATTERN FENCE

A single panel of ¼" or ⅜" exterior-type plywood provides enough diamonds for two 8' sections of this striking diamond pattern fence. Small inset shows how to lay out panel for cutting. Fence framing consists of 4" x 4" posts 54" long. Top and bottom rails are 2 x 2's. Panels are overlapped 1½" and joined by ⅜" bolts ¾" long and fastened to top and bottom rails with 1" screws. A brass angle is required on the inside of each corner of each section. Fabricate sections on the ground and nail to posts after assembly. Diamonds should be painted with a good quality exterior paint before assembling into fence sections. The few scraps left over from plywood panel can be made into a striking gate.

POOLSIDE SCREEN

Rustic grooved Texture 1-11 plywood provides shelter from wind and prying eyes in this unusual pool side screen utilizing full 8' panels of T 1-11 on a framing of 4" x 4" cedar posts with 2 x 4 top and bottom rails. The cantilevered 2 x 8 beams add a striking decoration on the street side and extend over the top to form a delightful pool side trellis. Posts can be sunk in concrete; if in soil, they should be buried at least one-third their length, with the portion in the ground preservative treated. Frame, including cantilevered beams and trellis should be completed and stained first. Then install T 1-11 panels and paint with a heavy pigmented stain or shake paint.

CHECKERBOARD SCREEN

Materials used in this double faced fence are: 4 x 4 posts spaced 8' on center, with 2 x 4 top, bottom and intermediate rails. Horizontal rails are spaced 16" on center. There are also five vertical 2" x 4" spacers per 8' section spaced 16" on centers. Four-by-eight-foot sheets of Texture 1-11 plywood can then be cut into eighteen 16" squares per panel. To achieve finished checkerboard look, every other square should be nailed to frame on one side of fence with grooved surface exposed. Reverse on other side of fence. Use dark colored shake paint for finishing grooved side of T 1-11, paint smooth sides with one or more bright colors. Frame should be stained before applying painted plywood. For stability of fence sections, be sure one-third of length of post is underground.

9

CHILDREN'S
PLAY WORLD
OF PLYWOOD

Sea-'n Sandbox

Child's Table and Stools

Giant Building Toy

Play Planks

Space Ship

Utility Table

Puppet Theater

Corner Study Area

Bed-Train Board

Flying Saucer

*All projects courtesy American
Plywood Association*

Exterior-type plywood is used to its versatile best here. The sea-'n sandbox is three units in one. During the daytime hours, the children can carry on their construction activities on one hand and splash to their heart's content on the other. After hours, drain the pool, invert it over the sandbox, and presto—the nocturnal pests that prowl in sandboxes are completely frustrated. As an added bonus, the inverted boxes make a fine patio or terrace table.

SEA-'N SANDBOX

MATERIALS

  2 panels ¾″ x 4′ x 8′ EXT-DFPA. AA
  or AB plywood
  1 piece ¾″ x 2′ x 4′ EXT-DFPA. AA
  or AB plywood
  2 pieces 2″ x 2″ x 8′ v.g. fir
  100—1½″ flat head galv. wood screws
  1—½″ cork
  1 pt. sealer 800
  ½ gal. paint
  2—4″ galv. handles

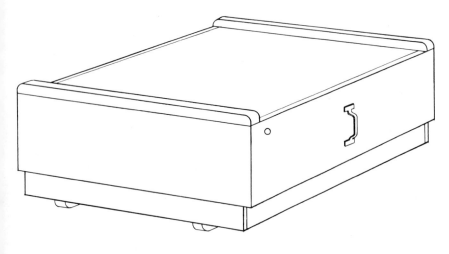

CUTTING DIAGRAMS

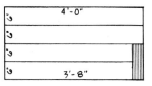

SEAT PANELS—1 - ¾″x2′-0″x4′-0″

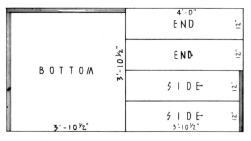

SEABOX PANELS—1 - ¾″x4′-0″x8′-0″

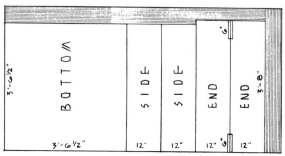

SANDBOX PANELS—1 - ¾″x4′-0″x8′-0″

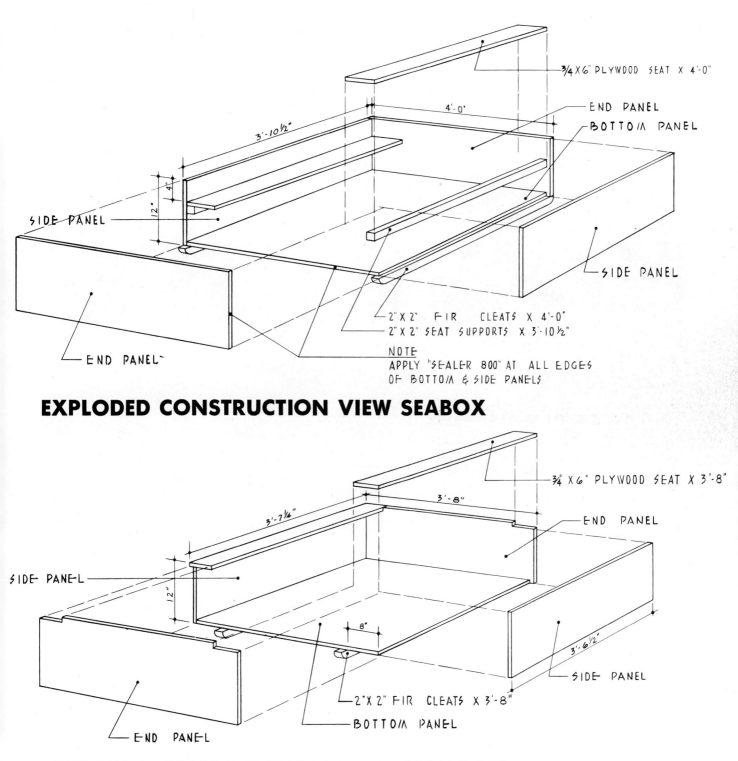

¾"X6" PLYWOOD SEAT X 4'-0"

END PANEL

BOTTOM PANEL

4'-0"

3'-10½"

SIDE PANEL

4"

12"

SIDE PANEL

END PANEL

2"X 2" FIR CLEATS X 4'-0"

2"X 2" SEAT SUPPORTS X 3'-10½"

NOTE

APPLY "SEALER 800" AT ALL EDGES
OF BOTTOM & SIDE PANELS

EXPLODED CONSTRUCTION VIEW SEABOX

¾"X6" PLYWOOD SEAT X 3'-8"

3'-8"

3'-7¼"

END PANEL

SIDE PANEL

12"

8"

SIDE PANEL

3'-6½"

2"X 2" FIR CLEATS X 3'-8"

BOTTOM PANEL

END PANEL

EXPLODED CONSTRUCTION VIEW SANDBOX

CHILD'S TABLE AND STOOLS

Your youngsters will love this sturdy table with stools designed just for them. Snacks and lunches are always more fun at a table of their own. Let them use it for roughhouse games, too. Fir plywood used in its construction will weather years of playful abuse.

Storage will be no problem, since the triangular stools slip into nest cut-outs of the table, in a clever tuck-away arrangement.

MATERIALS

As listed for one table and four stools

Code	No. Req'd	Side	Part Identification
A	2	23⅞″ x 23⅞″	Table top and bottom
B	2	19″ x 23½″	Table supports
C	4	11⅞″ x 19¼″	Stool back
D	4	11⅞″ x 13⅝″	Stool side
E	4	11⅞″ x 13⅞″	Stool side
F	8	See drawings	Stool top and bottom
	32 lin. ft.	¾″ tr. round	Nailing strip
	4 lin. ft.	2″ x 2″	Corner blocks

MISCELLANEOUS

4d finish nails as required
¾″ brads as required
Glue and finishing materials

CUTTING DIAGRAMS

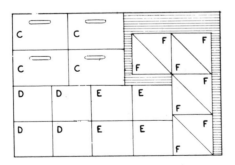

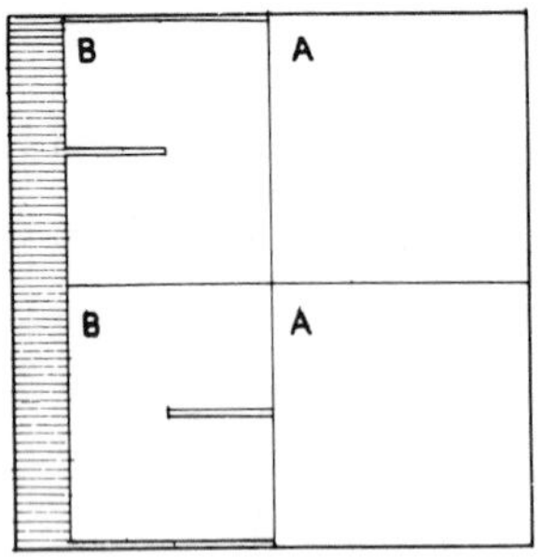

½″ x 4'-0″ x 4'-0″
EXT. - DFPA - A-A OR INT. - DFPA - A-A

¼″ x 4'-0″ x 6'-0″
EXT. - DFPA - PLYSHIELD A-C OR INT. - DFPA - PLYPANEL A-D

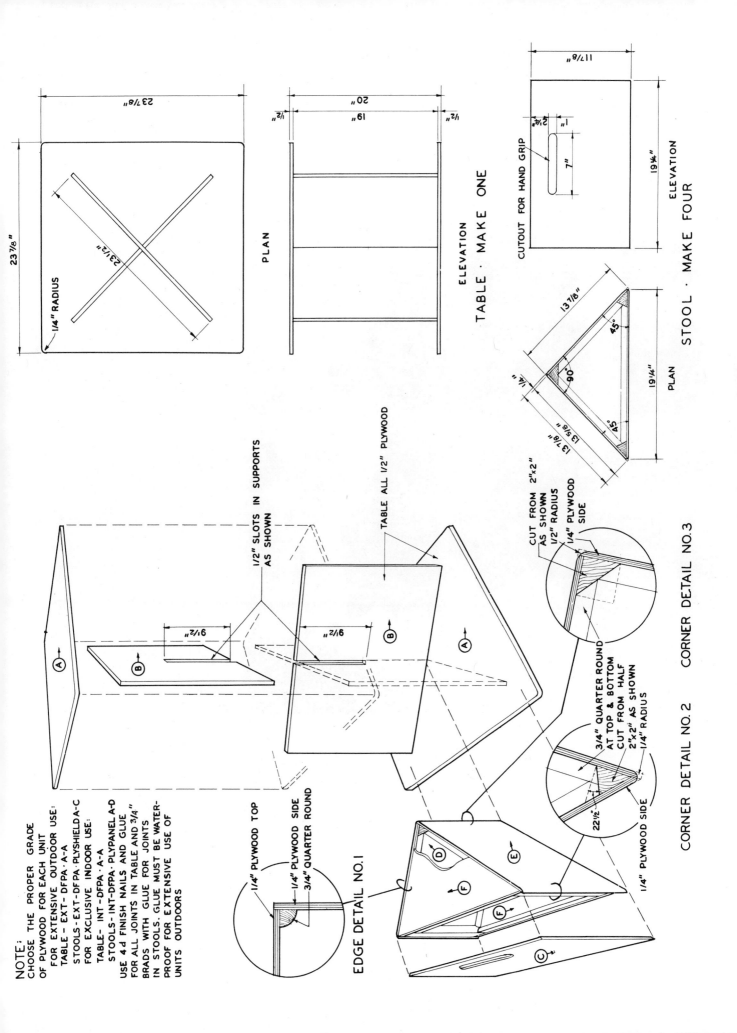

NOTE:
CHOOSE THE PROPER GRADE
OF PLYWOOD FOR EACH UNIT
    FOR EXTENSIVE OUTDOOR USE:
    TABLE - EXT - DFPA · A-A
    STOOLS - EXT-DFPA · PLYSHIELD A-C
    FOR EXCLUSIVE INDOOR USE:
    TABLE - INT -DFPA · A-A
    STOOLS -INT-DFPA · PLYPANEL A-D
USE 4d FINISH NAILS AND GLUE
FOR ALL JOINTS IN TABLE AND 3/4"
BRADS WITH GLUE FOR JOINTS
IN STOOLS. GLUE MUST BE WATER-
PROOF FOR EXTENSIVE USE OF
UNITS OUTDOORS

23 7/8 "
23 7/8 "
1/4" RADIUS
23 1/2"

PLAN

20"
19"
1/2"
1/2"

ELEVATION
TABLE · MAKE ONE

11 7/8"
2 1/4"
1"
7"
CUTOUT FOR HAND GRIP

19 1/4"
ELEVATION

STOOL · MAKE FOUR

13 7/8"
45°
90°
4"
13 7/8"
13 5/8"
45°
19 1/4"
PLAN

1/2" SLOTS IN SUPPORTS
AS SHOWN

TABLE ALL 1/2" PLYWOOD

9 1/2"
9 1/2"

Ⓐ
Ⓑ
Ⓐ
Ⓑ

1/4" PLYWOOD TOP
1/4" PLYWOOD SIDE
3/4" QUARTER ROUND
EDGE DETAIL NO.1

Ⓓ
Ⓔ
Ⓕ
Ⓕ
Ⓒ

CUT FROM 2"x 2"
AS SHOWN
1/2" RADIUS
1/4" PLYWOOD
SIDE

CORNER DETAIL NO.3

3/4" QUARTER ROUND
AT TOP & BOTTOM
CUT FROM HALF
2"x 2" AS SHOWN
1/4" RADIUS
22 1/2°
1/4" PLYWOOD SIDE

CORNER DETAIL NO. 2

GIANT BUILDING TOY

Your youngsters' imagination will enable them to make numerous and varying assemblies with this giant building toy. It is easy to build, for all major parts are simply cut from one panel of exterior-type fir playwood. Assemblies are held together with pins made from short lengths of ¼" dowels.

MATERIALS

    1 panel—exterior-type fir plywood (Grade A-A).
    6 pieces—4' length of 1" diameter birch dowel.
    1 piece—4' length of ¼" diameter birch dowel.
    Exterior primer and house paint, or
    Exterior trim enamel as required.

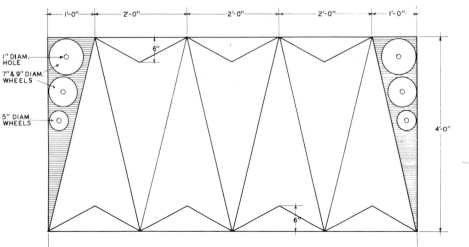

1" DIAM. HOLE
7" & 9" DIAM. WHEELS
5" DIAM. WHEELS

FIR PLYWOOD CUTTING DIAGRAM
1 PC. 5/8" x 4' x 8' EXT-DFPA-A-A

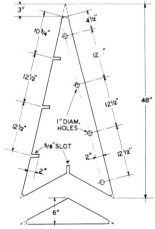

MAKE 7

PLAY PLANKS

They only amount to a few notched planks of plywood. But what wondrous castles your kiddies can build of these simple materials! Better make them a good supply. What builder, young or old, wants to run out of "lumber" just when he is ready to finish off the roof?

Plywood building planks make it easy for children to construct any number of walk-in size projects. No nails are needed; the notched planks alone build strongly and safely. For the complete set you will need three 4′ x 8′ panels and one piece 2′ long x 4′ wide. Use EXT-DFPA. A-A grade exterior fir plywood ¾″ thick. Saw each 4′ x 8′ panel into 4″ strips, 2′ long. Cut to these lengths:

4 doz. planks 6″ long   2 doz. planks 24″ long
3 doz. planks 12″ long   2 doz. planks 36″ long
2 doz. planks 18″ long   2 doz. planks 48″ long

Notch each plank as shown. Notch 6″ planks at center only; all others at ends. For accurate cutting use a circular saw with a sharp blade. A dado head simplifies notch cutting.

If they are going to leave these planks out in the rain, perhaps you should cut them of exterior-type plywood. Indoors, of course, the interior-type will do. And to avoid splinters, sand all the edges. If time permits, a coat or two of clear finish makes the planks nicer to handle —a consideration your midget builders will appreciate.

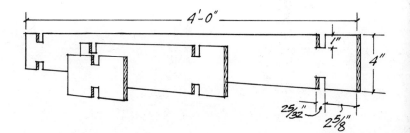

SPACE SHIP

If that youngster of yours is determined to blast off into orbit, here is just the space ship to take him there. Even if it is confined to the mundane precincts of your backyard, it makes a wonderful trainer for things to come.

Make the space ship of exterior-type plywood on 2" x 2" framing, as indicated on plans. A little imagination in painting can work wonders in getting it airborne. The space ship is sure to mesmerize your neighborhood, attracting midget Martians from ten blocks away!

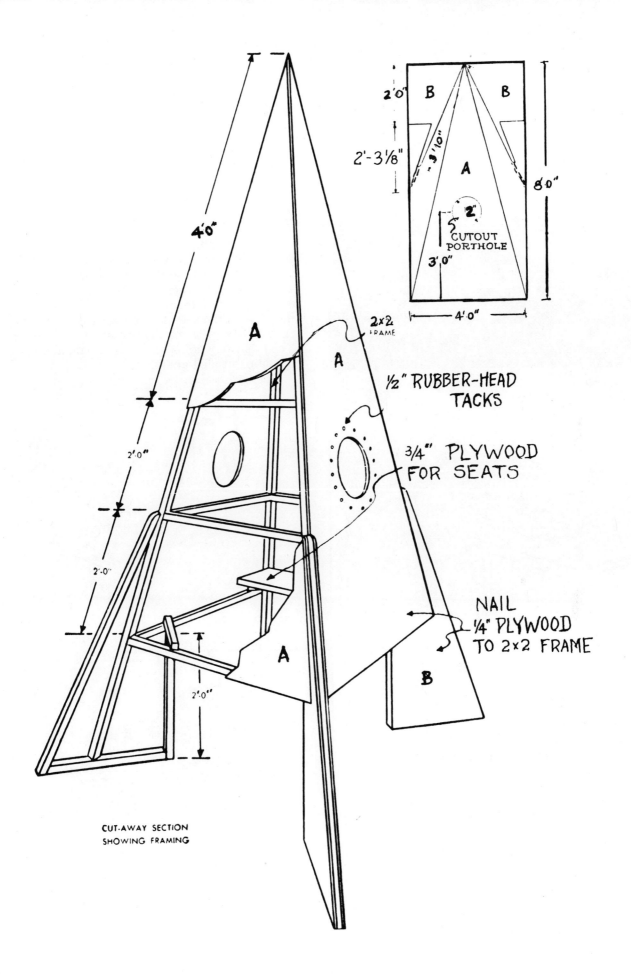

2'0"

B   B

2'-3⅛"

3'10"

A

2"

CUTOUT
PORTHOLE

3'0"

8'0"

4'0"

4'0"

A

A

2×2
FRAME

½" RUBBER-HEAD
TACKS

3/4" PLYWOOD
FOR SEATS

2'-0"

2'-0"

A

NAIL
¼" PLYWOOD
TO 2×2 FRAME

B

2'-0"

CUT-AWAY SECTION
SHOWING FRAMING

UTILITY TABLE

There are numerous ways in which this practical utility table can be put to use; in the playroom, basement, utility room, or outdoors. Even amateurs will find construction easy, using only ordinary hand tools. Simple lock joints made possible by the use of fir plywood, hold the base frame rigid without the use of any fastenings. The table may be readily taken apart and stored flat until needed again.

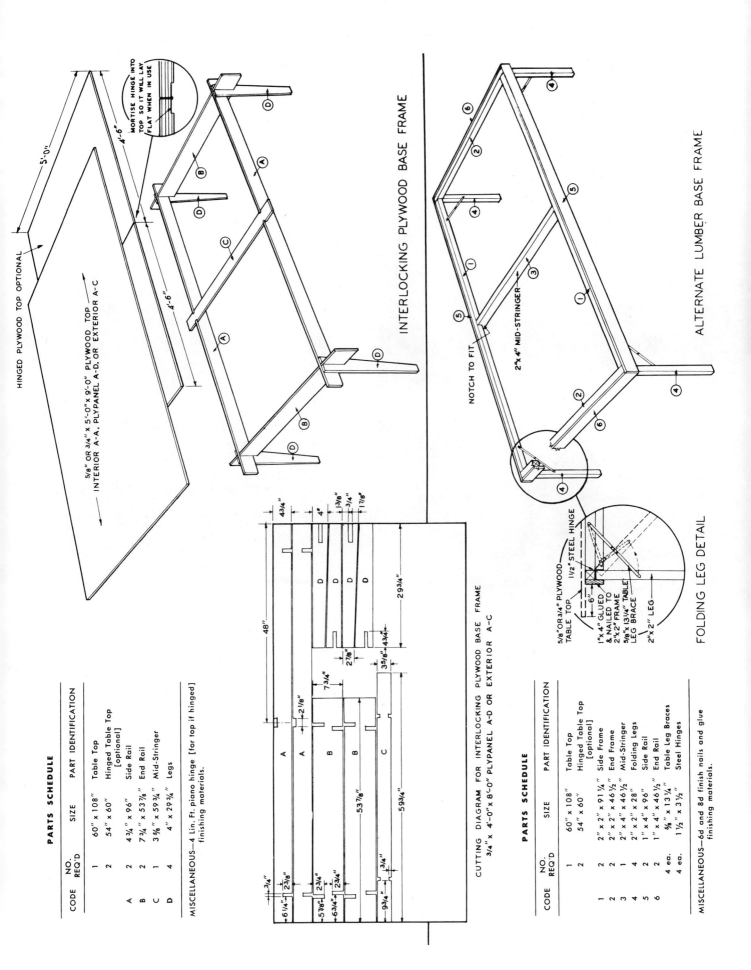

PARTS SCHEDULE

CODE	NO. REQ'D	SIZE	PART IDENTIFICATION
	1	60" x 108"	Table Top
	2	54" x 60"	Hinged Table Top [optional]
A	2	4 3/4" x 96"	Side Rail
B	2	7 3/4" x 53 7/8"	End Rail
C	1	3 5/8" x 59 3/4"	Mid-Stringer
D	4	4" x 29 3/4"	Legs

MISCELLANEOUS—4 Lin. Ft. piano hinge [for top if hinged] finishing materials.

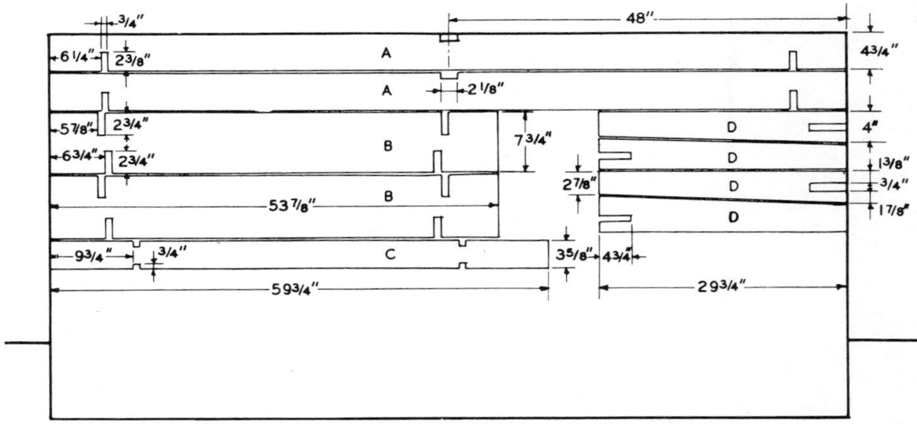

3/4"
48"
6 1/4"
2 3/8"
A
4 3/4"
A
2 1/8"
5 7/8"
2 3/4"
B
7 3/4"
D
4"
6 3/4"
2 3/4"
D
1 3/8"
2 7/8"
D
3/4"
53 7/8"
B
D
1 7/8"
9 3/4"
3/4"
C
3 5/8"
4 3/4"
59 3/4"
29 3/4"

CUTTING DIAGRAM FOR INTERLOCKING PLYWOOD BASE FRAME
3/4" x 4'-0" x 8'-0" PLYPANEL A-D OR EXTERIOR A-C

PARTS SCHEDULE

CODE	NO. REQ'D	SIZE	PART IDENTIFICATION
	1	60" x 108"	Table Top
	2	54" x 60"	Hinged Table Top [optional]
1	2	2" x 2" x 91 1/4"	Side Frame
2	2	2" x 2" x 46 1/2"	End Frame
3	1	2" x 4" x 46 1/2"	Mid-Stringer
4	4	2" x 2" x 28"	Folding Legs
5	2	1" x 4" x 96"	Side Rail
6	2	1" x 4" x 46 1/2"	End Rail
	4 ea.	5/8" x 13 1/4"	Table Leg Braces
	4 ea.	1 1/2" x 3 1/2"	Steel Hinges

MISCELLANEOUS—6d and 8d finish nails and glue finishing materials.

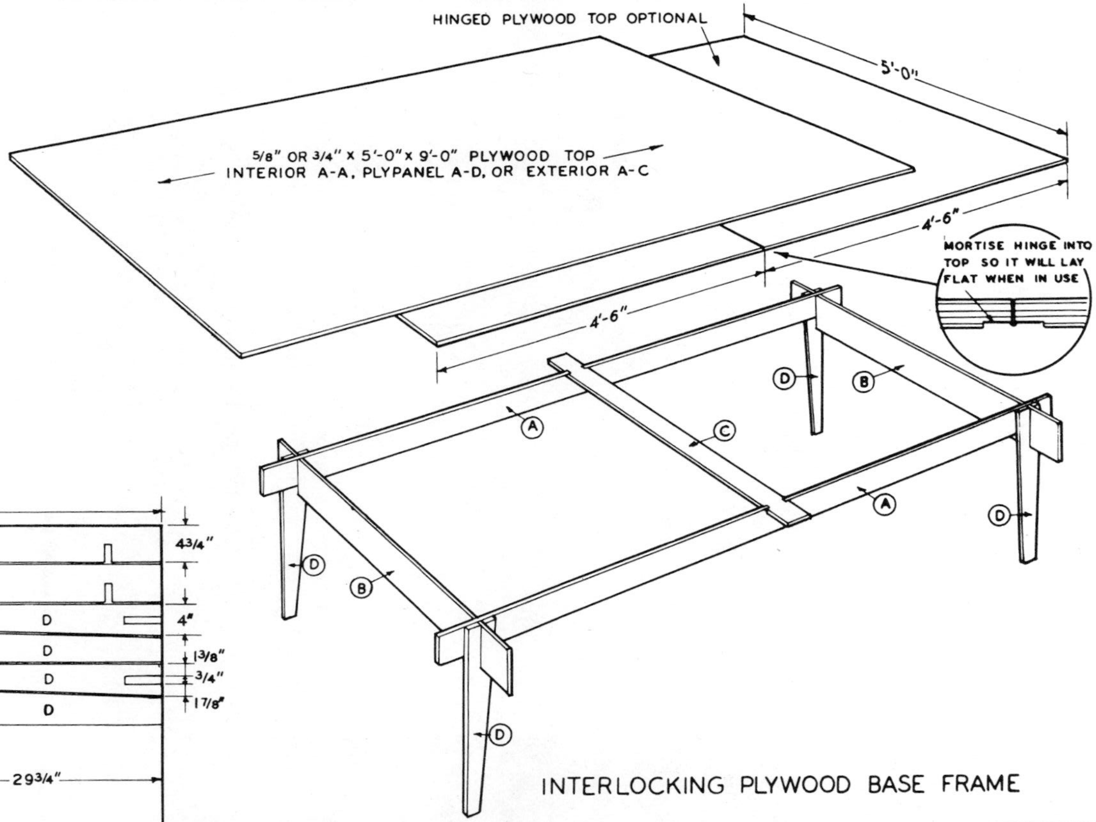

HINGED PLYWOOD TOP OPTIONAL
5'-0"
5/8" OR 3/4" x 5'-0" x 9'-0" PLYWOOD TOP
INTERIOR A-A, PLYPANEL A-D, OR EXTERIOR A-C
4'-6"
MORTISE HINGE INTO TOP SO IT WILL LAY FLAT WHEN IN USE
4'-6"
D
B
A
C
A
D
D
B
D

INTERLOCKING PLYWOOD BASE FRAME

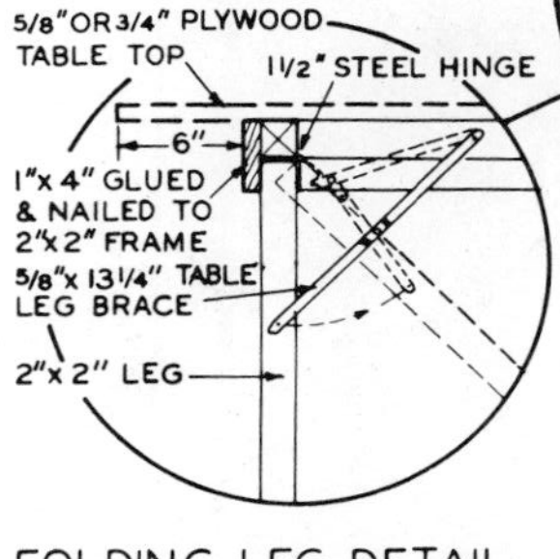

5/8" OR 3/4" PLYWOOD TABLE TOP
1 1/2" STEEL HINGE
6"
1" x 4" GLUED & NAILED TO 2" x 2" FRAME
5/8" x 13 1/4" TABLE LEG BRACE
2" x 2" LEG

FOLDING LEG DETAIL

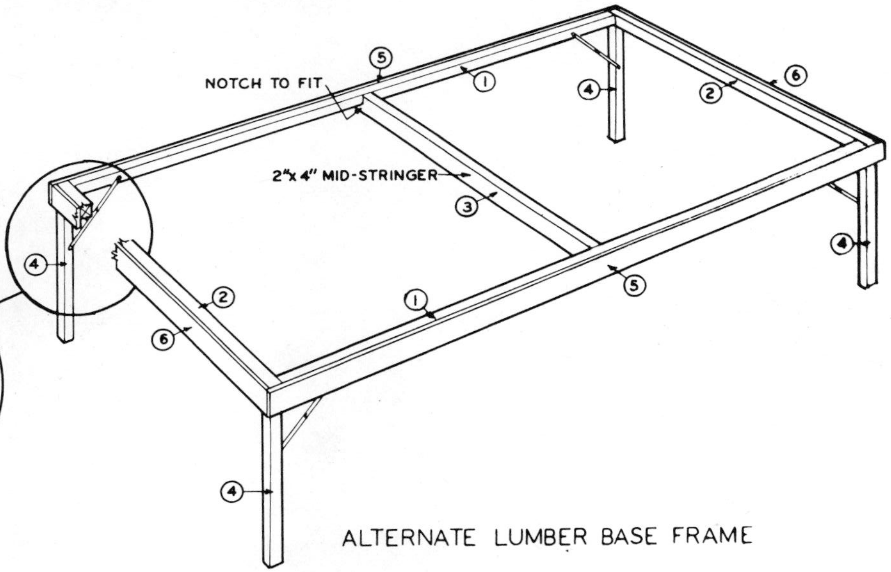

5
NOTCH TO FIT
1
4
2
6
2" x 4" MID-STRINGER
3
4
4
5
2
1
6
4

ALTERNATE LUMBER BASE FRAME

PUPPET THEATER

A few hand puppets, an imaginative youngster, and this home puppet theater will provide "live" entertainment for the whole family. With the large variety of hand puppets available today, the youngsters can enjoy do-it-yourself TV with clowns, villains, heroes, teddy bears, mice and many other animals.

Only one panel of ¼" interior fir plywood is required to build this simple project. Hinged sides are provided so it can be folded flat and stored away when not in use.

MATERIALS

FIR PLYWOOD

1 panel ¾" x 4'-0" x 8'-0" Plypanel A-D

Code	No. Req'd	Part Size	Use
A	1	35" x 54"	Front
B	2	12½" x 47"	Sides
C	1	13⅛" x 34"	Stage top
D	1	19⅝" x 32⅝"	Stage back

Use waste for cut-out decorations

LUMBER AND HARDWARE

No.	Size	Item	Use
5	1" x 2"-8'-0"	Framing	Stage opening & sides
1	¾" x ¾"	Stops	Stage opening
1½ pr.	¾" x 1½"	Surface hinges	Hinged sides
4 ea.	As req'd	Ballbearing casters	

MISCELLANEOUS

Crepe paper for curtains
4d finish nails and screws as required
Glue and finishing materials

CUTTING DIAGRAMS

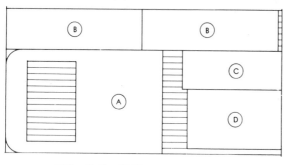

¼" x 4'-0" x 8'-0" INT • DFPA • A-D

DESIGNED FOR THE DOUGLAS FIR PLYWOOD ASSOCIATION, TACOMA 2, WASHINGTON

GET FIR PLYWOOD AND OTHER MATERIAL FOR
THIS PLAN FROM YOUR LOCAL LUMBER DEALER

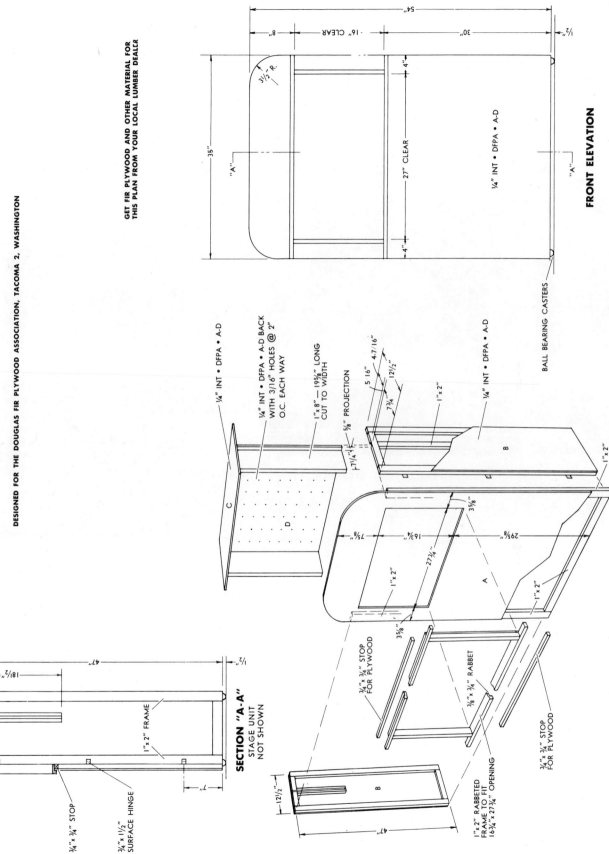

FRONT ELEVATION

SECTION "A-A"
STAGE UNIT
NOT SHOWN

CORNER STUDY AREA

Kids need a place of their own—for work, play and storing things. This wall desk will satisfy that need and easily fit into almost any corner of their room.

The two arms of the desk taper at the outer ends in a design calculated to provide the optimum amount of work surface without corners jutting too far out into the room. Drawers alternate with pigeon-holes to encourage youngsters to be neat by providing convenient and easily accessible storage space for their personal belongings.

MATERIALS

FIR PLYWOOD

1 panel ½" x 4'-0" x 8'-0" Int. A-A fir plywood
1 piece ⅛" x 2'-0" x 4'-0" tempered hardboard (drawer bottoms)

LUMBER AND HARDWARE

No.	Size	Item	Use
28 lin. ft.	½" x ⅝"	Facing strips	Edge facing
4 ea.	1" diam.	Wood pulls	Drawers
1 pc.	3'-0" x 6'-0"	Heavy gauge linoleum	Desk top
9 lin. ft.	1" x 2"	Wall cleat	Desk support

MISCELLANEOUS

6d finish nails and 1" brads as required
2" No. 10 f.h. wood screws as required
Glue, linoleum paste and finishing materials

CUTTING DIAGRAM

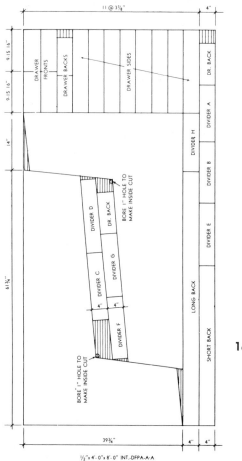

½"x 4'-0"x 8'-0" INT.-DFPA-A-A

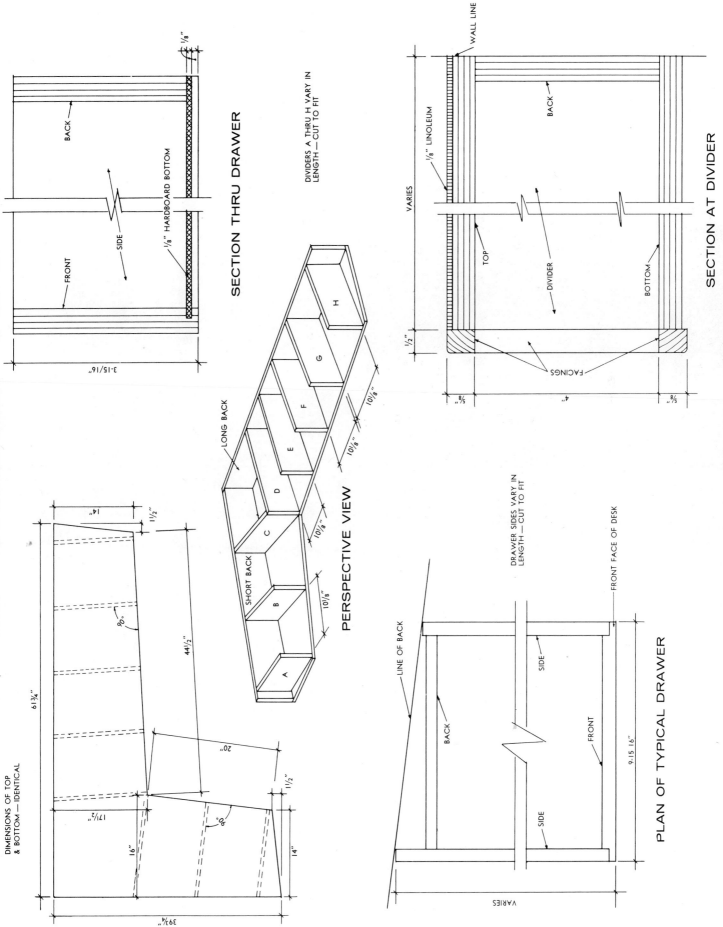

BACK

SIDE

FRONT

1/8" HARDBOARD BOTTOM

1/8"

3-15/16"

SECTION THRU DRAWER

DIVIDERS A THRU H VARY IN
LENGTH—CUT TO FIT

WALL LINE

1/8" LINOLEUM

VARIES

BACK

TOP

DIVIDER

BOTTOM

FACINGS

1/2"

5/8"

4"

5/8"

SECTION AT DIVIDER

LONG BACK

SHORT BACK

A

B   10 1/8"

C   10 1/8"

D   10 1/8"

E   10 1/8"

F   10 1/8"

G   10 1/8"

H

PERSPECTIVE VIEW

DIMENSIONS OF TOP
& BOTTOM—IDENTICAL

14"

1 1/2"

61 3/4"

44 1/2"

20"

90°

17 1/2"

16"

90°

14"

1 1/2"

39 3/4"

LINE OF BACK

BACK

SIDE

SIDE

FRONT

FRONT FACE OF DESK

DRAWER SIDES VARY IN
LENGTH—CUT TO FIT

9-15 16"

VARIES

PLAN OF TYPICAL DRAWER

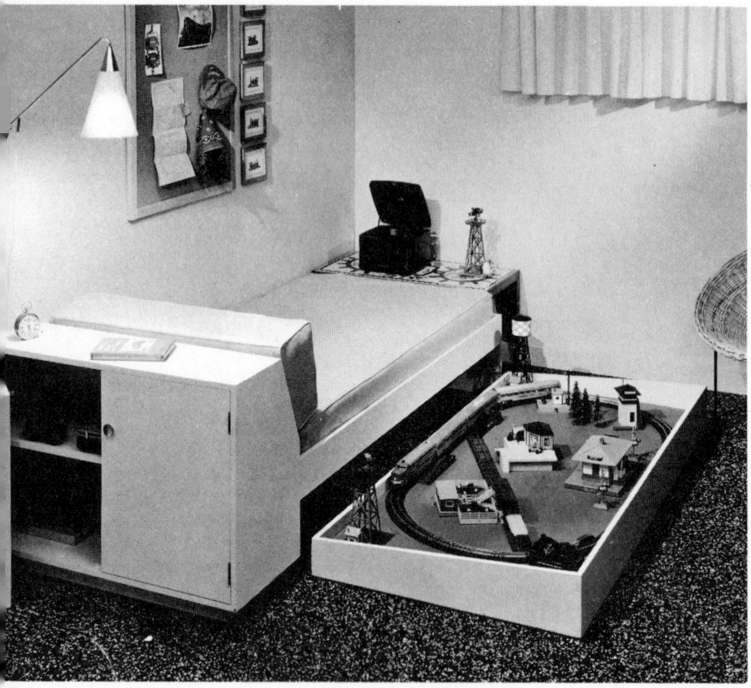

BED-TRAIN BOARD

If you are troubled by the problem of providing train board space in an average-sized child's bedroom, this design can be a practical solution. When not in use, train sets and accessories can be placed on shelves in the storage cabinet, which also serves as a headboard. The bed itself has been designed to accommodate an average, single-sized link spring and mattress. Fir plywood used in construction will withstand years of playful abuse by children.

MATERIALS

Code	*No. Req'd*	*Size*	*Part Indentification*
A	2	20¼″ x 24¼″	Cabinet door
B	1	12¼″ x 42⅛″	Cabinet top
C	1	11¼″ x 40⅝″	Cabinet headboard
D	2	14½″ x 40⅝″	Cabinet shelf and bottom
E	1	17″ x 40⅝″	Cabinet back
F	1	2¼″ x 13″	Cabinet base
G	1	2¼″ x 39⅞″	Cabinet base
H	1	See drawings	Cabinet side and rail
I	1	14″ x 41⅜″	Foot board
J	1	See drawings	Cabinet side and rail
K	1	5″ x 75½″	Train board, back rail
L	1	7″ x 75½″	Train board, front rail
M	1	39⅞″ x 74″	Train board, bottom
N	2	See drawings	Train board, side rail
O	1	40⅝″ x 75⅝″	Bottom, bed frame
	14 lin. ft.	¾″ x 1⅛″	Ledger
	14 lin. ft.	1″ x 2″	Nailer
	8 lin ft.	1″ x 3″	Runner
	29 lin. ft.	1″ x 4″	Frame and slats
	1 ea.	39″ x 74″	Link spring and mattress
	2 pr.	—	Semi-concealed hinges
	2 ea.	—	Friction catches
	2 ea.	—	Door pulls

MISCELLANEOUS

6d Finish nails and glue
Finishing materials

CUTTING DIAGRAMS

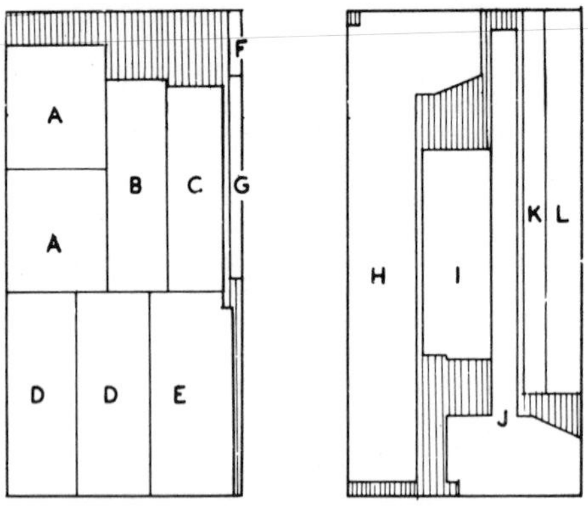

¾" x 4'-0" x 8'-0" ¾" x 4'-0" x 8'-0"
INTERIOR DFPA - PLYPANEL - A-D

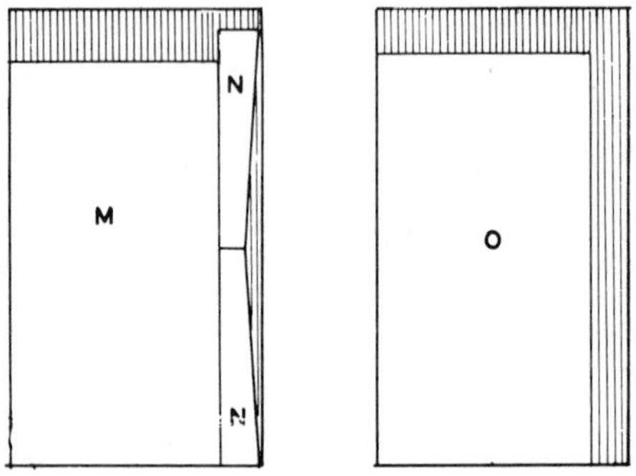

¾" x 4'-0" x 7'-0" ¼" x 4'-0" x 7'-0"
INTERIOR DFPA - PLYPANEL - A-D

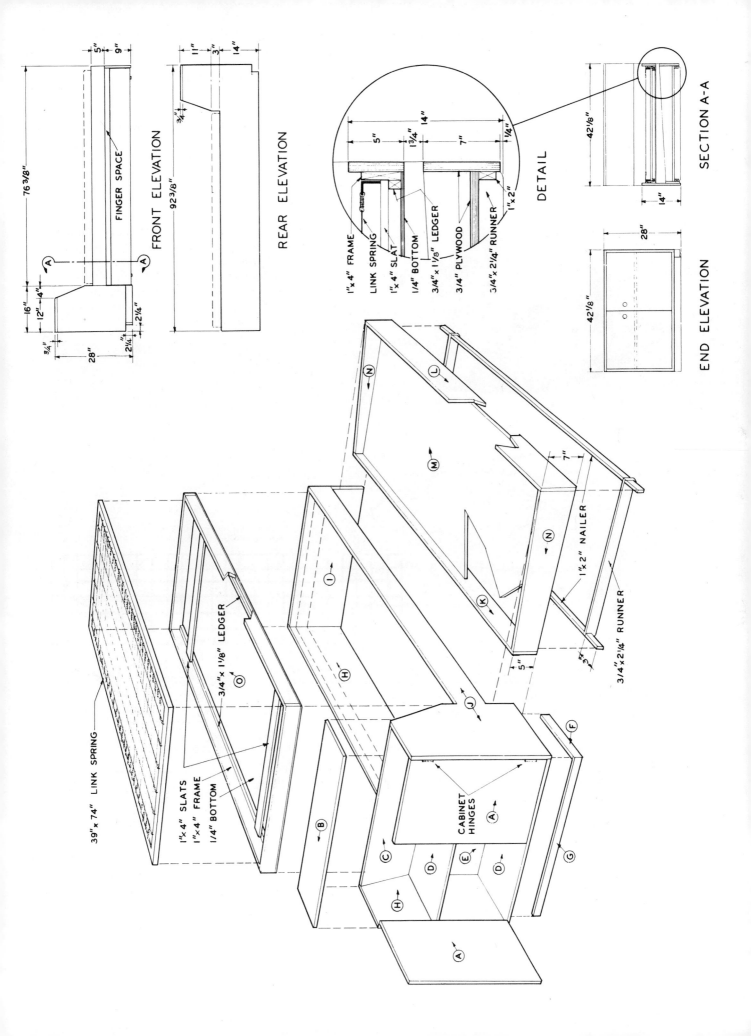

FRONT ELEVATION

76 3/8"

5" 9"

FINGER SPACE

16" 12" 4"

3/4"

2 1/4"

28" 2 1/4"

REAR ELEVATION

92 3/8"

11" 3" 14"

3/4"

DETAIL

14"

5" 1 3/4" 7" 1/4"

1" x 4" FRAME
LINK SPRING
1" x 4" SLAT
1/4" BOTTOM
3/4" x 1 1/8" LEDGER
3/4" PLYWOOD
3/4" x 2 1/4" RUNNER
1" x 2"

SECTION A-A

42 1/8"

14"

END ELEVATION

28"

42 1/8"

39" x 74" LINK SPRING

3/4" x 1 1/8" LEDGER

1" x 4" SLATS
1" x 4" FRAME
1/4" BOTTOM

CABINET HINGES

1" x 2" NAILER

3/4" x 2 1/4" RUNNER

7"

5" 3"

FLYING SAUCER

It may be land-rocked, but it's still a *Flying Saucer!* If there is any question about that, just ask those three-year-olds who, right now, are hovering over the planet Jupiter.

The greatest appeal of this rock-a-bye space vehicle lies in the fact that toddlers can rock in it to their heart's content with nary a chance of their getting hurt in the process. Mother Earth is close at hand, for the rockers are only 6″ high and spread so wide apart that it's practically impossible to spill the saucer.

You can make the entire vehicle from one panel of ¾″ exterior-type, A-C grade, plywood. A good, garish paint job goes a long way toward reinforcing its orbital status.

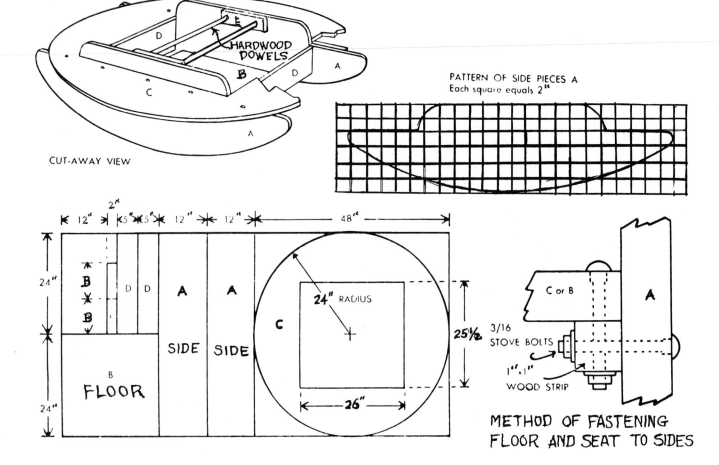

CUT-AWAY VIEW

HARDWOOD DOWELS

PATTERN OF SIDE PIECES A
Each square equals 2″

METHOD OF FASTENING
FLOOR AND SEAT TO SIDES

10

SPECIAL PLYWOOD PROJECTS

Courtesy of Hardwood Plywood Institute and Georgia-Pacific Co

HOW TO INSTALL PLYWOOD WALL PANELING

One of the most attractive home uses for plywood is as interior wall paneling. You can choose from a variety of beautiful wood veneers boasting exquisite graining effects and available in matched panels. These are less difficult to install than solid lumber. And since the plywood panels also come prefinished, they do not require the usual time-consuming chores of sanding, staining and finishing.

Perhaps the most significant virtue of plywood wall paneling is its ability to stay put. Unlike solid lumber, plywood has the inherent stability of cross-laminated construction and is only nominally affected by seasonal changes of indoor climate. It will not suffer from the wintertime furnace heat which causes substantial shrinkage and checking of solid woods. By the same token, you can be reasonably sure that the usual humidity of indoor climate in summer will not swell and bulge plywood as it does solid woods.

Plywood paneling is equally easy to apply to new or old construction. It can be installed directly over two by four wall studding; over furring strips, plaster, sheetrock, plywood sheathing or masonry. Wherever there is a flat surface—or wherever you can make a flat surface—you will find an area which can be covered effectively. Plywood's adaptability and versatility for improving and remodeling existing rooms is truly remarkable. In many cases (as shown in the how-to photo sequence which follows), plywood panels can be installed directly over papered and painted walls.

The following step-by-step photographs showing how to install plywood paneling were taken, especially for this book, in the author's home. In cooperation with the Hardwood Plywood Institute and the Georgia-Pacific Corporation, these rooms were actually paneled within a period of twenty-four hours. The photos show how it was done.

168

PREFINISHED PLYWOOD PANELING

FLAME GUM

HONEYTONE OAK

WALNUT

BIRCH

STRIATED
(FIR)

BROWN ELM

ROSEWOOD

MIST ASH

RIPPLEWOOD

Prefinished paneling courtesy of Georgia-Pacific Cor

Paneling Tools & Materials

Power tools can be used to speed your paneling project or you can get along nicely with the hand tools illustrated at the right. The portable circular saw and electric drill shown can be supplemented with a saber saw. But if you get into power be sure your sawing tools are equipped with fine-tooth blades. And do your power sawing from the back (unfinished) surface of the prefinished panels to reduce sawing damage on the finished side.

This reverse process of sawing with portable power tools can be confusing and can lead to inaccuracy. For this reason many home craftsmen prefer to use sharp (crosscut) hand saws which cut *on thrust* to markings on the finished side.

You will need a couple of horses (like those shown on page 26) to hold your panels in working position. If you intend to use power saws, be sure to pad the tops of the horses to avoid surface damage. Unlike raw, unfinished lumber, prefinished paneling must be protected at all times to guard against scratching and marring.

To determine how many plywood panels you will need for your job, measure your wall area carefully. Since each panel is 4' wide and 8' long, it is relatively easy to determine the number of panels needed in relation to wall space to be covered. You can deduct as much as one-half panel for each window opening and slightly more than that for each doorway. But scheme your paneling layout before making these deductions. You will find that remnants of paneling come in handy for making such items as the window valances shown on page 179.

Order the trim molding best suited to your job. This is also prefinished in tones compatible to your paneling. Ordinarily, 4d and 6d finishing nails are used. The smaller size is preferable, unless you have to go through unusually heavy plaster or material to reach the studding. Contact adhesive can also be used when paneling is applied over plywood sheathing, furring or fresh studding.

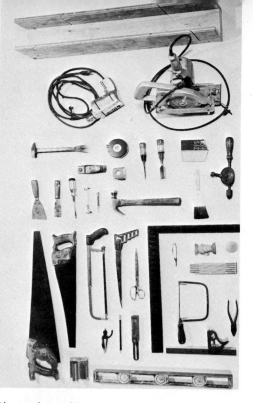

Plywood paneling tools

Plywood paneling materials

Courtesy of Hardwood Plywood Institute and Georgia-Paci *Corp.*

170

1 Prefinished panels are placed against the wall to match grain patterns. It is well to expose them to climate of the room for at least 24 hours prior to application. Thus they become adjusted to moisture content of the place where they are to be installed.

2 Old molding is gently removed to avoid damage to adjoining trim and painted areas. Work molding loose at one corner and then pry it free with a ripping chisel and hammer. Guard adjoining areas by prying against a large putty knife or strip of scrap plywood.

3 Measure and mark at 16″ intervals along wall. This should indicate approximate location of studding under plaster. For exact location, probe the wall with a small drill and make accurate markings near base and ceiling showing definite position of each side of every stud. A chalk line is then used to mark center of each stud.

4 When wall is uneven, furring strips of ⅜″ by 1-⅞″ plywood, may be required to produce a true surface. These strips are nailed to the wall over studding with horizontal spacers between them at 16″ intervals. They are then shimmed from behind with thin wedges to produce a true and level surface for paneling.

5 Trimming panels to required lengths is done with a fine-tooth crosscut saw. If a power circular saw or saber saw is used, saw from the back (unfinished) surface of the panel to avoid edge splintering of the prefinished side.

6 Try the trimmed panel in position on the wall where it is to be fitted. To fit snug behind existing trim of windows and doors, ¼" notches must be sawed behind projecting ends of head casing and window stool to receive edge of panel.

7 For exact fit, the shape of the window and door trim is scribed on panel. This compensates for irregularities of old construction around which new paneling must be fitted.

8 Coping saw is used to cut edges of panel to shape of existing trim. Block plane is used for longer edges. This can also be done with a power saber saw but caution must be observed to cut from back side of panel to protect finish.

9 Expansion space of ¼″ must be allowed on length of panel to avoid buckling during seasons of excessive dampness. Space is later covered by molding.

10 After panel has been fitted, it is lightly tapped into final position with a protective block of soft wood. Seams are closed with soft pounding of a rubber mallet, with caution observed to protect finish at all times.

11 Small, 4-d, finishing nails (1-½″), spaced approximately 12″ apart, suffice to nail paneling over plaster to studding. If paneling is applied directly to furring, or to new studding, it can be held with adhesive and a few nails.

12 Nail heads are carefully set with nailset of exact size to avoid enlargement of indentation. Holes are filled with matching putty stick in final treatment.

13 Corners are carefully checked for squareness and perpendicular alignment. When furring strips are used, true corner alignment can be obtained before attaching panels.

14 Adjoining corner panel is trial fitted and scribed to its corner mate prior to attachment. Care must be taken to maintain precise perpendicular alignment so that following panels will not slant and expose tapered seams.

15 Window casing is about to be enclosed as next panel is pressed into position. The projecting window head trim and stool have been slotted, against the wall, to receive and hold the panel.

16 Next panel encounters electric switch box where wall plate has been removed to facilitate exact measurements taken from edge of adjoining panel and up from base.

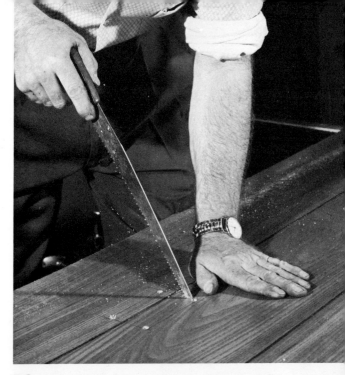

17 Measurements of switch box opening are carefully transferred to panel. All marking is done with soft pencil which does not mar finish and can later be erased from surface.

18 With switch box marking completed, ⅜" holes are bored at the corners to start and guide sawing of cutout. Sawing is performed with a keyhole saw or fine-tooth compass saw.

19 Switch box focuses into cutout opening as panel is fitted around door casing. Final panel encloses doorway and finishes the covering of this wall.

20 With only ¼" thickness of panel added to the wall surface, original switch plate can usually be returned to fit flush over new panel. Slightly longer screws may be required to close the box.

21 Prefinished molding, of compatible colors, is used to trim the wall paneling. This comes in a variety of shapes and sizes to suit your specific needs. Wrapped in cellophane, to protect the finish, this molding is easily worked.

22 Exact measurements are taken for cutting ceiling cove molding, base and corner cove. As well as the moldings used for this installation there also exists prefinished casing and trim, base, mullion, stop, and outside corner molding.

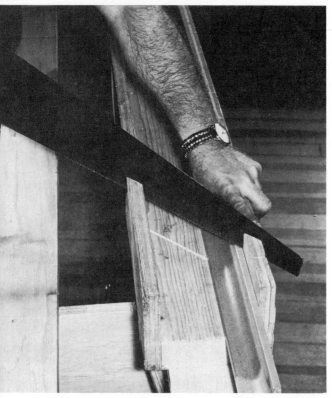

23 Ceiling cove molding is carefully mitered for exact fit at the corners. Prefinished molding comes in lengths adequate to the dimensions of average-sized rooms.

24 Flush fit of corner cove miter depends on accuracy of measurements and precision of miter sawing. It is nailed snugly around perimeter of ceiling with 6-d finishing nails.

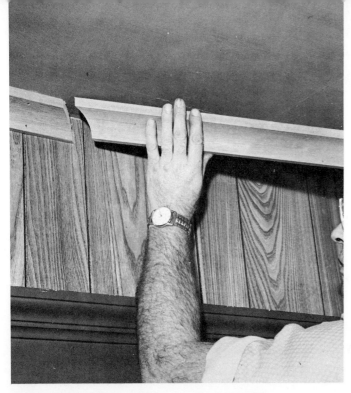

25 When molding splices are required, joining pieces should be mitered and overlapped for flush fit. Circular saw, precisely adjusted, may also be used to cut molding miters.

26 For this installation, ½" by ¾" "shoe" molding (quarter-round) was used as base trim over existing baseboard. Prefinished baseboard molding is also available.

27 Corner cove molding is scribed and shaped at ends to fit exactly between ceiling cove and base. Special, prefinished molding is also available for outside corners.

28 Slightly larger (6-d) finishing nails may be used for attaching molding. Heads are carefully set and all indentations filled with matching putty stick.

29 After prefinished paneling has been carefully installed, there is little left to do by way of finishing. But all nail holes should be filled with special putty stick of matching color. This comes with the finishing kit supplied with prefinished paneling.

30 If prefinished panels were scratched or marred while work was being done, damaged areas can be touched up with matching stain-filler.

31 While its application is seldom necessary on new work, a special plastic top coat (which also comes with the kit) may be used to refinish molding and paneling. This is also useful for matching other woods to your paneling.

32 With occasional polishing and waxing, prefinished paneling retains a warm luster over its beautiful graining. Harsh detergents and cleaning fluids should never be used as they are apt to damage the finish.

Photo sequence courtesy of Hardwood Plywood Institute and Georgia-Pacific Corp.

HOW TO MAKE PANELED WINDOW VALANCES

When you have finished your wall paneling job, you may discover that you have just enough prefinished plywood remnants left over to make window valances. In fact, if you have paneled around old fashioned window trim, you may welcome a way to camouflage such ancient casings with wide valances and drapes.

Valances like those shown above are easily constructed over a base box of pine or similar soft wood. Follow the construction drawing, butting the base parts together with 6-d finishing nails. The length of the valance is determined by the breadth of your windows. For a spacious effect, make them 12″ longer than the spread of your window trim. This allows a 6″ overlap for drapes on each side of the window.

After the box foundation has been made, veneer it with leftover paneling. Glue and clamp this over the base box, butting the front facing over the end pieces of matched paneling. When clamping, protect all prefinished surfaces with cardboard. The top lip of the facing veneer overlaps the base box ¼″, allowing room for the ¼″ top panel to be recessed in, and nailed along, top edges of the inner box.

Prefinished outside corner molding should be used to trim the bottom edges of the valance. This must be carefully mitered at the corners. Attach your curtain rods inside near the top of the valances before mounting. Since the valances are constructed with a top dust guard panel they are made as a six-sided box and will sit atop the window head even without nails while being adjusted. But they must be secured to the window head with a few partly driven nails, so that they may be readily removed for future cleaning.

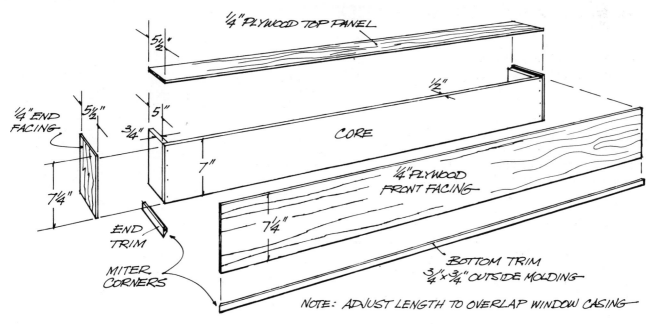

179

Courtesy of Weyerhaeuser Company

DOUBLE DUTY ROOM DIVIDER

Separate your living and dining areas with this functional room divider of rich warm wood —making each room look larger and, at the same time, seem more private.

Vertical plywood louvers with pleasing shadows and contrasting light add dramatic emphasis to both rooms. The louvers are supported by an attractive cabinet base that serves as a complete entertainment center.

Plywood paneling imparts a fine-furniture look to this handsome base, which is designed with space for AM-FM radio, roll-out turn-table and hi-fidelity speaker components. Doors mounted with piano hinges fold back to reveal a TV set, placed on a rotating turntable so that programs may be viewed from either the dining or the living areas.

In addition, the divider has shelf space for books, display, magazines and record storage. Beneath are drawers for cards and games. Select a plywood paneling that harmonizes with the rest of your home.

Obviously, the double duty room divider and the ten designs which follow, are more advanced than most of the other projects appearing in this book. But they are wonderful ideas and they are presented here to challenge the interest and ability of the more highly skilled home-craftsman or the professional woodworker.

These designs and material pertaining to them are presented through the courtesy of the Weyerhaeuser Company.

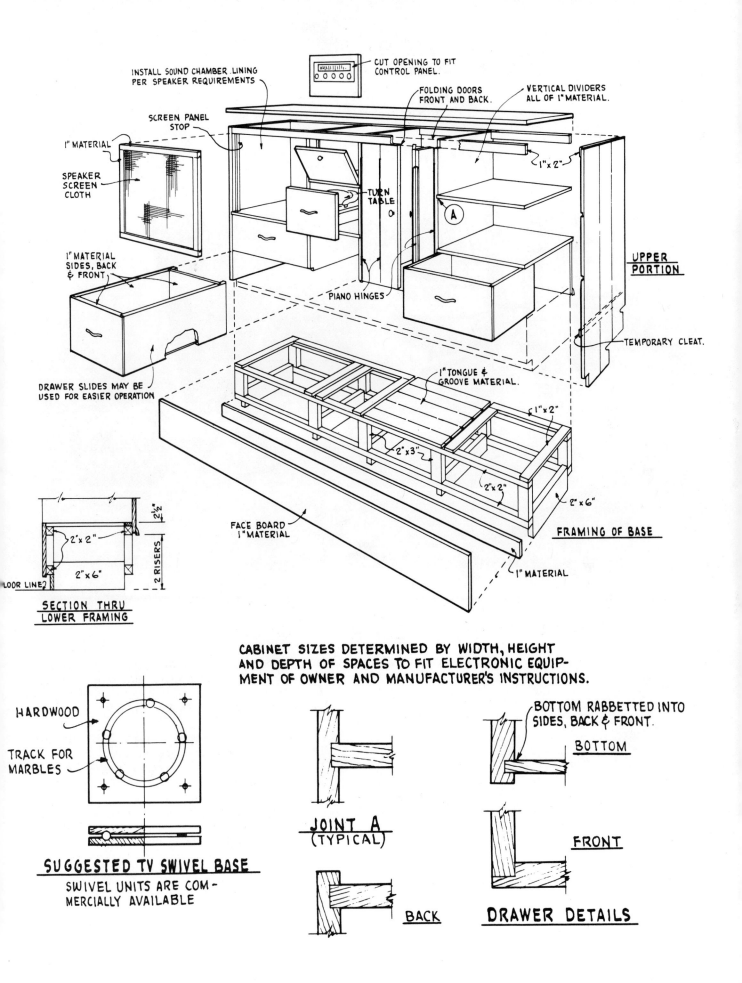

INSTALL SOUND CHAMBER LINING PER SPEAKER REQUIREMENTS

CUT OPENING TO FIT CONTROL PANEL.

FOLDING DOORS FRONT AND BACK.

VERTICAL DIVIDERS ALL OF 1" MATERIAL.

SCREEN PANEL STOP

1" MATERIAL

SPEAKER SCREEN CLOTH

TURN TABLE

1" x 2"

A

UPPER PORTION

1" MATERIAL SIDES, BACK & FRONT

PIANO HINGES

TEMPORARY CLEAT.

DRAWER SLIDES MAY BE USED FOR EASIER OPERATION

1" TONGUE & GROOVE MATERIAL.

1" x 2"

2" x 3"

2" x 2"

2" x 6"

FRAMING OF BASE

FACE BOARD 1" MATERIAL

1" MATERIAL

2½"

2" x 2"

2" x 6"

2 RISERS

FLOOR LINE

SECTION THRU LOWER FRAMING

CABINET SIZES DETERMINED BY WIDTH, HEIGHT AND DEPTH OF SPACES TO FIT ELECTRONIC EQUIPMENT OF OWNER AND MANUFACTURER'S INSTRUCTIONS.

HARDWOOD

TRACK FOR MARBLES

SUGGESTED TV SWIVEL BASE

SWIVEL UNITS ARE COMMERCIALLY AVAILABLE

JOINT A (TYPICAL)

BACK

BOTTOM RABBETTED INTO SIDES, BACK & FRONT.

BOTTOM

FRONT

DRAWER DETAILS

Courtesy of Weyerhaeuser Company

TWO-WAY GARDEN SHELTER

An inviting wood deck patio complete with cushioned settee is designed back to back with a convenient outdoor work and storage center. The areas are separated, yet compactly combined in this modern yet simple A-frame shelter.

A low wood deck provides the basic platform for the two-way garden shelter, which is adaptable to even the smallest of yards. Above it on one side is a colorful bench designed to seat three or more, where you can relax comfortably.

On the reverse side is a complete garden storage and working area. It provides plenty of room for your lawn mower, wall space to hang your tools, shelf space for plants and sprays, and a workbench for potting plants or for other outdoor projects. All outdoor equipment is conveniently close to the task at hand.

Overhead roof sections provide shade for both the patio and working area. In rainy weather, just lower the sections and the entire unit is sealed off for complete protection.

Construction is not too complex with exterior-grade plywood. Finish possibilities are many and varied. This plan may easily be adapted to the size of your yard, assuring that this "Fascinating Idea" will meet the needs of your entire family.

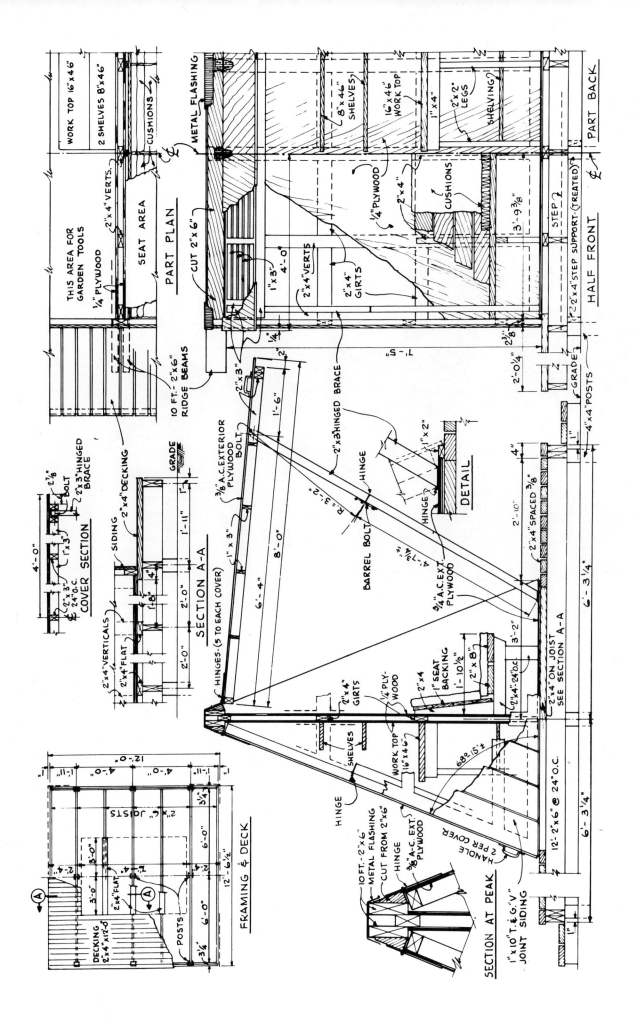

Courtesy of Weyerhaeuser Company

OUTDOOR STORAGE CENTER

Avoid those unnecessary trips to the garage or basement with this complete outdoor storage center of exterior-grade plywood.

A revolving storage closet of perforated hardboard provides hang space for tools, sporting goods, lawn equipment or fishing poles. Corner shelves are included for such necessary items as planting pots, work shoes or paint supplies.

Storage wells mounted on each door are handy for everything from seeds to sprays. Inside there is plenty of room for your lawn mower, wheelbarrow or portable outdoor barbecue.

The entire back wall may be used to hang hand tools, and the perforated hardboard also makes adjustable shelves easy to install and practical to use.

This unit will keep your yard and patio uncluttered . . . providing a handy place for children's toys as well as outdoor equipment.

The entire storage center will fit under a wide eave, or just build a simple roof extension. Paint to match the siding or trim of your home. All-wood construction contributes durability and economy.

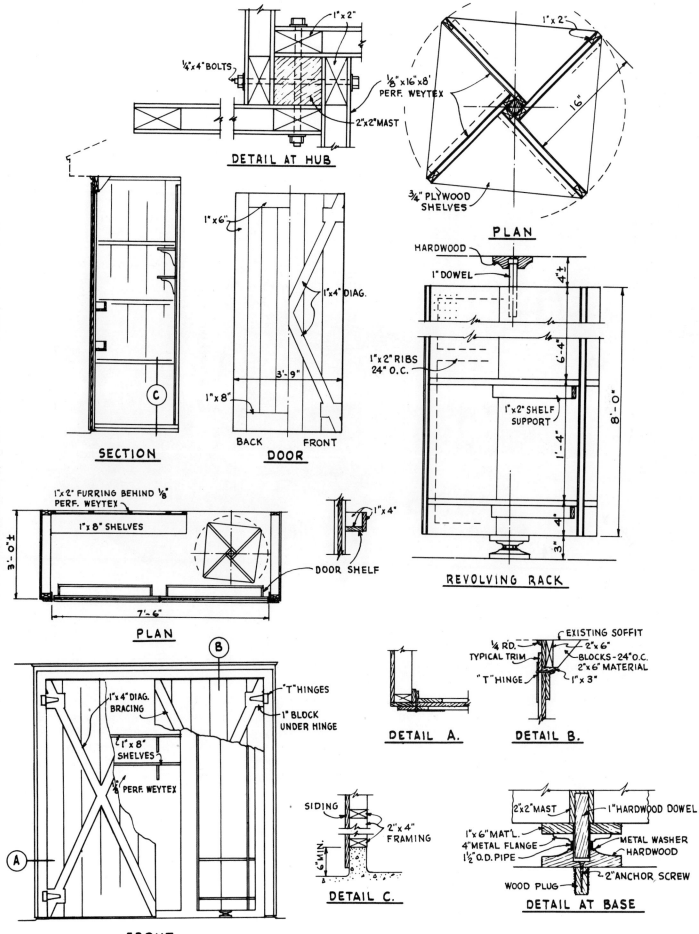

DETAIL AT HUB

1" x 2"

¼" x 4" BOLTS

⅛" x 16" x 8'
PERF. WEYTEX

2" x 2" MAST

1" x 2"

16"

¾" PLYWOOD
SHELVES

PLAN

SECTION

C

1" x 6"

1" x 4" DIAG.

3'-9"

1" x 8"

BACK   FRONT

DOOR

HARDWOOD

1" DOWEL

4"

1" x 2" RIBS
24" O.C.

6'-4"

1" x 2" SHELF
SUPPORT

8'-0"

1'-4"

4"

3"

REVOLVING RACK

1" x 2" FURRING BEHIND ⅛"
PERF. WEYTEX

1" x 8" SHELVES

3'-0"

1" x 4"

DOOR SHELF

7'-6"

PLAN

EXISTING SOFFIT

¼ RD.
TYPICAL TRIM

2" x 6"

BLOCKS - 24" O.C.
2" x 6" MATERIAL

"T" HINGE

1" x 3"

DETAIL A.

DETAIL B.

B

1" x 4" DIAG.
BRACING

"T" HINGES

1" BLOCK
UNDER HINGE

1" x 8"
SHELVES

⅛" PERF. WEYTEX

A

SIDING

2" x 4"
FRAMING

6" MIN.

DETAIL C.

2" x 2" MAST

1" HARDWOOD DOWEL

1" x 6" MAT'L.

4" METAL FLANGE

1½" O.D. PIPE

METAL WASHER
HARDWOOD

WOOD PLUG

2" ANCHOR SCREW

DETAIL AT BASE

FRONT

KITCHEN CENTER-ISLAND

This kitchen-island food preparation and serving center is designed to save you steps, and also to modernize your kitchen through the stylish addition of warm plywood paneling.

Your kitchen range tucks neatly into its own pre-cut recess, with plenty of counter-top working surface left over. Drawers may be partitioned to keep utensils right where they are needed. All the pots and pans normally used in everyday meal preparation are hidden behind distinctive wood paneled doors.

Roll out the serving cart and you have your china, crystal, linens and silverware ready for setting, plus a generous counter surface for carving and serving. Glide the cart to your dining area and eliminate as many as six normal setting and serving trips.

The serving cart and island, designed for easy construction and long life, are easily constructed of plywood.

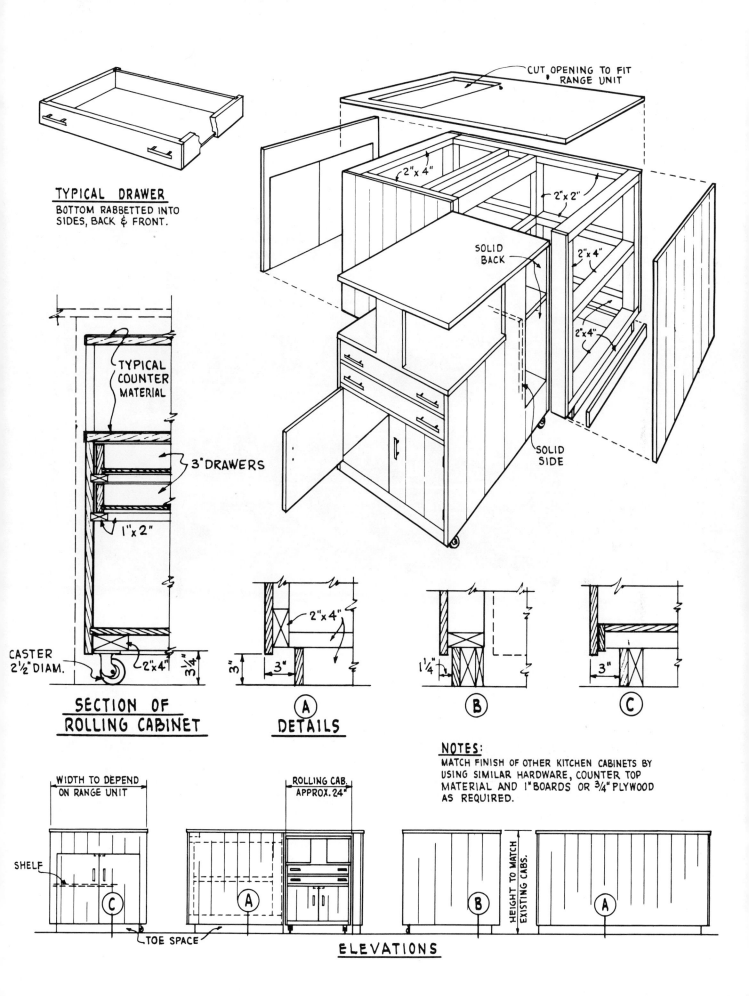

TYPICAL DRAWER
BOTTOM RABBETTED INTO
SIDES, BACK & FRONT.

CUT OPENING TO FIT
RANGE UNIT

2"x 4"

2"x 2"

SOLID
BACK

2"x 4"

2"x 4"

SOLID
SIDE

TYPICAL
COUNTER
MATERIAL

3" DRAWERS

1"x 2"

CASTER
2½" DIAM.

2"x 4"   3/4"

SECTION OF
ROLLING CABINET

A
DETAILS

2"x 4"

3"   3"

1¼"

3"

B

C

NOTES:
MATCH FINISH OF OTHER KITCHEN CABINETS BY
USING SIMILAR HARDWARE, COUNTER TOP
MATERIAL AND 1" BOARDS OR 3/4" PLYWOOD
AS REQUIRED.

WIDTH TO DEPEND
ON RANGE UNIT

ROLLING CAB.
APPROX. 24"

SHELF

HEIGHT TO MATCH
EXISTING CABS.

C

A

TOE SPACE

B

A

ELEVATIONS

Courtesy of Weyerhaeuser Company

FOLD-AWAY DINING CORNER

Here is an idea that will provide additional living space in your home without your having to add an extra room. It is a complete dining center that blends into your kitchen wall when not in use.

A plywood paneled section beneath the functional countertop swings downward to form the legs of this unique dining booth. Its brightly colored cushions create an atmosphere of gaiety that the entire family will love. A spacious dining table swings out from the plywood paneled wall, ready for instant use.

Choose your favorite paneling, available in a variety of species, patterns and grains. Construction is not too difficult. Just follow the working drawing on the opposite page.

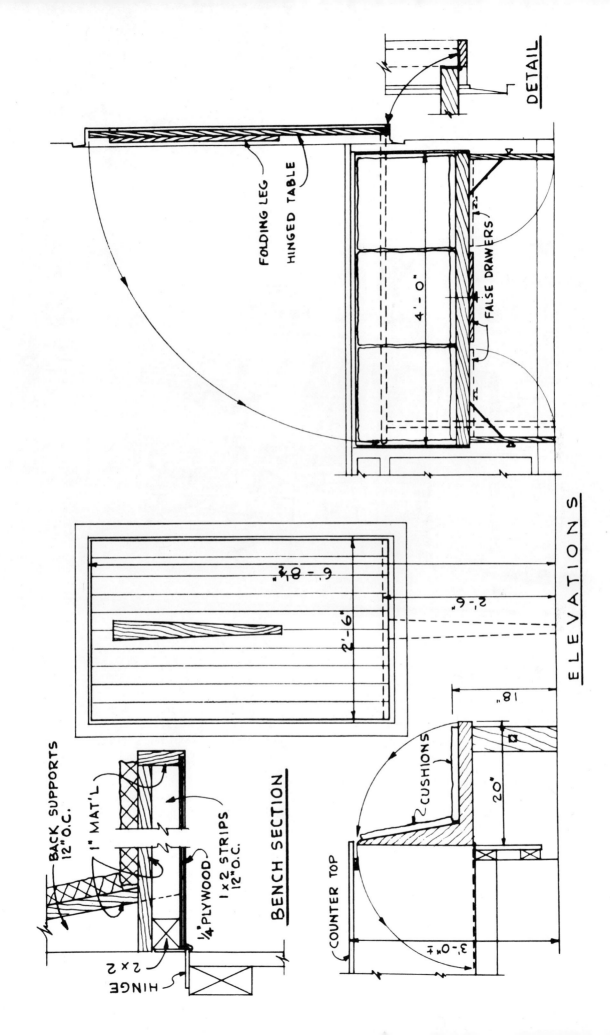

DETAIL

FOLDING LEG
HINGED TABLE

FALSE DRAWERS

4'-0"

2"

2"

ELEVATIONS

7'-8"

2'-6"

2'-6"

2'-6"

18"

BACK SUPPORTS
12" O.C.

1" MAT'L

¼" PLYWOOD
1 x 2 STRIPS
12" O.C.

BENCH SECTION

HINGE
2 x 2

CUSHIONS

COUNTER TOP

20"

3'-0"±

Courtesy of Weyerhaeuser Company

HOBBY HAVEN

Give your favorite hobbyist a place to work and his projects will form the decor for a distinctive family room.

This plan is adaptable to almost any hobby—photography, model construction, leathercraft or a gun collection. Tools and parts are readily available yet discreetly hidden behind the glowing beauty of plywood.

Sliding doors open to reveal the completed projects and may be locked for safety and protection. Below, shallow drawers and adjustable shelves help keep all parts in their proper working order.

Notice the built-in work station, which also doubles as a study. Above is a shelf for books or display. Behind, perforated hardboard or plywood paneling adds interest and utility to the entire wall area.

A storage cabinet handy to the work station blends harmoniously with the adjacent paneled wall, giving decorative continuity and added beauty to the entire room. This particular hobby haven was planned around a comfortable fireside setting.

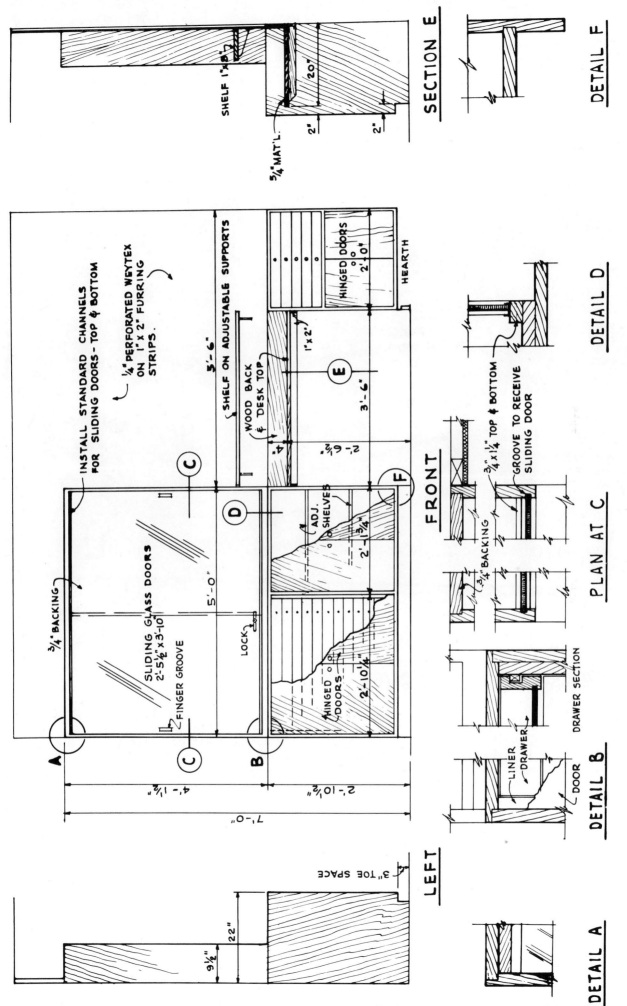

SECTION E

SHELF 1"x5½"

⁵⁄₄"MAT'L.

20"

2"

2"

DETAIL F

INSTALL STANDARD CHANNELS
FOR SLIDING DOORS - TOP & BOTTOM

¼" PERFORATED WEYTEX
ON 1"x 2" FURRING
STRIPS.

SHELF ON ADJUSTABLE SUPPORTS

5'-6"

WOOD BACK
& DESK TOP

1"x 2"

4"

3'-6"

2'-6½"

HINGED DOORS

2'-0"

HEARTH

DETAIL D

¾" BACKING

SLIDING GLASS DOORS
2'-5½" x 3'-10"

5'-0"

FINGER GROOVE

LOCK

ADJ. SHELVES

2'-3¼"

HINGED
DOORS

2'-10¼"

FRONT

¾"x 1¼" TOP & BOTTOM

GROOVE TO RECEIVE
SLIDING DOOR

¾" BACKING

PLAN AT C

A

C

B

F

4'-1½"

2'-10½"

7'-0"

DRAWER SECTION

LINER
DRAWER

DOOR

DETAIL B

LEFT

3" TOE SPACE

22"

9½"

DETAIL A

FINGER-TIP BUFFET SERVER

This built-in buffet will save you steps, help you serve both the dining and kitchen areas, set off your fine china and crystal, and enrich your home with the friendly warmth of natural grained plywood paneling.

Serve directly from the pass-through buffet counter. An accordion-fold screen along the kitchen side closes off the opening when it is not in use, providing an attractive background for decorative displays.

Above the pass-through is an adjustable shelf wall cabinet that allows you to remove or store china and crystal ware from either dining room or kitchen. Below, folding doors swing away to bring your best linen to your fingertips, with wrinkle-free, roll-away storage on individual rollers. Fixed shelves provide additional storage on the kitchen side.

A sliding drawer and hinged door hutch-type storage unit complete this unit, which combines beauty with function and is easily built with plywood.

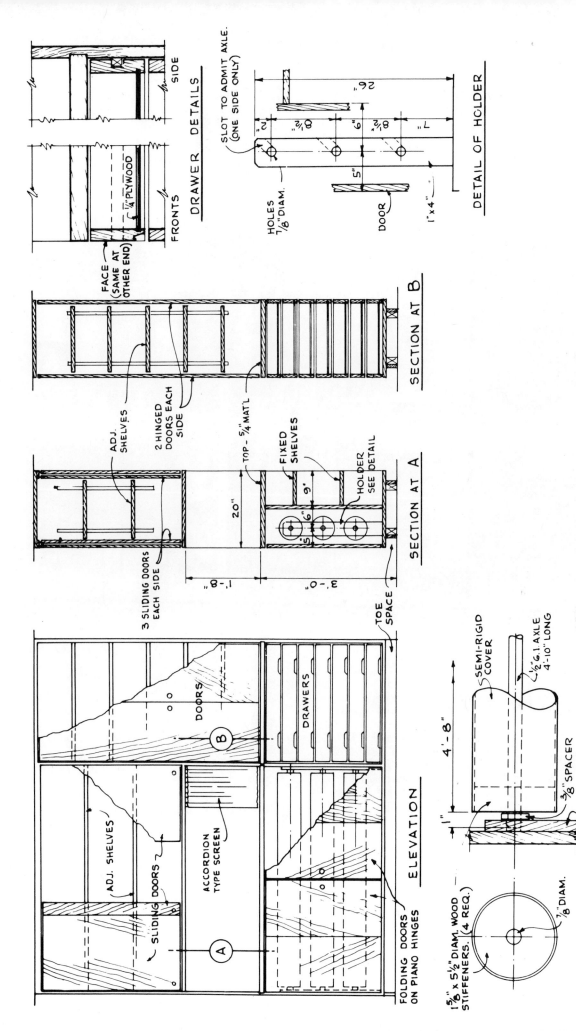

DRAWER DETAILS

SIDE

FRONTS

¼" PLYWOOD

DETAIL OF HOLDER

SLOT TO ADMIT AXLE. (ONE SIDE ONLY)

26"

2"
2½"
6"
3½"
L"
5"

HOLES ⅞" DIAM.

DOOR

1" x 4"

LUMBER   62 B.F.
PLYWOOD   250 S.F.

SECTION AT B

FACE (SAME AT OTHER END)

ADJ. SHELVES

2 HINGED DOORS EACH SIDE

TOP - 5/4 MAT'L

SECTION AT A

20"

9"
6"
5"

FIXED SHELVES

HOLDER SEE DETAIL

3 SLIDING DOORS EACH SIDE

1'-8"

3'-0"

TOE SPACE

ELEVATION

DOORS

B

DRAWERS

A

ADJ. SHELVES

SLIDING DOORS

ACCORDION TYPE SCREEN

FOLDING DOORS ON PIANO HINGES

1⅝" x 5½" DIAM. WOOD STIFFENERS. (4 REQ.)

TABLE CLOTH BOLSTER

SEMI-RIGID COVER

½" G.I. AXLE 4'-10" LONG

4'-8"

1"

⅜ SPACER
1" x 4" HOLDER

⅞" DIAM.

Courtesy of Weyerhaeuser Company

LAZY SUSAN WARDROBE

Separate your wardrobe by season or by formal and informal ensembles, or group your accessories according to wear, all with this beautiful and practical lazy Susan wardrobe.

The natural color and complementing texture of plywood paneling will make the entire unit the focal point of your bedroom, a conversation piece to be admired by family and guests.

There is plenty of room in each wardrobe compartment for wrinkle-free hanging, and right next door are shelves for hats, shoes,

purses and gloves. Each storage section contains three bins with hinged wood paneled covers on the front to shelter hankies, lingerie and sweaters.

At the touch of a finger an entire new wardrobe comes into reach, with free-wheeling casters rolling smoothly on a strong base. A folding door insures complete dust-free protection.

Construction is simple for the skilled craftsman. Do it yourself, or arrange to have it professionally built.

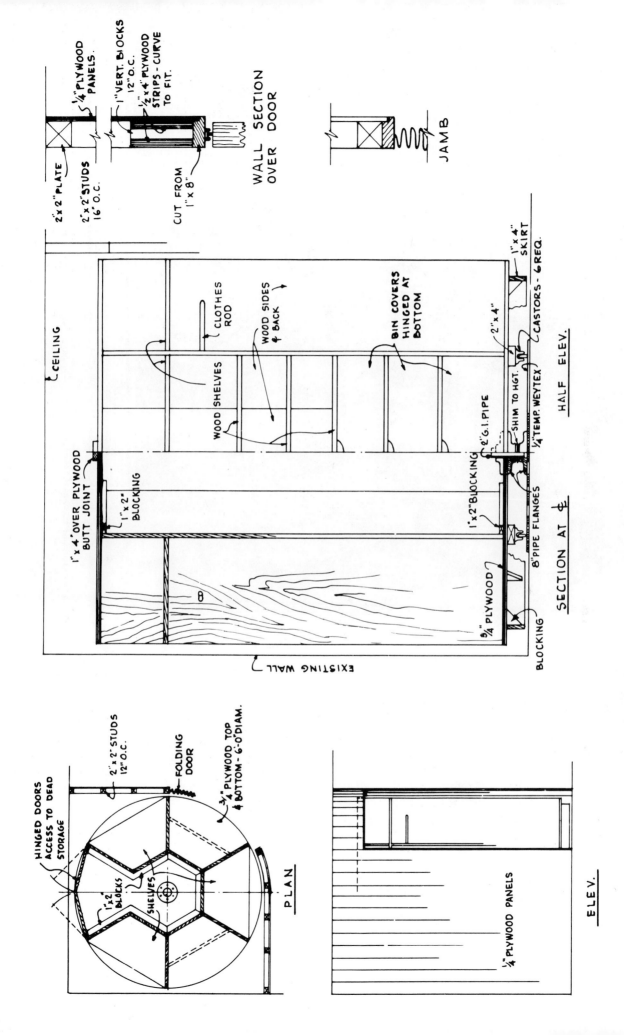

¼" PLYWOOD PANELS.

1" VERT. BLOCKS 12" O.C.

½" x 4" PLYWOOD STRIPS - CURVE TO FIT.

2" x 2" PLATE

2" x 2" STUDS 16" O.C.

CUT FROM 1" x 8"

WALL SECTION OVER DOOR

JAMB

CEILING

CLOTHES ROD

WOOD SIDES & BACK

WOOD SHELVES

BIN COVERS HINGED AT BOTTOM

1" x 4" OVER PLYWOOD BUTT JOINT

1" x 2" BLOCKING

1" x 2" BLOCKING

2" G.I. PIPE

SHIM TO HGT.

¼" TEMP. WEYTEX

1" x 4" SKIRT

CASTORS - 6 REQ.

2" x 4"

8" PIPE FLANGES

¾" PLYWOOD

BLOCKING

BLOCKING

θ

EXISTING WALL

SECTION AT ℄

HALF ELEV.

HINGED DOORS ACCESS TO DEAD STORAGE

2" x 2" STUDS 12" O.C.

FOLDING DOOR

¾" PLYWOOD TOP & BOTTOM - 6'-0" DIAM.

1" x 2" BLOCKS

SHELVES

PLAN

¼" PLYWOOD PANELS

ELEV.

Courtesy of Weyerhaeuser Company

HIDE-AWAY SEWING CENTER

Begin with your family room or laundry room, add the beauty of plywood paneling, and you have the basis for a complete hide-away sewing center with many unique and practical features designed for the woman of the house.

Plywood paneled folding doors set the decorative scheme for the entire room. When opened they disclose a fold-down ironing board, fold-down cutting table, and a built-in cabinet to store patterns, threads, bolts of fabrics, yarn and books.

Just roll out the sewing desk for more working room. Your machine may be recessed into the top, or placed on the surface. Plenty of drawers keep shears and spools close to the project at hand.

Notice how the entire sewing center is included within only 6' 8" of space. Build it into your present home or include it in the design of your new home.

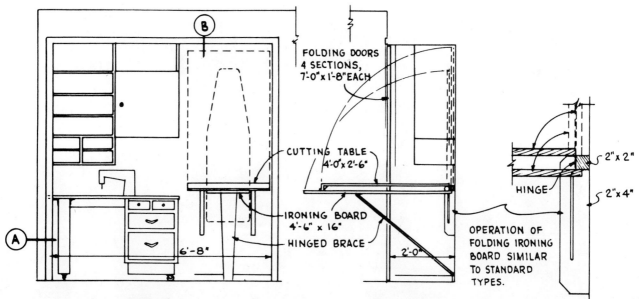

FOLDING DOORS 4 SECTIONS, 7'-0" x 1'-8" EACH

CUTTING TABLE 4'-0" x 2'-6"

IRONING BOARD 4'-6" x 16"

HINGED BRACE

6'-8"

FRONT

2'-0"

SECTION

HINGE

2" x 2"

2" x 4"

OPERATION OF FOLDING IRONING BOARD SIMILAR TO STANDARD TYPES.

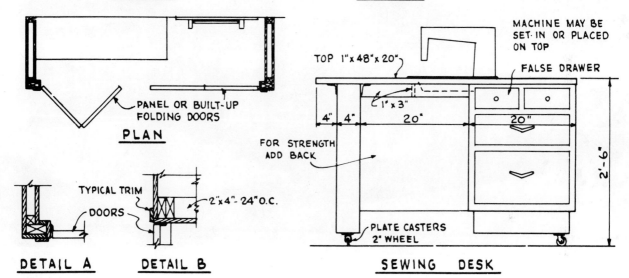

PANEL OR BUILT-UP FOLDING DOORS

PLAN

TYPICAL TRIM

DOORS

2" x 4"- 24" O.C.

DETAIL A   **DETAIL B**

MACHINE MAY BE SET·IN OR PLACED ON TOP

TOP 1" x 48" x 20"

FALSE DRAWER

1" x 3"

4" 4"   20"   20"

FOR STRENGTH ADD BACK

2'-6"

PLATE CASTERS 2" WHEEL

SEWING   DESK

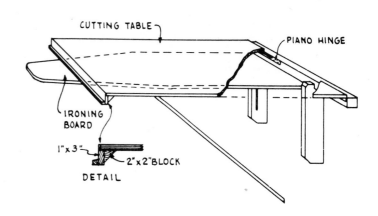

SHELF

DOOR

24"   24"   15"

FRONT   **SECTION**
STORAGE CABINET

CUTTING TABLE

PIANO HINGE

IRONING BOARD

1" x 3"

2" x 2" BLOCK

DETAIL

BUILT-IN BED WALL

Additional closet space plus the luxury of a paneled bedroom, with valanced bed alcove, come with this built-in plywood wall.

You can adjust the depth of alcove and closets to your requirements. A large room will suggest deep storage. But you need not deny yourself the convenience of this attractive arrangement even in a small room where space is limited. Simply move your paneling closer to the wall and make do with what space you have.

As noted on the plan, the construction of this bed wall is not too complicated. The paneling is attached to two by four framing secured at ceiling and floor. The folding doors give full access to shelves and drawers. Fluorescent lighting can be installed in space above the closets and bed alcove.

While plans are not included for construction of the shelved headboard of the bed, the clever craftsman will undoubtedly figure out a scheme of attack. For your paneling, use prefinished plywood of type and tone to suit your taste. You will be pleased with both the practical and decorative aspects of your handiwork.

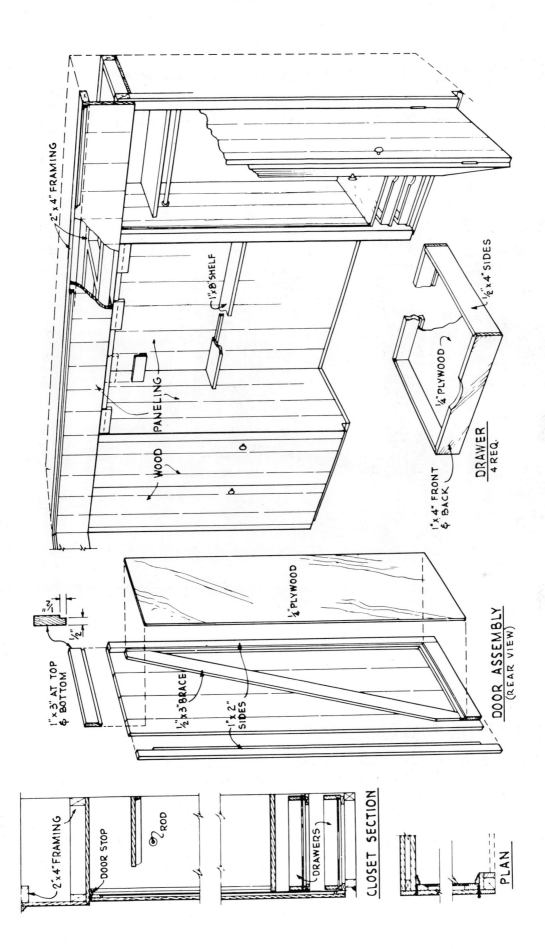

2" x 4" FRAMING

1" x 8" SHELF

WOOD PANELING

1½" x 4" SIDES

¼" PLYWOOD

1" x 4" FRONT & BACK

DRAWER
4 REQ.

¼" PLYWOOD

1" x 3" AT TOP & BOTTOM

½"

½" x 3" BRACE

1" x 2" SIDES

DOOR ASSEMBLY
(REAR VIEW)

2" x 4" FRAMING

DOOR STOP

ROD

DRAWERS

CLOSET SECTION

PLAN

FOLD-UP HOME WORKSHOP

For Dad only—a complete, self-contained home workshop with tools, lumber, shop equipment, and supplies locked into his own fold-up craftsman's center.

Although this unit may be expanded if space is available, the complete workshop pictured above fits into an 8' wide area.

Place your power tools and storage cabinets flush against the wall and all tools, lumber and supplies are just an arm's-length away.

Two storage walls of ¾" plywood provide plenty of room for paints and other supplies, plus additional surface for tool display. These 2' 6" deep storage partitions swing inward on all directional casters, enabling you to lock and secure the entire workshop.

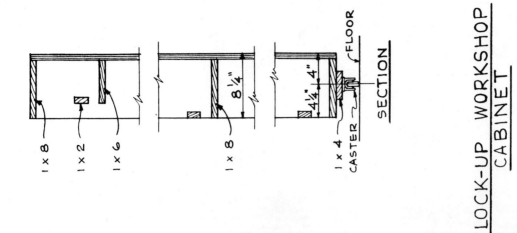

1 x 8
1 x 2
1 x 6

1 x 8

1 x 4
CASTER
FLOOR

4¼" 4"
8¼"

SECTION

LOCK-UP WORKSHOP
CABINET

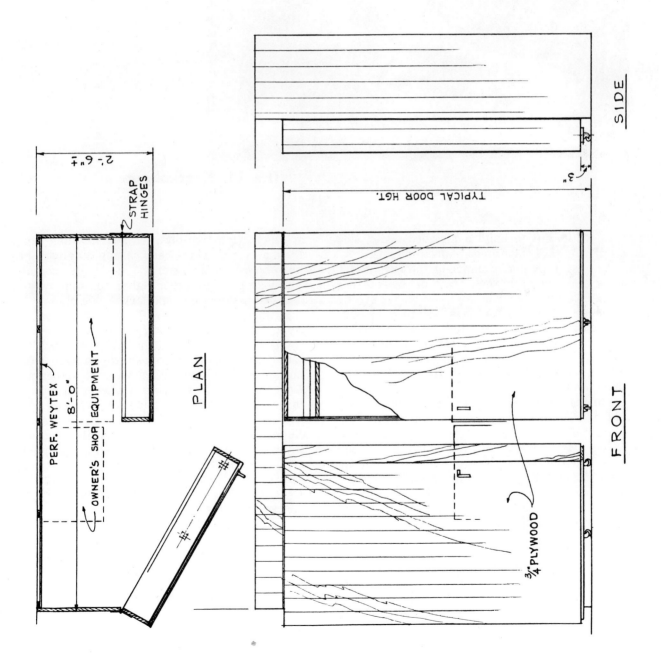

2'-6"±

STRAP HINGES

PERF. WEYTEX
8'-0"
OWNER'S SHOP EQUIPMENT

PLAN

SIDE

3"

TYPICAL DOOR HGT.

¾" PLYWOOD

FRONT

PLYWOOD BOAT BUILDING

The 15' Knockabout

Do you want to build a plywood boat? You can if you have the proper plans and tools.

As proven by performance of the famous PT boats and other plywood craft of World War II, exterior-type, marine plywood makes strong and enduring boats. And it is easy to work. Unlike the old-fashioned, individual planking methods, large plywood panels go on all in one piece. As shown in photo-sequence at the right, this convenience saves much time in hull construction.

Illustrated above is a 15' knockabout sloop which was designed for the American Plywood Association by the noted naval architect, Edwin Monk. Generous freeboard and clean lines distinguish this well-designed sailing craft. Though its performance delights experts, this is essentially a safe and stable sailboat designed for day sailing and family fun. You can get plans for building it from the Plywood Association.

But the knockabout is only one of a fine fleet of sail and power craft which outstanding naval architects commissioned by American have designed for do-it-yourself boat builders. Dozens of other attractive plywood boats, which range from a 5' "pumpkin-seed" sailing dinghy to big, live-aboard, cruising craft, are made available for boat builders with elaborate, step-by-step, detailed instructions and large-scale plans.

In fact, the American Plywood Fleet has become famous in boating circles all over the country. For example, the "Thunderbird" 26' racing and cruising sloop, shown on page 205, is now one of the fastest growing class boats in American and Canadian waters. More than three hundred of these have already been built.

While dimensions of these book pages preclude presentation of the large-scale American Plywood boat plans, the step-by-step photographs at the right and on the following page, demonstrate procedures of plywood boat construction. These pictures show how the 15' knockabout was actually built.

A sampling of four other fir plywood boat designs is illustrated on page 205. And there are dozens of other designs waiting for your selection. You can get the complete list by writing to the American Plywood Association, Dept. PWFE, 1119-A Street, Tacoma 2, Washington.

1 Establish a level working plane with sawhorse jigs. Spike parallel stringers on sawhorses and attach spacer blocks to stringers to spot locations of frames.

2 Pre-assemble the frames and mount them in order at block locations on stringers. Attach stem to forward frame. Stem is nailed to brace block on floor.

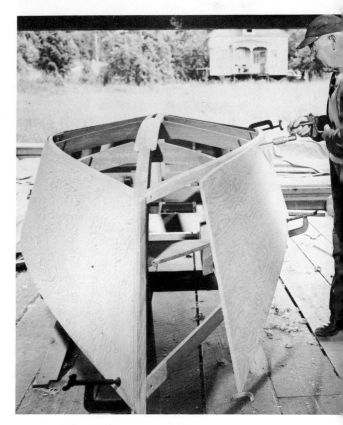

3 Now fair the assembled framework by planing bevels along the keel and chines to conform to bottom slope of frames.

4 One-piece plywood side planks go on with waterproof glue and non-corrosive, flat head screws. "C" clamps are used to hold planks in position while screws are driven.

5 When you have planed the side planks flush with the chines, fit and fasten the bottom planks. Then plane the bottom edges flush with the sides.

6 Trim the bottom planking for the centerboard slot. Plane the V-bottom flat along keel line for flush fit of centerboard slot molding and keel.

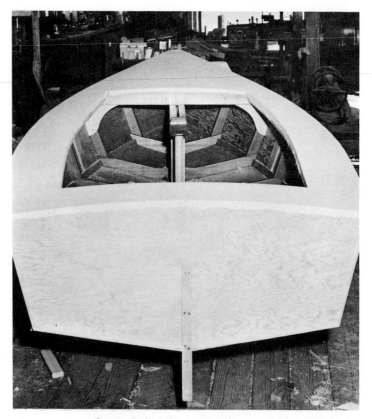

7 Now the hull is taken off the jig and rolled right side up. Leave the crossbands on the center frames until you have fitted the deck beams.

8 With deck beams in place and plywood decking attached, the knockabout is ready to have her mast stepped. Painting and final fitting will follow.

Photo-Sequence Courtesy of American Plywood Association

The 5' Sailer

The Plywood Rowing Dinghy

The 18' Day Cruiser

The 26' "Thunderbird"

INDEX

SP
EDUC
SEAS

Sean M.
West Virg

Derek J.
Appalachiar

Richard M. Kairigh, MS
Meredith College

J. Scott Townsend, EdD
Appalachian State University

Library of Congress Cataloging-in-Publication Data

Sport education seasons / Sean M. Bulger ... [et al.].
    p. cm.
   Includes bibliographical references.
   ISBN-13: 978-0-7360-4639-8 (soft cover)
   ISBN-10: 0-7360-4639-9 (soft cover)
  1.   Physical education and training.   I. Bulger, Sean M., 1969-
   GV341.S597 2006
   796.071--dc22

                    2006011798

ISBN-10: 0-7360-4639-9
ISBN-13: 978-0-7360-4639-8

Acquisitions Editor: Bonnie Pettifor; **Developmental Editor:** Amy Stahl; **Assistant Editors:** Bethany J. Bentley, Martha Gullo; **Copyeditor:** Joyce Sexton; **Proofreader:** Sarah Wiseman; **Permission Manager:** Dalene Reeder; **Graphic Designer:** Fred Starbird; **Graphic Artists:** Denise Lowry, Angela K. Snyder, and Dawn Sills; **Photo Manager:** Sarah Ritz; **Cover Designer:** Keith Blomberg; **Photographers (cover):** Brenda Williams, Tom Roberts; **Art Manager:** Kelly Hendren; **Illustrators:** Kelly Hendren, Denise Lowry, Roberto Sabas, Michael Richardson, Keith Blomberg, Patrick Griffin, Titus Deak, Keri Evans, Mic Greenberg, Argosy, Kareema McLendon, Brian McElwain, and Tim Offenstein; **Printer:** Sheridan Books

Printed in the United States of America   10 9 8 7 6 5 4 3 2 1

Human Kinetics
Web site: www.HumanKinetics.com

United States: Human Kinetics, P.O. Box 5076, Champaign, IL 61825-5076
800-747-4457
e-mail: humank@hkusa.com

Canada: Human Kinetics, 475 Devonshire Road Unit 100, Windsor, ON N8Y 2L5
800-465-7301 (in Canada only)
e-mail: orders@hkcanada.com

Europe: Human Kinetics, 107 Bradford Road, Stanningley, Leeds LS28 6AT, United Kingdom
+44 (0) 113 255 5665
e-mail: hk@hkeurope.com

Australia: Human Kinetics, 57A Price Avenue, Lower Mitcham, South Australia 5062
08 8372 0999
e-mail: liaw@hkaustralia.com

New Zealand: Human Kinetics, Division of Sports Distributors NZ Ltd., P.O. Box 300 226 Albany, North Shore City, Auckland
0064 9 448 1207
e-mail: info@humankinetics.co.nz